MAMA,
YOU ARE
ENOUGH

PAGE STREET
PUBLISHING CO.

MAMA,
YOU ARE
ENOUGH

How to Create
CALM, JOY, and **CONFIDENCE**
Within the Chaos of Motherhood

Claire Nicogossian, PsyD

Clinical Psychologist and Founder of Mom's Well Being

PAGE STREET
PUBLISHING CO.

For all the mothers in my life:

Barbara Nicogossian, Ann Gallagher, Claudia Nicogossian, and Parandzem Hacopian, and the generations of mothers that came before me, and my loving and supportive father, Arnauld Nicogossian. Your sacrifice, love, and devotion to family has impacted generations and carved a path of many opportunities—thank you.

Contents

preface

I love my children, but I hate being around them.
I can't wait for them to be in school all day.

I wanted nothing more than to be a mom, but the thing is,
I never expected it to be like this. I've lost myself,
and I don't even know who I am anymore.

I yell at my children all the time, and I feel so guilty
for losing control.

These are some of the countless statements I've heard in the therapy room from overwhelmed and stressed mothers. Becoming a mother is a life-changing event, and as a licensed clinical psychologist with more than two decades of clinical experience supporting mothers, I've seen that, on the journey of mothering, many women are neither prepared for nor expect the stress and strain that come with raising a child.

Years ago, I noticed a trend in the therapy hour: mothers needing support, compassion, and skills to cope with the stress of motherhood. They were experiencing many challenging emotions but were apprehensive to share these feelings with friends or family for fear of judgment. It was in response to these hundreds of women in different stages of mothering that I wrote this book.

The goal of this book is to help mothers identify, label, and manage the challenging emotions of motherhood, which I call *shadow emotions*—feelings ranging from sadness and tearfulness to guilt, anxiety, loneliness, burnout, frustration, resentment, disgust, and shame. The reason I call them shadow emotions is because when we label emotions—or even experiences, interactions, or people—as good or bad, positive or negative, right or wrong, we create very rigid and distinct ways of thinking. Labeling this way creates judgment, and when we judge something or someone, we break the connection between ourselves and that emotion or person and create a decision, a fixed belief. By letting go of the common "good" versus "bad" labels and instead viewing our challenging emotions as more neutral shadows, we create an opportunity to be curious, to look beyond surface details, to be openhearted, and to connect on a deeper level with ourselves, our emotions, our experiences, and other people.

In my private practice, mothers who were stressed, depressed, or anxious would sit on the couch and share with me the shadow emotions they were experiencing. In the confines of a safe, nonjudgmental space, they felt enormous relief hearing that it's normal to experience shadow emotions in mothering. It's okay to feel shadow emotions in motherhood for several reasons: (1) Feeling shadow emotions doesn't mean you have to act on the emotion; (2) feeling shadow emotions doesn't mean that you don't love your children enough; and (3) feeling shadow emotions in motherhood does not equate to being a "bad" mother.

Without this assurance, though, many mothers continue to leave their shadow emotions unmanaged. They put a lot of effort into protecting and shielding these feelings, lest they ever be revealed. As mothers, we've crafted a narrative at home, at work, and within our children's schools and neighborhoods: Everything is fine. Everything is perfect. We're happy, satisfied, and loving every minute of every day of mothering. But there is a hidden cost to not being honest. Mothers are often left feeling isolated, judged, worried, and concerned that they are failing at parenting.

Almost two decades ago, when I became a mother to twin girls, I experienced firsthand what I had been hearing from clients for years in the therapy room: Parenting is a never-ending giving of oneself. Today, I am a mother to four children, and I too have experienced many of the shadow emotions described in this book. Inspired by mothers in the therapy room, in addition to what I was hearing from friends and moms in my community (and often experiencing myself), I began to explore the trends I observed. I found research supporting what I was seeing and experiencing: In today's fast-paced world, mothers are overwhelmed and stressed juggling the demands of work, home, relationships, and family.

In moments of stress, moms experience a range of shadow emotions—but seldom talk about their feelings. And when they do talk about the hard stuff in mothering, they almost always preface their confession of the shadow emotions by trying to reassure and persuade their listener that they really do love and care for their children. Part of this disclaimer comes from fear of judgment and wondering what others may think when they share something like, "I love my children more than anything, but some days I wonder how I can keep on giving myself. I'm losing myself, and I hate how I feel being around my kids. I just need a break."

These are what I call the *shadow moments* of motherhood, moments that cast a shadow on experiencing happiness, as well as connecting and nurturing our child, ourselves, and other significant relationships. The truth is that shadow moments are part of motherhood. When we normalize these feelings by talking openly and honestly, without judging what mothers are

3

feeling, we accomplish multiple things: We create a response of compassion without judgment; we help moms move from a place of being ashamed for what they feel to accepting their feelings; and we help moms open up to finding solutions and skills to manage shadow emotions, which I believe is the path to thriving in motherhood.

I like to use impressionist art as a metaphor for motherhood. Using small dabs of bold paint in ways that can often appear to be "messy" layers, the artist creates a visual effect of light and form depicting a subject from their personal point of view, or their impression. Standing in front of an impressionist painting, if you were to focus on one area of the painting close up, all you'd be able to see is dabs of colors, messy and layered. To fully appreciate what the painting is about, you have to step back and get some perspective.

It's the same in motherhood: Experiences and moments are the paint, and motherhood is the canvas. Shadow moments are dabs of darker colors, messy and chaotic at times. Focusing too closely on the shadow moments, we can get lost in them, believing that we're *not good enough* or that we're failing when, in fact, we're having a shadow moment—a dab of messy paint— all of which contributes to your canvas in motherhood.

You don't have to know what the canvas is going to look like. These shadow moments are not all of you, they are part of you: variations of light and dark in bold, vibrant, illuminating patterns that together create a beautiful, unique work of art on your path and journey through motherhood. Throughout this book, we will explore the authentic, vulnerable, and very real shadow sides of motherhood, embracing them and learning from them, which creates a mosaic of healing as we move beyond them.

introduction

Every hour of the light and dark is a miracle.
—Walt Whitman

On a fall morning many years ago, I set out to plant tulip bulbs with my two-and-a-half-year-old daughter, Anna. Her older twin sisters were at school and her five-month-old baby sister, Lauren, was taking a nap. Relishing an opportunity for sacred one-on-one time with just a single child, I gathered all of the supplies needed for Anna and me to spend some time planting on this particular October morning: bulbs, hand shovels, and gardening gloves, a set for each of us.

If you've raised a child through ages two and three, you know all too well the challenges that come with this developmental age: wild mood swings, a quest for independence and autonomy, blossoming personality interests, and will. And the all-too-familiar response to many requests: "No!" Anna must not have gotten the memo that we were supposed to have a pleasant morning of bonding, because she had one epic meltdown.

At first, all seemed to go well as we kneeled on our gardening mats, digging holes and placing bulbs into the moist soil. About five minutes into gardening, as she was digging into the soil, Anna spotted a squirming worm. The worm startled her and sent her running to the driveway. No coaxing or reasoning could get her back to my side. I asked Anna to sit on the steps close to me while I finished planting the row of bulbs. She refused. Instead, Anna ran across the street to see a neighbor's cat. Leaving my spot, I ran to get Anna and brought her back across the street, telling her about safety and not crossing the street without an adult. And here is where the power struggle began, a power struggle that waged pretty consistently over the next six months.

Bringing her back to our house and asking her to sit on the steps while I finished planting was a futile request. Anna started making demands to visit the neighbor's cat, eat apples, change her clothes, go inside, you name it—she wanted nothing to do with our morning of gardening. I ignored her, trying to go about my planting, hoping she'd burn off some energy and come around. No such luck. It was as if on that day a switch was flipped and Anna decided that for the next six months, everything I suggested she'd reject, challenge, or argue about. It was an exhausting time for both of us.

As a mother of four daughters, I count myself fortunate that this was the first time I had experienced such an intense, scary *shadow moment* of not wanting to be around my child. Of course, I loved her and treated Anna with kindness and nurturance, but I dreaded mothering her because I felt *so ineffective*. The parenting skills that I used with my twins and that had worked for nine years at this point—quite well, I might add—did not work with Anna. When the same parenting skills didn't work with Anna, I felt exhausted, overwhelmed, and inept at caring for her. And these feelings lasted on and off for six months. Call it the terrible twos or threes, whatever it was, this was a difficult time in mothering.

Then one morning in April, as Anna and I returned home after walking the twins to the bus, Anna approached our walkway and squealed with delight as the tulips we planted six months before were blooming. Excited, she said, "Mommy, those flowers we planted last Halloween! They came up!"

6

"Yes, Anna, they did. Those bulbs we planted are becoming beautiful flowers," I said.

"That was a fun day, Mommy. We should plant more flowers!" And off she went running in the yard.

I stood there staring at the red teacup-shaped tulips, tears welling in my eyes, and thought, *She thought it was a fun day, while I felt it was the beginning of a super challenging time with so many shadow moments mothering her. What a different place we are in compared to last fall!*

Around this time, it was as if the switch that had turned on and started the difficulty between us turned off just as quickly. The irrationality, tantrums, and meltdowns subsided. I had my sweet, loving, agreeable, and full-of-wonder Anna back. I share this story with you because it was a powerful time in mothering, when I felt so many intense shadow emotions. Of course, I had many shadow moments before this period, but those six months with Anna, as I cared for four children under the age of nine (one of whom was a very strong-willed two-year-old), were some of the most challenging experiences of motherhood I had experienced up to that point.

As a person who sees the world through metaphors, I can't help but see the comparisons and similarities between planting and motherhood. As a mama for almost two decades, I've come to see motherhood as a cycle of growth, much like a tulip's: darkness, anticipation, uncertainty, change, joy, celebration, and reward. As different as our mothering journeys may be, we all share the similarity of growing through uncertainty and the unknown, learning about ourselves and our children along the way as we nurture and care for tiny humans.

Think back to when you first knew you were going to be

a mother. Whether your child grew in your body or your heart (if you're a mama who has fostered, adopted, or surrogated), the beginning of motherhood is filled with many unknowns. We begin motherhood in the dark, unaware of the range of emotions we're going to experience: anticipation, shock, surprise, fear, worry, joy, and many more. So much of our emotional experience in motherhood starts in the dark and the unknown.

My journey as a mother to my twins began with many shadow emotions, along with major physical challenges from complications in my pregnancy and their birth. The first year of motherhood was incredible—I was overwhelmed with love, joy, and gratitude, as well as stress, exhaustion, frustration, sadness, fear, and worry. Despite my two advanced degrees, I felt emotions that no one had ever warned me about, nor had I heard such feelings being talked about. When I began to experience stressful and confusing emotions—such as overwhelm, irritability, exhaustion, and boredom—I felt ashamed to have such feelings in the midst of my gratitude for being a mother. How could I feel shadow emotions when I had two healthy, thriving babies? I was conflicted, feeling intense emotions along with profound gratitude and love.

I remember feeling myself go through the motions of caring for my babies, bored, lonely, and unfulfilled. I wondered if other new moms felt this way, juxtaposed between gratitude and exhaustion, love and overwhelm. I was apprehensive about voicing my feelings—I had tested the water by bringing up my feelings to other mom friends and family members to see if honestly sharing my emotions about motherhood was acceptable. For example, when someone would ask how things were going with the twins, I would say, "Well they're sleeping through the night and doing great, but I'm so tired. I'd love some time to myself." In response, I would hear phrases like, "Oh, all moms feel that way, but enjoy these moments— they grow up so fast!" Or, "They're such a blessing. You're so fortunate." Or, "I didn't feel that way—I loved every minute with my children!"

Well-intentioned friends, family, or other moms would reassure me, dismiss my feelings, or give me an ominous warning about my children being babies for a short time. I quickly learned it was socially unacceptable to talk about the truth of shadow emotions in motherhood.

Toni Morrison, the American author and editor who won a Nobel Prize in Literature in 1993, once said, "If there's a book that you want to read, but hasn't been written yet, then you must write it." This is one of my core motivations to write the book you are now reading. This is the book I wanted to read when I first become a mother, a book to help me understand the shadow emotions I was experiencing in motherhood that I knew other moms must be experiencing but were apprehensive to voice at playdates, school drop-offs, and social gatherings.

I wanted a realistic portrayal of the range of feelings, from positive to negative and everything in between, to be brought out of the *shadows* and *into the light*. As a psychologist, I was hearing some of the same feelings I experienced expressed in the therapy hour. And I found myself repeating, not only to myself but to moms, "Just because you experience certain feelings doesn't mean you have to be defined by these feelings, nor do you have to act on your feelings. You can have shadow emotions and continue to be a competent, loving, grateful mother."

As a mother who is in the midst of raising a family and as a clinical psychologist supporting mamas, I want you to know this:

It's okay to feel irritable, depleted, and lonely in motherhood. It's okay to feel sad, frustrated, and bored. It's okay to feel so overwhelmed or angry that you don't know how you'll find the energy to get up and do this all over again tomorrow. You can experience these shadow emotions and love and adore your children with every cell and breath in your body. You are not alone, and this book is going to help you learn to manage your shadow emotions and thrive in motherhood.

I'm so glad you've found this book, because here you will learn about yourself and your emotions: the awesome ones we all imagine when we become mothers—joy, gratitude, love, adoration, contentment, appreciation—and the *shadow emotions* that catch us off guard, such as anger, sadness, fear, disgust, and embarrassment. In these pages, you're going to find the whole experience of motherhood, not just the moments we anticipate and look forward to, intentionally portray when we leave the house, or carefully curate on social media. The journey of motherhood is a great unknown, unfamiliar at times. We don't always know what to do with, how to react to, or how to manage the emotions we experience. But over time, if we stay committed to caring for ourselves, nurturing our relationships, and managing our feelings, thoughts, and behaviors, we can get through the challenging times in motherhood. We can start to feel more brightness, happiness, gratitude, and well-being. This book is going to inspire you to appreciate yourself and embrace the whole experience of motherhood without judging yourself, which in turn will bring more compassion and understanding into your life so you can thrive in motherhood!

This book is divided into five main shadow emotions: sadness, fear and anxiety, anger, embarrassment, and disgust. With each section, there is a general description of the shadow emotion in motherhood, and chapters that explore the variations of these shadow emotions, and how these feelings can present in motherhood. Each chapter is structured with helpful information including how to reframe negative self-talk, termed as *shadow mantras*, to positive and compassionate self-talk, called *thriving mantras*. There are also specific skills and strategies for each shadow feeling called Moving Beyond the Shadows, which will help you manage and move past the shadow emotion you're experiencing. And at the end of each chapter is an inspiring Thriving Mama Reflection to help you feel inspired to bring self-compassion for yourself into motherhood.

The cornerstone of therapy is trust, connection, and confidentiality. In this book there are some examples in motherhood of moms experiencing shadow emotions. None of the descriptions identify any specific individuals. To illustrate examples in motherhood, all names are fictitious, and clinical issues and presentations have been combined to create an illustration for the emotion or struggle highlighted. Any recognizable details have been altered; therefore any resemblance of an individual for a case example to any actual person is entirely coincidental.

PART I

learning to thrive in modern motherhood

chapter 1

the key to thriving in motherhood: understanding and managing your emotions and feelings

Every emotion has a source and a key that opens it.
—Rumi

I can think of no role in life that compares to the emotional experience of motherhood. Before becoming a mother, with two advanced degrees in mental health and psychological functioning, I thought I knew a lot about emotional states impacting thoughts, behaviors, and experiences in a person's life. Then I became a mother, and all that prior experience and education no longer applied. Becoming a mother creates a heightened awareness of the intensity of human emotions. Think back to the time before you were a mom. Think about the feelings or thoughts you had. Now think about becoming a mother. Wouldn't you agree that you've felt more emotions and have had more thoughts and experiences that intensified what it means to be human in the role as a mother?

Motherhood is an ever-evolving journey, one in which we

learn about ourselves via nurturing and caring for our children. Motherhood is not an isolated experience built on one moment or event; it's a process of self-discovery and understanding that provides an opportunity to experience astounding love, compassion, and understanding for ourselves, our child, and our partner. Motherhood is sacred. But it's not immune to the ups and downs of life or to life's emotions—happiness and anger and every emotion in between. Motherhood isn't one experience; it's all of these things. And like anything complete, there will be moments (often many moments) that force us to stop, pay attention, and refocus.

Being a mother involves being a caregiver, protector, nurturer, teacher, nurse, counselor, chef, chauffeur, and advocate. With so many roles, motherhood can feel tiring, demanding, and overwhelming. Of course, motherhood is a lovely, inspiring, and divine gift. Motherhood can be and is not limited to being:

divine and superficial
a blessing and a strain
joyful and enraging
peaceful and chaotic
happy and depressing
connected and lonely
confident and uncertain
a source of love and disdain

And in these extremes, there is a range from mild to severe emotions that make up a continuum of emotional experiences in motherhood. But all of these contrasts make up the whole of motherhood, just like a beautiful impressionist painting. Motherhood is a series of shadow moments and lovely moments;

dabs of paint both light and dark. Focusing on only one part of motherhood—for example, the shadow moments with your child—takes away the perspective of viewing motherhood as a whole, which is beautiful and unique.

To be a mother is a sacred calling, not given to everyone. And the surprising thing about motherhood is we can never truly anticipate the role of a lifetime until we are in the position of nurturing a beautiful soul. And that's why it's critical to understand the *shadow side* of mothering. Because when we learn of a baby or child coming into our lives, whether we planned and worked for our child or they came as a surprise, we are forever changed.

When I was pregnant with my babies, I'd have thoughts and dreams of what they would look like and who they'd become. I'd imagine what it would be like to feel their hands hold mine or their arms hug me. I didn't think about how they wouldn't sleep for days, refuse to eat, or be difficult to soothe. I didn't anticipate the fear and helplessness I'd feel when they were sick and I couldn't do anything to make them feel better as they cried in pain. I didn't imagine how tough it could be to find time to shower, eat a meal, or spend time with my husband and friends.

And when I was pregnant, I could hardly imagine a day when my child would be disrespectful or lie, much less hurt a peer, a sibling, or me with an unkind word. I also never dreamed about the time my teenagers would roll their eyes at me, talk back, and blatantly ignore a request made of them. One of the most surprising things about motherhood is you can never fully know what to expect or how to manage the role until you're experiencing it. Which is why I believe mamas need support and guidance to understand the range of emotions experienced in motherhood, from the positive ones we expect (like love, joy, gratitude, awe, and contentment) to the *shadow emotions* that catch us off guard (like sadness, fear, disgust, anger, and embarrassment), which I call shadow emotions.

Understanding Shadow Emotions in Motherhood

We live in a world where it's natural to put things in categories: good or bad, healthy or unhealthy, strong or weak, happy or sad, positive and negative. Placing things in categories can be helpful at times, but often, doing so is a rigid and inflexible way of looking at things. Describing situations or experiences in such extremes is quick and streamlined but a tad judgmental, decreasing an opportunity to understand something and yourself in more depth and with curiosity. I prefer to see things on a continuum, in a range of variations, and emotions are a perfect example.

Emotions are often labeled as positive or negative; the positive ones bring us joy, happiness, and contentment, and they're the ones we strive to feel. On the other hand, the negative emotions are the ones we want to avoid, push away, ignore, diminish, and remove from our experiences. But I see avoiding or suppressing our emotions as problematic. Our desire not to experience the "negative" emotions prevents us from understanding ourselves on a deeper level. Here is what I know from two decades of being a therapist: No feeling or emotion is negative or bad. All emotions and feelings—even shadow emotions—are simply pieces of information about what we are experiencing or responding to in any given moment. Just like actual shadows created by clouds on a sunny day, emotions are neither good nor bad—they are simply part of life.

Shadow emotions are the challenging emotions and feelings we experience, the ones that push us outside of our comfort zone or feel unpleasant. Experiencing a shadow emotion creates an opportunity to pause and check in with ourselves as to what we are experiencing. Instead of reacting without intention or awareness, when we experience a shadow emotion, we can pause, take a compassionate and curious approach to understand what we are feeling, and use skills and strategies as outlined in this book, deciding on how we'd like to respond. Managing shadow emotions is an act of self-care.

Putting this in greater context, if you are a mother of an older child, I'm sure you have heard them say, "I'm afraid of the dark." And what do we usually say to this child? "There is nothing to be scared of; you are safe, and I'm right here." If the child persists, perhaps you offer a night-light or rub their back and stroke their head and hair. Maybe you sing a lullaby or give a hug and kiss for reassurance. Perhaps, if the child continues to need more because of their fear, you listen to them and ask what you can do to help. Maybe they'll request that you check under the bed, close the closet door, or give them a cherished stuffed animal, all gestures that bring comfort to them.

Now think for a moment about when you were scared of the dark. But this time, the darkness is not at night. (I know plenty of moms who relish the hours in the evening when children are asleep, the house is quiet, and they finally have a moment to themselves!) I'm talking about the darkness of having felt afraid or judged when you experienced a shadow emotion. Perhaps it was a time when you felt overwhelmed, exhausted, or stressed, and you could barely handle all of the responsibilities of your life. Or maybe it was a moment of loving your child so much but feeling so unfulfilled as a person. Or those moments in motherhood when you lose your temper with your child and say hurtful things out of frustration, and while your child accepts your apology, you lament in the guilt for having lost your temper and the fear you have permanently damaged your child with your rage.

As a mother and a psychologist, I can say this: *You can experience dark moments and shadow emotions in motherhood and still be grateful for your child, adore being a mother, and continue to be a good mother.* Motherhood is seldom defined in one moment. It is a series of events and years of nurturing, protecting, teaching, and guiding your child through development and life. By bringing light and awareness to the shadow emotions in motherhood, we can make changes and improve not only our children's lives but also our own lives. So while you may feel an emotion, it doesn't mean you have to dwell on that emotion, it doesn't mean you're defined by the emotions you feel, or that you have to act on the emotion. Instead, you can be informed and pause for a moment, reflect and choose how to respond. This is the core component of managing emotions: choosing a healthy way to respond instead of an unhealthy way of reacting.

In this book, five categories of shadow emotions are explored: (1) sadness, (2) fear, (3) anger, (4) embarrassment, and (5) disgust. Because emotions exist on a continuum, within each broad shadow emotion you will read about a range of specific feelings in varying intensities, from mild and moderate feelings to more intense and severe emotional reactions. Refer to the MotherMood Wheel of Emotions on page 20 to see how I approach our main emotions, including both the shadow emotions and joy, broken down into their more specific and intense feelings. You can also download it on MomsWellBeing.com

Some of the feelings will be familiar to you, and others you may seldom experience, if you experience them at all. And that is okay. Remember, there is no judgment; rather, you must simply open up to awareness and understanding about what you experience.

Over my years of clinical experience, I have developed the following ten truths that, when deeply understood, can lead to powerful transformation in your journey through the emotions of motherhood.

Ten Truths about Emotions and Feelings in Motherhood

1. Emotions and feelings are neither good nor bad.

2. An emotion or feeling does not define you or your abilities as a mother.

3. Experiencing an emotion or feeling doesn't mean you have to act on it.

4. Feelings and emotions provide opportunities for awareness and reflection, which leads to self-growth.

5. Emotions and feelings can be experienced along a continuum from mild, to moderate, to intense, to severe.

6. Emotional states can be temporary, linger for short amounts of time as well as be more lasting and pervasive states of being.

7. Judging an emotional state with phrases like, "I shouldn't feel this" or "I wish I didn't feel this," blocks self-compassion and understanding and delays an opportunity for personal growth.

8. Emotions and feelings are wise parts of ourselves; when we do not acknowledge or pay attention to them, they will find a way to be seen, whether we want them to or not.

9. Even when it's challenging, showing compassion for our emotions and feelings creates opportunities for growth and healing.

10. Taking care of your emotional state is a crucial component of thriving in motherhood.

mothermood wheel of emotions

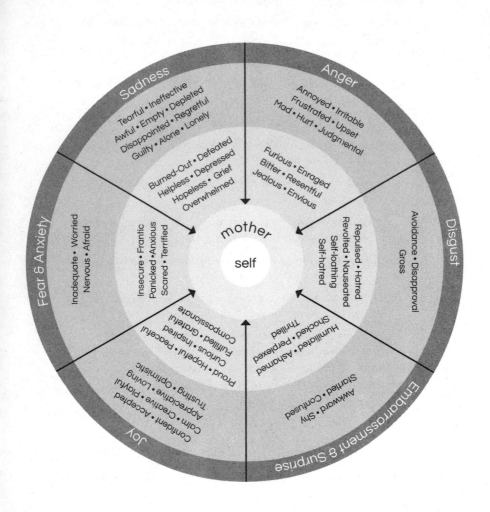

Breaking Down Emotions and Feelings

In my work and through my experience as a mother, I have come to believe one of the most essential skills needed to thrive in motherhood is emotional self-care, which is being able to identify, understand, label, and manage your emotions and feelings. And while emotions and feelings sound like similar things, there are significant (albeit subtle) differences. Knowing these differences will help you be more aware and compassionate with yourself and what you're feeling and experiencing. Let's start with the basics.

An emotion is something our human brains are hardwired from birth to experience. No one teaches us how to experience emotions; we're born with the capacity to experience them. Emotions are powerful responses to how we interpret, respond, and act in life. And while there is a lot of debate about how many emotions we're hardwired to experience, I embrace the model of eight primary emotions: sadness, anger, fear, disgust, joy, surprise, interest, and embarrassment (shame).

Emotions contain three components: (1) a physical component, (2) a cognitive component, and (3) a neurological component. The physical component of experiencing an emotion happens when we have a physical reaction to a situation and begin to feel changes in our body; we may experience a racing heart, tense muscles, sweating, tearfulness, and so on. The physical reaction alone doesn't identify the emotion; for example, think about tears, which you might cry for many reasons (such as sadness, exhaustion, fear, relief, or joy).

The physical component of an emotion or feeling is scanning what you are experiencing in your body. The physical sensations cue us into what we may be experiencing. For example, emotional responses often create some combination

21

of the following physical symptoms:

- Stomach distress
- A rush of energy
- Muscle tension
- Sweating
- Tiredness or fatigue
- Racing heart or palpitations
- Tearfulness or crying
- Shortness of breath
- Racing thoughts
- Jitteriness or restlessness

Think about a racing heart and changes in breathing. Many things can create a racing heart and change your breathing: exercising or carrying your child (exertion), seeing your child walk (excitement), hearing a loud thud (fear), or catching your child climbing out of the crib for the first time (surprise). A racing heart and changes in your breathing are emotional responses to something, but what emotion do they indicate?

The answer is that we could be experiencing many emotions. This truth is why we also need to understand the cognitive component of emotional responses, which is understanding how our thoughts and appraisal of the situation can decrease or increase our emotional response. Our thoughts help us understand what we are experiencing. What we think about, perceive, and experience influences the kind of thoughts we all have, which in turn contributes to our emotional health. Thoughts also influence how we respond to situations and the environment.

For example, your elevated heart rate and breathing make sense when you're going for a brisk walk while pushing your child in a stroller. But if your heart races in the middle of the night and wakes you out of a deep sleep, it may take you a minute to figure out why you're having this physical experience. Was it because you heard a noise? Did you have a bad dream? Or are you having panic episodes? A physical response requires a mental or cognitive component to label, decode, and decipher in order to understand what is happening.

Third, emotions have a neurological (or brain chemistry) component. Our bodies produce hundreds of chemicals in the brain called neurochemicals, which influence feelings, thoughts, and behaviors. For example, dopamine, serotonin, and oxytocin have been called the happy hormones. Oxytocin, for instance, is referred to as the "bonding hormone," responsible for empathy, intimacy, and trust. This chemical is released in the brain during physical contact and intimacy (e.g., hugging, cuddling, sexual activity, or nursing a baby). Disruption in the levels of these neurochemicals, such as dopamine and serotonin, can impact everything from sleep to appetite and mood, to energy levels and the kind of thoughts we have.

All three of these components work together to create the emotions and feelings we experience.

Emotional Responses: Why Feelings Matter

Generally speaking, an emotion is an automatic response to something we experience. This means you don't have to do anything; the emotion happens in response to an internal or external situation.

In session, I often use this example to describe an emotion: Let's imagine you're driving home from an evening outing.

All of a sudden, a deer jumps into the road from the ditch, crossing your path close to your car. In response, you automatically slam the breaks to miss hitting the deer. As you do, everything in the front seat—your purse, a few groceries—falls to the floor from the passenger seat. In a matter of seconds, your heart is racing, your stomach drops, your arms and shoulders are tense, and your knees are shaking as the deer darts off into the darkness and you resume driving home. The emotion you're feeling is a combination of surprise (initiated by how fast the deer ran into the road) and fear (initiated by a threat of danger). This example illustrates the automatic response of an emotion.

A feeling is an emotional response to an internal or external situation or event that is influenced by our thoughts, experiences, culture, and personal history. Feelings are emotional responses personal to us, based on our individual differences and experiences.

To illustrate, let's think about the example of the deer darting in front of your car. You made it home safe after the stressful drive and go right into the evening routine with your family: making dinner, getting ready for the next day, bathing your child, reading them a bedtime story, and putting them to bed. As you lay down to sleep, your head hits the pillow, and although you're tired, you can't drift off, because all you can think about is the "what-ifs" that could have happened with the deer:

- What if your children had been in the car?
- What if you had been on the phone?
- What if your little ones had been asking you to play music and you didn't see the deer?

- What if you had hit the deer?
- What if you had been injured?
- What if your child had been hurt, or worse?

All of these thoughts create so much distress that you can't sleep. This is an example of a *feeling* of worry and panic fueled by your thoughts of how potentially dangerous the situation could have been.

In contrast, let's say for the past few months, you've been working hard to reduce your distracted driving. Instead of talking on the phone in the car or checking your texts at stoplights, you've made an effort not to touch your phone when driving. After the deer darted in front of your vehicle and you stopped in time, you head home and go into the evening routine. As your head hits the pillow, you have a profound sense of gratitude and appreciation for your new practice of not driving distractedly and go to bed with a sense of peace and relief for changing a once problematic behavior.

Same situation, two different feelings, based on an individual's thoughts, experiences, and personal history.

In summary, an *emotion* is an automatic response that we don't control. A *feeling* is an emotional response influenced by our thoughts (which we can control), our experiences, and our personal history. Let's dive deeper into how thoughts influence our feelings.

How Negative and Self-Critical Thinking Increases Shadow Emotions and Feelings

Our thoughts can be tricky. Thoughts are always with us; we can have them anytime and anywhere, and it's challenging to make them go away. If I tell you not to think of a pink elephant, I can almost guarantee you will immediately think of a pink elephant!

And not only are thoughts hard to get rid of but also, on any given day, we have thousands of them. Some experts estimate we have between 60,000 to 80,000 thoughts a day! I think when you're a mom, the number is even higher (closer to 100,000), and I think the number of thoughts increases by several thousand with each additional child! So whatever your estimate, if you're a mom, you have a lot of thoughts every day.

Moms think about what everyone needs, often multitasking and juggling so many things at once for their family, work, and responsibilities. When a mom is thinking about what her family needs *all the time*, she is bearing what is called the mental load. The mental load is composed of all the behind-the-scenes responsibilities, from scheduling and attending doctor's appointments, signing permission forms for field trips, and making it to social events to buying gifts for parties, organizing playdates, and balancing sports practices and activities. The mental load and the to-do list of what her family needs—it never stops! When a mom's mind is too full, continually thinking and doing for everyone, this can be a perfect breeding ground for stress.

A mama's thoughts don't stop at what her family needs; throughout the day, she has many thoughts that can be described in the following categories:

- **Positive:** Moments of appreciation and gratitude, and caring thoughts toward herself, others, and the larger world
- **Neutral:** Neither positive nor negative thoughts, which include thinking about to-do lists, tasks that need to be accomplished, things to do or places to go, as well as any narration describing what she is doing, where she is going, or what she may need to do

- **Negative:** Critical judgments, statements, and observations about herself, others, or the larger world

When the majority of a mother's thoughts become negative—whether she thinks negative thoughts about others or whether she is self-critical and engages in negative self-talk—if she believes every thought as true and does not challenge the negative thinking and manage it, everyday life has the potential to become fraught with problems. Think back to the example of your not being able to sleep because of all the "what-ifs" that could have happened had you hit the deer. Not challenging your thoughts created distress, and you weren't able to sleep because you were worrying about all of the possible scenarios of danger. Negative self-talk (the negative statements, beliefs, or phrases we say to ourselves) has been shown to increase physical stress and arousal, creating challenging physical states and sensations, and fueling more negative thinking.

As a psychologist, I spend a significant portion of my time educating and helping clients understand the power of thoughts.

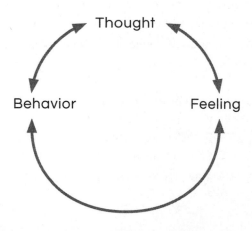

What we feel will influence the types of thoughts we have, the memories we recall, and the ways we choose to respond. And what we think about and focus on mentally will influence how we behave and what we can feel. Our thoughts influence our feelings, which in turn influence how we act and behave, which can create more emotional reactions, thoughts, and behaviors. Our thoughts-behaviors-feelings are interrelated and impact and influence one another. The diagram on the previous page illustrates this cycle well. And it makes sense; if you're feeling sad, chances are you have more sad thoughts, recall more sad events, and in response tend to react to others and your environment in sad behaviors/actions. Which, in essence, then has the potential to create an increase in sad thoughts and more intense sad feelings and behaviors.

Part of understanding our emotions and feelings is taking into account the thoughts we have associated with our feelings. And there's a good reason for this: Our thoughts can fuel and intensify our emotional reactions or they can reduce a feeling.

If the majority of our thoughts become negative and self-critical about ourselves or others, chances are those thoughts are going to increase feeling shadow emotions as well as impact how we interact and function during our day. And this isn't just a matter of opinion. Here are some interesting findings from research on our thoughts:

- People who are depressed have more negative thoughts about themselves, other people, the world, and the future.
- A mood state, whether positive or negative, will impact the type of memories a person recalls.
- A person who is in a negative mood state will more readily

recall negative memories, whereas an individual in a positive mood state will remember positive memories.

- People who are under pressure with many cognitive demands have increased thoughts of dying, one of the most reported unwanted thoughts.

- Listening to aggressive and violent songs can increase aggressive thoughts and feelings. (For example, a research study of five hundred college students showed that when the students spent time listening to violent musical lyrics, they had more violent and aggressive thoughts.)

- Being engrossed in violent interactive video games is associated with increased aggression.

- Most people report intrusive and upsetting thoughts; individuals with anxiety, OCD (obsessive-compulsive disorder), and worry believe the invasive thoughts as accurate and true, whereas those without anxiety, OCD, and worry can let the thought go.

Being able to understand and identify the thoughts you have when you're experiencing an emotional reaction is an essential part of learning to thrive in motherhood.

At this point, you may be thinking, *So I have negative thoughts a lot—now what?* The good news is this—the first step in changing anything in your life is to be aware of and understand your thoughts. The next step is to challenge the thoughts using a skill called reframing.

Reframing is a technique used to manage negative or inaccurate thoughts by considering a different point of view or an alternative perspective. One way to reframe is to ask yourself the following questions:

- Is this thought true? If so, where is the evidence for this?

- Is there another possible explanation for what may be happening in this situation?
- Am I taking this personally?
- If someone I cared for came to me with the same thought, how would I respond?

Positive reframing is an important skill in thriving in motherhood because it takes away the judgment of yourself or another person, a situation or an event. Instead of categorizing someone or something as good or bad, reframing moves your thoughts into a broader understanding seeking alternative explanations. Positive reframing is a skill that builds resiliency, helps manage stress, and allows you to move into a place of mental well-being. The chapters on the shadow emotions will help you learn this skill of reframing by sharing specific negative thoughts you may relate to and how they can be reframed to a positive perspective. These are called shadow mantras and thriving mantras; you'll see more in the chapters that follow.

Now that you have an overview of the shadow emotions and how thoughts impact feelings and behaviors, we will lay the foundation for moving into thriving mama mode through self-care. If your goal is to thrive in motherhood, then think of self-care as the steps that will get you there!

chapter 2

a guide to self-care in modern motherhood

Thriving in motherhood is not about being perfect, never making a mistake, or having every moment of mothering go smoothly. Let's be real—motherhood is challenging, exhausting, and full of mistakes and conflict! At the same time, however, being a mother is amazing and rewarding.

Being a mama in the modern world is a whole new way to parent. It requires navigating demands and pressures faced by no other generation in history. Compared to what our ancestors experienced, family life has changed dramatically. Almost half of American mothers are working full-time. It is less common for moms *not* to be in the workforce—only a quarter of American families have one parent who does not work outside the home.[1] And with these changes in family structure, modern family life means parents not only share the financial responsibility, but they're also sharing more of the household responsibilities. But things are slow to change, with mothers continuing to shoulder more of the day-to-day parenting responsibilities, household management, and the children's schedules, activities, academics, and medical needs (including taking time off from work when a child is sick).[2]

Another stressor I've seen over the past twenty years of practice as a psychologist (and as a mama raising children) is the fact that more families are living farther away from their extended family, which means less support with raising children. And with both parents working, there is the added stress of daycare, after-school care, cleaning, cooking, and spending quality time together as a couple or a family. It's understandable why families take advantage of two-day delivery from Amazon, meal subscription services, grocery delivery, and restaurants—families are maxed out and trying to streamline managing a household. By the time families come home after work, school, and activities, there is only a small window of time—often just a few hours—for dinner, homework, baths, and bedtime. Then families start all over the next day.

Then there's the added layer of the modern world being connected 24/7 to news, information, and social media through smartphones and screens—we have created a culture focused on productivity with little downtime. Parenting through the digital era is complex; parents are navigating screen time and social media and striving to keep childhood going as long as possible while kids are getting phones and devices earlier and earlier. There is so much modern parents have to keep up with and be on top of in addition to the demands of working and raising a family.

Some parts of parenting will never change, but modern parents have to juggle issues and concerns previous generations did not have to face. These are *not better or worse* from my perspective; it's a matter of complexity in modern parenting. Modern parents have the same number of hours in a day as parents of previous generations, but slowing down for family time, couple time, and self-care is more challenging than ever!

I believe the two most valuable resources in parenting are *time* and *energy*. So many parents are exhausted, stressed, and overwhelmed—but they're not taking care of themselves. Many parents believe *there's no time* for self-care, *do not understand* the importance of self-care, or have *difficulty transitioning* out of "production mode" because there's a seemingly endless to-do list when raising a family.

You may belong to the group of parents who wonder, *Is self-care really enough to fix the stress and overwhelm?* Self-care won't lift all of life's burdens, but the intentional self-care that I'm sharing with you in this book is a great place to start! And you may point out another dilemma with self-care: *How do parents fit in self-care with an already demanding and packed schedule?*

Believe me, I get it. As I raise my girls, finding the time and making self-care a priority can feel overwhelming. What I encourage clients (and remind myself) is that self-care is possible if you plan it and break it down into small steps you can take each day.

Self-care doesn't have to be overwhelming and stressful or cost money. Self-care is a practice of *knowing yourself* and *what you need* to feel healthy and happy to thrive in motherhood.

Self-care, at its simplest definition, is any activity or behavior that creates and maintains health and well-being. Self-care is made up of the intentions, actions, and behaviors you use to add joy and happiness to your life as well as help you manage the stress of raising a family, the demands of work, and the responsibilities you're obligated to fulfill. I believe there are six primary dimensions of self-care in motherhood: (1) physical, (2) emotional, (3) mental/cognitive, (4) social, (5) spiritual, and (6) personal.

PHYSICAL SELF-CARE

Physical self-care is any action or behavior focused on taking care of your body and physical health, including getting enough sleep, staying hydrated, eating healthy and nutritious food, being active, and exercising regularly. Physical self-care also includes routinely showering and grooming yourself, consuming caffeine and alcohol within healthy limits, going to medical appointments, and following recommended preventive care and interventions for your health-related issues and concerns.

Physical self-care skills are the most crucial part of health and well-being because our physical health creates the foundation from which all other parts of well-being flow. And when we're not taking care of our physical health, nothing seems to go smoothly. A body that is exhausted, dehydrated, depleted of nutrients and minerals, and not fueled by proper energy does not run efficiently. When our body is out of balance, there is a high likelihood that our emotions, thoughts, and behaviors are also out of balance. As a mama, I know you've been there. Sleepless nights, skipping meals, and not being able to get dressed until the afternoon because of chaos with a child can be a setup for incredible stress, overwhelm, and impatience. But after getting a good night's sleep and taking care of your physical needs, you can feel like a whole new person the next day.

EMOTIONAL SELF-CARE

Emotional self-care is being able to identify, label, and acknowledge your feelings and take the necessary steps to care for and manage those emotions. Emotions are powerful and influence our thoughts and behaviors. Our emotions can be our best allies, helping us navigate situations and relationships. They

34

can also be our worst enemies when we give in to every feeling without thoughtfully taking the time to understand and manage the emotion.

In the best-case scenario, our emotions become beacons of information to help us navigate our responses to situations, other people, and ourselves. This is why being able *to care for* and *manage our feelings* is essential to support overall well-being. It's normal to experience a range of emotions, from positive (e.g., happy, calm, grateful) to neutral (e.g., bored) to stressful (e.g., angry, depressed, frustrated). Emotions range from pleasant to unpleasant and include everything in between. No feeling is "wrong" or "bad" or even "negative" for that matter. Instead, it's how we deal with the emotion that is important. It's about how well we manage stress and what coping mechanisms we choose to use during times of stress and strain.

Emotional self-care can include going to therapy to understand yourself and manage a mental health issue, journaling your feelings to increase self-awareness and release stress, and taking medication for a mental health issue or diagnosis. I see reading this book as an act of emotional self-care, so give yourself credit—you're already beginning the journey of caring for yourself!

MENTAL AND COGNITIVE SELF-CARE

Mental and cognitive self-care activities are behaviors that keep your mind engaged, challenged, and stimulated in healthy ways. Mental self-care also includes being mindful and aware of the internal dialogue going on in your mind, also known as *self-talk*. Self-talk can range from positive to neutral to negative thoughts and statements.

Thoughts are powerful. Self-talk creates a reaction, whether through a feeling or behavior, and it becomes a cycle of influence, which is why healthy mental and cognitive self-care includes managing negative self-talk and thoughts. Some negative self-talk is expected. But what's unhealthy is when self-talk is frequently negative, judgmental, and left uncorrected.

Over the decades in my practice, many mothers have shared with me the ways they engage in negative self-talk, what I call shadow mantras: comparing themselves to other moms, being incredibly hard on themselves for making a mistake, or harboring guilt, doubt, and shame by believing they are failing at motherhood. Part of mental self-care is reducing, managing, and eliminating negative self-talk or statements.

Finally, healthy mental and cognitive self-care includes using sound judgment in situations and interactions, having a good memory and recall, and regularly engaging in personally enriching activities, hobbies, and interests.

SOCIAL SELF-CARE

Social self-care is being connected and spending time with those who are important to you. Social relationships are an essential component of well-being. In the age of social media, where the emphasis is on the number of "friends" and "followers" a person has, the real importance is the quality (not the quantity) of your social relationships. Healthy relationships involve kindness, support, companionship, trust, respect, and compassion in times of celebration as well as times of stress and crisis.

Not all relationships require the same level of connection, support, and companionship. Social relationships are often varied and unique. What is essential is having a balance between what is internally important to you and what is created in genuine relationships; that is, we need to make an effort to nurture the beneficial, supportive social relationships we need and want. Finally, healthy social relationships contribute to overall well-being by creating a sense of connection, purpose, and community.

PERSONAL SELF-CARE

Personal self-care is taking care of your goals and dreams and creating meaning and purpose in the life you want to live. This area of self-care involves learning about yourself, knowing yourself, and planning and creating the life you want to live. Personal self-care is all about the person within the mother, the person who often gets pushed to the side or placed low on the priority list because of all of the giving to her children and family. Some personal self-care acts can include setting goals and working toward meaningful accomplishments or activities, such as changing careers, going back to school, volunteering, pursuing a creative endeavor, or starting a new business. Personal self-care is cultivating self-understanding, growth, goals, and interests.

One of the biggest challenges for first-time moms is adjusting to the sense of self that seems like it's gone away forever—many new moms struggle with feelings of *loss of personal identity and freedom*, even as they recognize how meaningful being a mother is. The adjustment to motherhood can seem so overwhelming because no longer are you as a mama thinking about yourself; you are organizing every waking moment around what your child needs, which can place personal self-care on hold for some time.

I want to remind you that just because you put personal self-care on hold doesn't mean you don't or won't have the future chance to develop personal interests and goals that are meaningful to you. One of my personal goals (which I had held since I was in elementary school) was to pursue writing. Life took me on a different path as a psychologist. Around the time my youngest was a year old, I wanted to reconnect with an interest I had always wanted to pursue: writing children's books. I joined a writer's group, began writing picture books, took a class or two on the craft of writing, and submitted my picture books to publishing houses—and received many rejections. About a year into writing, I found myself wanting to write fewer picture books and more about what I'm most passionate about in my life: motherhood and helping others. Long story short, eight years later, after many rejections and obstacles counterbalanced with lovely moments, you're holding what was once a personal dream that started with one step of personal self-care. So even if now isn't the time, remember that if you hold in your heart your goals and dreams, there will be a time to pursue them!

SPIRITUAL SELF-CARE

Spiritual self-care is composed of the actions and behaviors that bring you a sense of connection, meaning, and purpose in your life. *Spirituality* is a word many immediately associate with religion. However, a broader definition of spirituality is having a sense of connection to other people, including those in your community, those in the larger world, your ancestors, your relatives, and/or the divine or a higher being. Spiritual self-care is also feeling connected to nature, expressing gratitude, and having compassion toward yourself and others. Spiritual moments can include having a sense of purpose in your life through a role connected with your skills, abilities, and life experiences. And if

self-care in motherhood

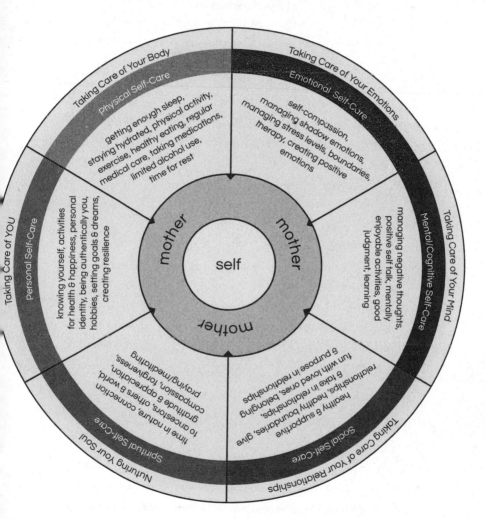

Here is an example of a self-care wheel in motherhood. You can go to MomsWellBeing.com and download your free Motherhood Self-Care Wheel to personalize your self-care wheel.

you're practicing religion, then participating in religious ritual, prayer, and services can deepen your spiritual well-being.

One of the most important parts of understanding self-care is knowing there is *no one way* to practice self-care. There are vast differences among us, including what each of us needs to feel healthy and happy and to thrive. What works for me may not work for you or your best friend or partner. But there is some common ground for laying a foundation of health through self-care behaviors that are focused on taking care of your physical and emotional health.

I often use the analogy of building a home when I talk about self-care. There are endless possibilities of what a home can look like. However, most homes share this: a *solid foundation*. When you build a house, you don't put the roof on first. Instead, the first step is to clear the land and establish a strong foundation. Once the foundation is established, you can build the rest of the house in many different ways. This analogy holds true for self-care as well. Begin by creating a foundation of good physical health: how you rest, move, and restore and what you consume. Physical health is the foundation of self-care from which all other self-care is built.

What Self-Care Isn't

Many of my clients have expressed confusion about what self-care is and isn't. Self-care is neither optional nor selfish and is hardly a one-time event. And self-care is different than pampering or indulging in pleasurable activities. Self-care is a daily discipline, a skill, and a practice to committing to one's overall health and well-being.

Self-care can include going to get a manicure or massage, but these acts will not help you manage a toddler meltdown in the supermarket. Self-care, from a mental health professional's perspective, helps you manage stress, cope with emotions, and improve happiness and well-being. Self-care is different than self-pampering, which is to treat yourself to or gratify yourself with kindness, care, or indulgences. Some examples of self-pampering are getting a massage, having your nails done, sleeping late, or ordering takeout.

There is nothing problematic or wrong with self-pampering, but it needs to be in proportion with other self-care behaviors. Who doesn't want a break from routine by ordering takeout or getting a massage? But if the only way you take care of yourself is through self-pampering, you may find these behaviors do not sufficiently help you cope with day-to-day stress in motherhood.

Self-care is also different than self-indulgence, which is the inability to resist excessive gratification of one's appetites, desires, or whims. Examples of self-indulgence include eating a rich or expensive meal that you would not normally eat and binge-watching TV. Extreme forms of self-indulgence include overeating, shopping excessively, and drinking alcohol excessively. Again, there is nothing wrong with self-indulgence now and then—but if you are using self-indulgence as a way to cope with stress and take care of yourself, then over time, self-indulgent choices can harm your physical, emotional, and mental well-being. I like to think of self-indulgence as a spicy seasoning: A little bit of self-indulgence goes a long way!

Self-care is not optional. Over the years in the therapy room, I've worked with moms who believe that self-care is optional, that it's something they'll get to when the kids are older, or that it's reserved for the few times a year when they're on vacation. Sometimes, I even hear that self-care is not needed. It upsets me when moms tell me they've been told to put their children first and sacrifice self-care. I passionately respond that mothers are *not martyrs* and that if a mom doesn't take care of herself first, she has little left to give her family. Parents' overall well-being (including their mental, physical, emotional, and social health) is essential to caring for and raising a child. When parents take care of their needs in a healthy way, they can deal with the inevitable stress and demands of life and family.

You may have the belief that taking care of yourself is selfish and that all of your energy needs to be focused on your children. The reality is this: *If you take care of yourself, you have more energy to be present and take care of your children.* Even small, daily efforts of self-care add up to help balance, restore, and create a solid foundation of health and well-being for you to draw from in times of stress. Self-care is not selfish. It's self-preservation!

And finally, self-care is not a one-time event. Balancing the demands of raising children can be overwhelming. And when you consider that motherhood is a journey and lifelong commitment, you can see that taking care of yourself isn't something that can wait for eighteen years or more. Have you ever noticed the only way some people will slow down is when they have to, such as when they get sick? Or others take care of themselves only on breaks or holidays, seeing self-care as something to pursue just a couple of times a year.

Instead, I view self-care as a process, a practice of committing to your well-being and caring for yourself daily, even if it's only in small amounts. Self-care takes time, effort, planning, commitment, and energy.

Start Where You Are: Leveling Up Your Self-Care

Depending on where a mama is in her motherhood journey and the age of her children, she'll need to be aware of what she needs for self-care. And if she has multiple children of different ages and stages, her self care needs are going to be unique to her. I think of increasing self-care as leveling up: After physical and emotional self-care, what is the next area of self-care that needs to increase or level up?

When I had four children under the age of eight, I was in survival mode. Most days, all I could accomplish were the basics of survival: feeding and bathing the older girls and taking them to school; trying to keep the younger two on a sleeping and nursing schedule; and going back to work to earn a living. Social self-care, such as spending time with friends or going on a date with my sweetie, was the last thing I could think of. At the end of the day, all I wanted to do was try to catch up on sleep. My social self-care was a low priority. But what *was* a high priority was getting enough sleep, eating, and hydrating as best as I could (as well as occasionally getting in a workout if the little girls would sit in the stroller long enough for a walk).

Fast-forward to today: All my girls are in school all day. Instead of working part-time, I'm working full-time (which comes with a different set of challenges). But I'm able to focus on personal and spiritual self-care through finding meaning and purpose in my work, writing, and teaching—something that was simply not possible eight years ago when I needed to focus on my physical health. I'm also much more focused on emotional self-care. I have to focus on taking care of my emotional health in ways I've never had to before as a mother, because raising tweens and teens is intensely emotional (for all involved)! The point is, self-care in motherhood is ever changing and evolving and highly individualized to you, your life, and the ages and stages your children are in.

Wherever you are in your mothering journey, start with physical and emotional self-care as the foundation. Do what you need to do to achieve as much health as is possible in your life right now. Then pick *one* area of self-care that is a top priority and level up in that area. Focus your energy and effort on strengthening this area of self-care in your life to the best of your ability. If you have the time and energy to choose more than one area, that's great. Still, my recommendation is to focus on one area that will have the most positive impact on your overall well-being.

When we mothers give so much, we have to replenish through self-care skills what we've given to our families in order to thrive. Thriving in motherhood involves managing stress, coping with shadow emotions, taking care of ourselves, and sharing our gifts and abilities in small and large ways, all while raising a family. Thriving isn't about simply getting through the day; thriving is about enjoying your life, connecting with your family, and feeling contentment and joy. This can show up in small ways, such as enjoying spending time with your child in conversation during a shared activity (like going for a walk, eating dinner together, playing, or bathing) and feeling grateful for everyday blessings (like appreciating the rhythm of family routine, having time to prepare a meal for your family, or having a smooth day with your child).

If thriving is the goal for mamas, then self-care skills and strategies are the steps to get there, and the information in this book will help! From a clinical psychologist's perspective, thriving in motherhood is about:

- being open and vulnerable in order to learn about yourself;
- being willing to look at your thoughts, feelings, and behaviors with curiosity instead of judgment;
- letting go of perfection and high and unrealistic standards and embracing vulnerability, self-compassion, and understanding;
- making mental, physical, emotional, social, personal, and spiritual self-care a practice in your everyday life, even in small amounts;
- not idealizing the absence of stress, strain, and overwhelm but *knowing what you need* and putting things in place to move from distress to health;
- having an awareness of how you handle stress as well as the coping skills you use to manage stress levels;
- shifting self-observations from "right" or "wrong" to curiosity and interest to learn more about yourself and how to create personal health and well-being; and
- seeing mistakes not as failures but as opportunities to learn, grow, and develop wisdom in motherhood.

Now that you have the framework, let's dive into the shadow emotions of motherhood. As you take care of your emotional health by deepening your understanding of the shadow emotions, remember to be compassionate and to hold off judging yourself. Motherhood is an emotional journey, and when we care for our emotions, we create health and well-being, which is truly thriving in motherhood.

PART II

embracing sadness on the path to thriving

I love being a mom, but I feel so sad all the time.

*There are so many things I want to do, but I have no energy—
I'm so exhausted.*

*So much has happened since becoming a mom, I feel like I've
lost myself and barely even know who I am anymore.*

*I wanted to be a mom so much, but I had no idea how hard it
would be. Does it ever get better?*

The joy of becoming a mother is like no other! Those first days
with your baby can feel surreal. This is everything you ever
wanted, and a space is filled that you never knew was empty, and
it's now overflowing with emotions you can't quite put into words.
Perhaps it's love, but more often, I think it's awe, overwhelm, and
shock as you scan every surface of your sweet baby, breathing
in the reality that this little human in your arms has already
changed you in ways words can never fully describe. And as the
minutes and hours pass, it begins to sink in: *You are a mother, a
protector, a nurturer. A part of your heart will live outside of you
for as long as you walk this earth.*

When we rise to greet the role of being a mother, we
anticipate the moments of joy, love, connection, and fun in caring
for and guiding our child through life. Which is why it can be
so hard for moms when, in the midst of their awe and gratitude

for having a baby, the shadow emotion of sadness pops up in unexpected ways, propelling mamas into uncharted waters. They wonder if they'll ever return to those initial blissful moments when they first met their child.

The shadow emotion of sadness comes in many forms in motherhood. Sometimes it can feel like a passing summer storm and other times like the endless, cold, gray, and brutal days of winter. It's almost as if nature hardwires mothers to prepare for the shadow emotion of sadness and all the delicate variations of this emotion when, within a few days postpartum, the baby blues set in. They last for a few days for some mothers and for others these symptoms last up to a few weeks, as a new mother's body adjusts to the dip in hormones. The change wrought by the baby blues is notable, ranging from mild to disruptive when they take the form of sadness, irritability, tearfulness, trouble sleeping, problems with concentration, and fatigue. Statistically speaking, 50 to 80 percent of new moms postpartum will experience some intensity of the baby blues. And for some new mothers, the baby blues last longer than two weeks, developing into more significant and intense variations of the shadow emotion of sadness, like postpartum depression or anxiety, which requires mental health support, intervention, and treatment.

And if a mama made it through the postpartum time with mild baby blues and minimal postpartum issues, then it's just a matter of time before nature gives her another opportunity to experience the shadow emotion of sadness: when she's sleep deprived. When a mama is up every two to three hours for days, weeks, and often months at a time, she experiences levels of exhaustion she never thought possible. Sleep deprivation causes significant mood changes, often intensifying feelings of guilt, ineffectiveness, exhaustion, and tearfulness.

It's as if nature is sending mothers a message: Sadness and all the variations of this shadow emotion are part of motherhood, so be prepared, embrace it, learn to identify it and acknowledge it, and most importantly, manage it, because on the journey through motherhood, sadness comes in many forms. Regardless of when it appears, sadness can catch us completely off guard by the surge of its intensity, propelling us into an emotional place we never expected in the role we wanted more than ever.

Sadness in motherhood doesn't always show up the way a mother expects (such as crying and feeling unhappy). Sadness can be experienced as boredom, loneliness, guilt, exhaustion, and burnout. The common theme with all variations of this shadow emotion is loss: loss of personal freedom, relationships, interests you once enjoyed, effectiveness, and energy. Loss can also result from a stressful life situation (such as the loss of a relationship, job, pregnancy, person, and so on) not always directly related to motherhood.

Loss of personal freedom is one of the top stressors in motherhood. Personal freedom is your ability as a mom of finding ways of doing things that used to come with ease, such as taking a shower, using the bathroom, eating a meal, and getting out of the house in order to go to the supermarket, work, exercise, or spend time with your friends or partner. In order to have time to yourself or to work and manage your home (let alone time to spend with those you care about), you have a few choices: You can share childcare responsibilities with your sweetie, enlist the help of a friend or family member to care for your child, hire a daycare, or take your child with you. All of these options take mental energy, cooperation, and resources.

It can feel as if there are many barriers to the luxury of personal freedom.

Loss of personal freedom directly impacts all of a mother's relationships. This incredible shift can contribute to motherhood being lonely at times because of the loss of support and connection. A lot of emphasis is usually placed on finding a community or group of mom friends, but that isn't as easy as it sounds, especially when you feel isolated, left out, or excluded.

Another source of sadness in motherhood is the shadow emotion of exhaustion. Motherhood is a constant giving of oneself in ways that can push a mother to physical, emotional, and mental extremes. Sadness can show up when we feel overwhelmed from constantly giving to our child and pushes us to our limits of exhaustion, depletion, and burnout.

Guilt can also follow on the heels of sadness in motherhood. Many of us mothers feel a sense of sadness expressed through guilt for things we did or forgot to do. We wonder if we're good enough as moms. Guilt crops up when we evaluate our actions through unrealistic, perfectionistic, and, at times, unattainable standards we hold for ourselves—standards that we'd never place on another mother. Making mistakes is part of being human and *being a mother*. But the problem is, when guilt and regret become disproportional, this causes us to question our worth and value. Left unmanaged, guilt and regret can develop into the shadow emotion of shame. Shame results from believing that our negative self-talk is true and internalizing our mistakes (for example, yelling at our child and thinking, *I'm a bad and unloving mother*) instead of focusing on the error of the behavior (for example, rephrasing our self-talk to something like, *I feel guilty for what I said and did*).

Sadness is concerning when you have many of the following symptoms in your life: difficulty sleeping (e.g., sleeping too much or too little), tiredness or inability to sleep, increased or decreased appetite (e.g., weight gain or weight loss), low energy, or lack of motivation, paired with tearfulness or hopelessness. When some or all of these symptoms are present and disrupting your everyday life, then you need to reach out to a medical or mental health provider for evaluation. These symptoms signal a mental health issue, and treatment and support will be incredibly beneficial. You don't have to suffer, and feeling this way does not mean you're failing at motherhood—it means you need medical attention, support, and treatment.

The chapters that follow examine how the shadow emotion of sadness shows up in motherhood. And while none of it is easy, or comfortable for that matter, here is what I want you to know as you read the following pages: You may feel alone on your journey, but you are not alone in the emotions you experience in motherhood.

chapter 3

soothing the tears

how to embrace sadness and move toward hope

Tears are the words the heart cannot express.
—Anonymous

There are so many experiences in mothering to make us tearful—
we may cry tears of joy, happiness, awe, and gratitude or tears of
frustration, stress, anger, and sadness. In this chapter, we are not
discussing tearfulness that comes from the beautiful moments
in motherhood, such as the first time your baby smiles, or says
"mama," or wraps their arms around you. The tears described here
are the ones asking us to pause, pay attention, and understand what
is going on beneath the surface, pushed down because of lack of
time, lack of support, or fear. Often behind tearfulness is sadness,
hormonal changes, stress, exhaustion, overwhelm, and frustration.
Maybe your tearfulness is a combination of all of these!

Tearfulness and crying is our body's way of releasing
tension, showing us there is something we need to pay attention
to. Tears are often the physical manifestation of releasing
emotional discomfort, such as pain, stress, frustration, worry,

sadness, anger, or concern.

Recall a time when your child was a baby and cried. When they cried, they were communicating one of their needs to you. You'd go through the decision tree of what it could be: Are they hungry? Do they need to be changed? Are they hurting? Do they need me? And if, after you went through all of the possibilities, making sure your baby was fed, dry, safe, and warm, they still cried, you likely did a few things: You held them, comforted them, handed them to someone else, or let them "cry it out." Here's what all new parents know: Babies cry, and sometimes they cry for reasons we don't know or can't understand. Babies cry to communicate something to us and the world, whether we understand their cries or not. As moms, when our baby or child cries, it can be incredibly frustrating if our efforts to console them or make it better don't work. We are left feeling helpless, not knowing what to do next. And still, we often react with compassion and warmth and do our best to soothe our child and make it better.

This level of compassion we have toward our child is the same compassion we need to focus on when we feel tearful and upset. To experience tearfulness or to cry is part of the experience of being human; it's a universal experience of vulnerability regardless of gender, age, religion, and culture. Feeling tearful is a little flag asking us to look deeper into what may be going on, what we need to do more or less of, or what we need.

Motherhood opens us up to experiencing tearfulness at a whole new level. Think back to a time before you were a mama, and ask yourself this: *"Was I ever this tearful before I was a mom?"* For me, that would be an emphatic no! Mothering is an emotional experience, an act of immersing yourself in the needs of another and the responsibility of caring for a little human you've committed to raising for at least eighteen years and are connected to for the rest of your life! When motherhood is framed this way, of course tearfulness seems natural.

As a mom to four girls, I've been tearful often, both in the past and present: every time I found out I was pregnant, at each birth, as I navigated the baby blues with each pregnancy, and even now when I'm hormonal and see pictures of my girls at younger ages, when I'm sleep deprived, or when I'm overwhelmed with parenting and work. (I'm sure you can make your own list of tearful moments too!) Take comfort, because regardless of where we are in our mothering journey, all of us mothers have experienced tearfulness in some way.

But how do you handle tearfulness? Do you acknowledge it? Do you push it down and ignore it? Do you dwell in it and get swept away by it? I want you to understand why you're tearful. I want you to embrace it, acknowledge it, and allow yourself to feel. (However, if you notice tearfulness happening often, paired with feeling sad, down, with low motivation and loss of interest in things you once enjoyed, paired with just not feeling like yourself, then what you may be experiencing could be more than a shadow emotion; it could be a symptom of a mental health issue.)

Sadness, expressing itself as tearfulness, is a shadow emotion that does not always lead to depression. Depression in motherhood is very real. But it is more than sadness. Depression is a mental health issue brought on by variations of loss, distress, grief, and untreated maternal burnout and is influenced by hormonal changes (such as fluctuations in a woman's menstrual cycle) and life stressors (such as delivering a baby and adjusting to postpartum life).

You Are Not Alone: Bri's Story

Bri scrolled on her phone as she nursed her baby girl, while her three-year-old son, Eli, played on the floor in front of her. Bri felt like most days she was going through the motions of caring for her kids—nursing felt like a chore, playing with her son was exhausting, and most days she'd watch the clock until naptime or until her partner came home. Mentally, she was grateful to have two healthy and happy kids and that she could be at home with them; but she was bored, lonely, and had a lot of guilt. She felt guilty for using the kids' naptime to scroll on social media instead of attending to all of the things she knew she could be doing and for dreading the time when her kids would wake up. Bri realized she needed more support after she dropped her phone on her baby girl's head, causing a small bruise, which in turn created in Bri a surge of sadness, a feeling of ineffectiveness, and a sense of overwhelm and guilt that turned into incredible stress.

Our work together focused on decreasing her loneliness, structuring her day with a routine of activities for herself and the children, and using naptime as a chance to restore and take care of herself with things that brought her joy and meaning. We also worked on her perfectionistic and negative self-talk through reframing and self-compassion. In addition, Bri set some personal goals to do things unrelated to the kids, like crafting and taking a dance class at night. I encouraged Bri not to dwell on what happened with her daughter but to forgive herself and to use the experience as a learning opportunity. And we came up with a plan for times when Bri felt bored or stressed, she wasn't to use social media or screen time, as it often triggered feelings of sadness, irritability, and anxiousness.

Being mindful of what you are experiencing, how often you experience it, and what you need to feel better is the first place to start when you have shadow moments. I want you to read through the suggested tips that follow to help you grow from this experience.

At the Heart of Tearfulness

At the heart of tearfulness is shifting into/embracing compassion for what you're feeling and experiencing. When you're feeling tearful, instead of judging yourself or telling yourself you shouldn't be feeling this way, be more compassionate with yourself. Acknowledge what you're experiencing, be curious about what the tearfulness is about, and take care of your emotions with the same compassion, understanding, and love you would express to your child.

Reframe Your Mantra

Thoughts are powerful. Your self-talk has a deep impact on what you feel and how you respond. Keep this principle in mind and reframe problematic thoughts that increase your shadow emotions.

SHADOW MANTRA If you're saying this . . .	THRIVING MANTRA Positively reframe to say this . . .
The smallest things make me cry. I've been teary most of the day. What's wrong with me?	Tears are one way to express stress, fatigue, sadness, and pain. While I may not know why I'm feeling this way, it's acceptable to feel this. Nothing is wrong with me. It's okay to explore what else may be going on right now that may be making me tearful.

SHADOW MANTRA If you're saying this . . .	THRIVING MANTRA Positively reframe to say this . . .
I cry all the time! I don't feel sad or upset. This isn't like me. I wish it would stop.	My tears are showing me I need to pay attention to my physical and emotional health. Maybe the reason I feel so tearful is because I need to increase my self-care, take care of myself, and explore what's going on. What has been missing in my self-care routine?
If I stop and think about it, I'm going to cry.	What I need most right now is to allow myself to feel what I'm experiencing. If now isn't the best time to cry, I need to create a space soon that allows me to express myself.
I'm crying for no reason. I get so emotional over anything and everything.	There's always a reason for crying: tension release, fatigue, sadness, hormonal issues. Taking time to understand what is going on and what is stressful to me is important. I need to be compassionate and caring toward myself instead of judging my feelings or dismissing them.

Moving Beyond the Shadows

TIP #1: ASK QUESTIONS TO CREATE SELF-AWARENESS.

When it comes to our emotional experiences, giving ourselves the space to understand what is going on helps us move from discomfort to awareness and gives us solutions to foster a state of contentment, harmony, and peace. Begin by asking yourself the following questions.

- **Is there a reason why I'm tearful?** Do I have a specific reason for feeling tearful and crying? Am I tearful because of a situation, event, or circumstance?

- **Am I tearful because of fatigue?** Have I been losing sleep or not sleeping well, and could I be feeling this way because I'm exhausted? Has my sleep deprivation resulted in my being more tearful, with limited energy to do things or solve problems compared to when I am rested? Is there a reason for my fatigue? Could there be an issue with how I'm taking care of myself—am I getting adequate sleep, nutrition, hydration, and exercise?

- **Am I tearful because of stress?** Am I feeling this way because I've been so stressed out? Do I have too much to deal with? Too little time and help? Is there a situation that has been causing stress in my life?

- **Am I tearful because I'm relieved?** Am I feeling tearful because I've made it through a stressful time? Now that I finally feel better, am I letting it out and feeling a lot of things that I was pushing down? Was my daily life in such a state of stress that I'm more tearful out of relief that things are settling down?

- **Am I tearful because I'm hormonal?** Am I tearful because of hormonal issues like PMS (premenstrual syndrome) or PMDD (premenstrual dysphoric disorder)? Is my period right around the corner? Am I feeling tearful because I recently had a baby or recently changed or stopped my nursing routine? Is it possible I'm going through perimenopause?

- **Am I tearful because of mental health concerns?** Could my tearfulness indicate a larger problem, such as depression or anxiety? (See the next tip to check whether your tearfulness may be a signal of a bigger issue.)

TIP #2: NOTICE THE TRENDS.

A key skill for thriving in motherhood is being able to notice the patterns and situations that take you out of balance or disrupt your daily life. There's nothing problematic about being tearful every now and then. However, tearfulness that happens frequently or every day for a few weeks or more, for no apparent reason, *and* causes distress is something to pay attention to. And if tearfulness is paired with trouble concentrating; a feeling of constant exhaustion; persistent feelings of guilt, sadness, or hopelessness; sleep issues; and/or appetite changes, please reach out to a medical or mental health provider for evaluation, as this can be depression or another health issue.

TIP #3: HOW IS YOUR SELF-CARE?

As mamas, we can focus on productivity, doing everything for everyone at the cost of taking care of ourselves. When you're feeling tearful, it's good to check in and ask yourself: *How are my self-care skills recently?* Remember, the foundation of well-being is physical self-care (sleep, nutrition, exercise, and hydration). But have you been taking the time to do activities you enjoy, which creates a sense of happiness, fulfillment, and restoration (for example, eating a meal and actually focusing on the food in a mindful way, listening to your favorite music or an encouraging podcast while you nurse your baby, or taking a walk in nature)? If you haven't been taking care of yourself and having fun, chances are that if you start adding healthy habits and enjoyable activities to your routine, you may find your tearfulness decreases or goes away altogether.

TIP #4: WHEN WAS THE LAST TIME YOU HAD A PHYSICAL?

So many changes happen to our bodies as we get older and when we have children. If you've been crying or feeling tearful more than usual (or more than makes sense to you, meaning there's no reason or explanation to it), make an appointment with your primary care doctor or OB/GYN and discuss with them what you are going through. Hormonal imbalances, nutritional and vitamin deficiencies (like a lack of vitamin D, vitamin B$_{12}$, and iron), and medical conditions (such as a thyroid imbalance, Lyme disease and diabetes) can all impact your overall health and well-being. Remember, when an emotional response shows up and stays around for a while, it's important to pay attention to it!

TIP #5: GIVE YOURSELF PERMISSION TO FEEL AND EXPRESS YOURSELF.

When you can point to a reason or you have an understanding of why you've been tearful, take a deep breath and allow yourself to feel. Remember, no feeling is bad. The shadow emotion of tearfulness is your body and mind's way of asking you to pay attention to something—to stop and take a moment to allow yourself to feel. And when you do, embrace what you're feeling. Don't push it away. Remember what happens when we dismiss, ignore, or try to push away a feeling? It comes out stronger and in unexpected ways, forcing us to pay attention to what we're experiencing. So when you feel tearful or begin to cry, take a deep breath in, hold it, and release it through exhaling. Acknowledge and honor your feelings by saying, *"It's okay that I'm crying. I need to feel this and just be. I don't need to fix this feeling or push it away. I just need to sit with this feeling of tearfulness."* And when you feel ready, you can try some of the remaining tips in this section—but only when you're ready.

TIP #6: REACH OUT FOR SUPPORT.

When we're feeling tearful or going through a tough time, one of the best things we can do is to reach out to supportive friends, family, or a therapist. Letting caring and supportive people know what you're going through is one way to move from discomfort and suffering to connecting and thriving. Think back to the earlier example of a baby crying—we naturally go to the baby and pick them up in an effort to comfort. As adults, we need comfort too. And while it may not come in the form of someone being right there to take care of us and know what we need, reaching out and letting supportive people in our life understand what we're going though is an attempt at comfort, which creates connection. And know that if you're nearby someone who loves and supports you, ask for a hug. Sometimes the smallest gestures can make the biggest impact as a step towards feeling better.

Thriving Mama Reflection

Tearfulness and feeling sad are the ways our body communicates that the heart and mind need attention and care. These shadow emotions can be uncomfortable, causing us to react with avoidance, dismissal, or concern. When your child gets hurt, has a concern, or is crying, you respond by offering comfort and reassurances. You embrace them until they're soothed and in a calmer state. Which is why the simple act of meeting your child where they are and just being there is sometimes all that is needed for them to feel better. You are no different than your child. Acknowledging what you are feeling, allowing tears to flow if needed, and responding to yourself with compassion and kindness is a courageous act of self-care.

there's no manual in motherhood

ways to handle feeling ineffective and defeated and increase your confidence

A person who never made a mistake never tried anything new.
—Albert Einstein

When you became a mother, did you wonder, *How is it possible I'm responsible for this little human, who doesn't come with a handbook or instruction manual?* Mothering is like not knowing how to swim, being thrown into the deep end of the pool and asked to figure it out. So much of motherhood is simply keeping our heads above water. Becoming a mother is stepping into the great unknown, learning as you go, teaching yourself how to parent. This learn-as-you-go scenario creates fertile ground to feel ineffective—a lot!

What contributes to mothers feeling ineffective is the mental load of motherhood. Moms have so much pressure on their shoulders; they act as the timekeeper, schedule maker, chauffeur, home chef, and organizer, all while raising and nurturing a child. With all of this pressure, there are lots of opportunities to have well-intentioned plans and goals crumble due to lack of cooperation, efficiency, organization, or knowledge of a needed parenting skill. And the emotional response to this chaos is feeling ineffective; and if left unmanaged, this feeling of ineffectiveness can develop into its more intense cousins, defeat and helplessness.

A common stressful scenario in motherhood is bedtime. Let's say that one night your child begins challenging bedtime; they refuse to get dressed, use the potty, or brush their teeth. Night after night, you dread bedtime, because your efforts feel ineffective. As a result, your self-confidence in your parenting diminishes, and you're left feeling insecure, frustrated, irritable, overwhelmed, and sad about the situation. Being able to identify moments of feeling ineffective is important because in doing so, you can pause, assess the situation to determine what's working and what needs to be changed, and put a plan in place to manage these feelings. In turn, being aware of what you feel is an act of self-care, which can help prevent this feeling from progressing to defeat and helplessness.

When feelings of ineffectiveness are not managed, when they become more pervasive and frequent, defeat is the emotional response. Defeat in motherhood is more than when your intentions, goals, and behaviors don't have the outcomes you want or expect. Defeat is a super stressful emotional response teetering on the edge of distress—you may want to give up and not try anymore because you feel your efforts are wasted. Moments of defeat in motherhood can include the following:

- Cleaning and organizing your child's toys, only to have your hard work completely disorganized moments later.

- Going shopping and letting your child pick out new clothes, only to have them refuse to wear anything they picked out once you're home.

- Making a wonderful chicken dinner, only to hear from your teenager that they have decided to become a vegetarian while your six-year-old is having a meltdown because the chicken and rice are "touching" each other.

All of these situations can leave a mother thinking, *Why did I even try?* That is a core mental thought when we're feeling defeated.

We plan things with the best of intentions for our children. We can see the path ahead that our child may not, whether for an outing (e.g., putting on sunscreen or wearing a coat), a routine (eating healthy foods or keeping a bedtime routine to feel rested), or life skill (doing homework or being able to clean up after oneself). But when children don't cooperate or when they defy our requests, we perceive we lost a battle we didn't even know we were in. Feeling defeat every now and then is part of motherhood; the concern is when this shadow emotion becomes a pervasive pattern.

Feeling defeat over and over again for a prolonged period of time can result in our losing confidence in our parenting skills, giving up on the hope that things will ever get better, and being afraid of what the future holds for our child. But when we make choices to learn from defeat and problem-solve in healthy ways, we take one more step forward on the path to thriving in motherhood. It's okay to experience the feeling of defeat, but do not feel defeated with yourself, your child, or motherhood.

You Are Not Alone: Lena's Story

Lena dreaded 5:00 p.m., since this was the time she would be responsible for her son Ian. Lena worked from home and a sitter picked up Ian (age eight) and his sister, Beatrice (age ten), every day from school, and took them to after-school activities. Lena loved both of her children, but she felt incredibly ineffective with Ian. He was a completely different person than Beatrice: high-energy, strong-willed, constantly needing to be entertained or engaged in an activity, and unable to play independently.

Lena came to me for support because she felt ineffective as Ian's mom; he rarely listened to her and bedtime battles were lasting for hours at night. Our work first focused on normalizing how challenging parenting can be, especially when one parenting style works great with one child but not another. As I explored Lena's family structure and routine, what became clear was that Lena was lacking consistency in her parenting responses, which created confusion for what Ian was to expect as well as inconsistent consequences for not cooperating. When Lena became overwhelmed, she gave in to Ian's demands or yelled at him to get him to pay attention and comply with the routine. Adding to the mix, Lena's partner traveled a lot, making her the sole parent to handle Ian's behaviors during the week.

Our work focused on adding peaceful parenting skills to Lena's approach paired with establishing clear expectations and consequences when Ian did not follow family rules. Lena also added one-on-one time for her and Ian to experience connection and positive time together. After several months, the changes Lena made to her family routine helped improve her connection with Ian and decreased her feelings of ineffectiveness.

This is just a moment, a stretch of time that is challenging. Don't make it bigger than it is!

If feelings of defeat are not managed—if they become frequent, persistent, and pervasive to most situations in mothering—this feeling can develop into severe helplessness. A mother who feels helpless does not believe in her abilities and skills. She does not believe that her behaviors will have any impact. Chronic feelings of helplessness, with beliefs that nothing we do matters, raise a red flag (if you are experiencing this combination, get support from family and mental health professionals, as pervasive helpless feelings signal a deeper mental health issue that needs attention).

Mothers have the biggest hearts with which to forgive, in addition to well-springs of energy: As mothers, we continue to give to our family even when we have nothing left. Somehow we find the energy to love and provide for our children through the most difficult, exhausting, and terrifying moments of motherhood. So when we feel any variety of these shadow emotions (ineffectiveness, defeat, helplessness), it means we are going through a lot and need a break to increase our self-care, to reset and restore our energy, and to receive additional support from our family.

At the Heart of Feeling Ineffective, Defeated, and Helpless

At the heart of the shadow emotions of ineffectiveness, defeat, and helplessness is sadness, frustration, and disappointment about an outcome that we did not expect or about efforts that failed to produce our desired result. From the outside, these feelings may look like varied forms of giving up. In reality, a current of doubt flows below the surface as we wonder if we have what it takes to be a good mother, fearing we're somehow failing at mothering. Here's the reality: *There are many moments of feeling defeated in motherhood, and very often, it has nothing to do with us. It just is.* I want you to read that again: *Very often (more often than you would think) a stressful and challenging situation with your child has nothing to do with you—it just is.*

Instead of keeping this reality in mind, though, we often take our child's behavior personally, believing our child initiated a battle specifically to defy, harm, or upset us over the simplest requests (for example, to clean up, put on their shoes, or do homework), when in actuality, our child is likely going through a developmental phase impacting their social, emotional, and cognitive behaviors. Or our child may be upset with something that happened at school or with a friend and isn't ready to share it yet, so rejecting dinner is easier than expressing their pain. The details beneath the surface are why it's essential for moms to develop *curiosity* about their child's behavior instead of taking the behavior personally. Children communicate through behavior what is difficult or impossible to put into words or even understand. And when moms become *detectives*, looking for alternative explanations for a pattern of behavior, instead of believing they are failing as mothers or that their child is being disrespectful, a whole new way of connecting with compassion happens between mom and child.

Reframe Your Mantra

Thoughts are powerful. Your self-talk (the things you say to yourself) has a deep impact on what you feel and how you respond. Keep this principle in mind and reframe problematic thoughts that increase your shadow emotions.

SHADOW MANTRA If you're saying this . . .	THRIVING MANTRA Positively reframe to say this . . .
I give up! I can't do it anymore.	Things didn't turn out the way I wanted, but my intentions were good. I need to pause, regroup, and increase my self-care. When I'm in a calmer mental space, I will be able to find ways to work through this.
Why bother? There's no point in trying.	I'm going to have these reactions from time to time. I can look at what I may need to do differently. With some rest, healthy distraction, and self-care, I'll feel better. I need to not be so harsh with myself.
It will always be this way no matter what I do.	While life feels hard right now, there's no evidence it will always be this way. What is the one thing I can do right now to take care of myself and move into a more positive frame of mind?
I failed again. What's the point in trying?	Using words like *fail* is going to make me feel stuck. I can learn from this situation and take what I learn to do something different next time. I need to focus on my future efforts and be more encouraging to myself.

Moving Beyond the Shadows

TIP #1: ASK QUESTIONS TO CREATE SELF-AWARENESS.

These shadow emotions of ineffectiveness, defeat, and helplessness are uncomfortable. Be compassionate with yourself and acknowledge that these feelings are tough. Shift into a mindset of curiosity. Try to figure out what's going on right now.

Begin by asking yourself the following questions:

- Do I feel defeated often? Is this something that happens every now and then, or is this a pattern I experience frequently?

- What developmental stage is my child in? Have I overlooked something related to their emotional, social, cognitive, and physical development stage and age?

- Is this emotional reaction related to the situation, or is something else in my life contributing to how I react? Am I taking things too personally in this situation? What can I do to find out what is going on beneath the surface for me and my child?

- How do my thoughts or beliefs contribute to feeling defeated? Do I often think, *Everything should go smoothly all the time*, or, *My child should listen to me all the time*? Are my thoughts and beliefs centered on perfectionism, or are other beliefs contributing to this reaction?

TIP #2: TRY PERSPECTIVE-TAKING.

Perspective-taking is an important skill to learn if we are to thrive in motherhood. The past is just that—in the past. And the future hasn't happened yet. All you have right now is the moment you're in *right now*. Just breathe into that thought! Take some pressure off yourself and begin by asking yourself, "Will this matter tomorrow? Next week? In a month?"

If you can say, "No, it won't matter," then it's time to learn from this moment and let it go. If it's hard to let it go and move on through perspective-taking or distraction, then review the following tips.

TIP #3: NOTICE AND MANAGE YOUR THOUGHTS.

Our feelings can be a lot like a fire, perhaps a campfire or fire pit on a chilly day. Fire provides protection, warmth, and the ability to do things throughout our day. Keeping with this metaphor, if our feelings are the fire, then our thoughts are like fuel: If we don't add fuel to the fire, it decreases in intensity. If we add fuel, it keeps burning. Or, if we spray it with lighter fluid, it may even rage out of control!

Let's apply the campfire metaphor to a scenario. Imagine you have a very challenging outing with your child while at the supermarket. There's barely any food in your house, and you need a few basics, such as fruit, cereal, and milk. It's almost time for lunch, and you realize you're pushing the clock by shopping now because your toddler's naptime is in thirty minutes. Halfway through the shopping trip, your toddler has a meltdown. Frustration begins to rise as you swiftly make your way to the checkout. While your child screams in the cart, you reach into your bag and realize you forgot your wallet. Your mind starts to race: *You've got to be kidding me! Why did I even bother? I didn't need this today. I just need things to run smoothly.*

Let's examine two possible paths to take in this scenario, one in which the thoughts fuel and intensify the feeling and another where the feeling is reduced by balanced thoughts and positive reframing.

Scenario #1: *You leave the groceries in your cart and carry your screaming and wriggling toddler out of the store. You feel a surge of frustration and defeat as you struggle to put your child in their car seat. Once you're in the driver's seat, your keys in the ignition, you sigh and grip the steering wheel, your eyes closed. Negative self-talk starts inundating your mind: I'm so disorganized. If only I were like other moms. Yet another example of how I'm failing. What was I thinking, shopping so close to naptime? I did* *this to myself. I'm so embarrassed. The clerk looked so annoyed. She probably was thinking, "This mother is a hot mess. That poor child." I have no one to blame but myself.*

Scenario #2: *Leaving the market, you feel frustration and defeat. As you turn on the car and grip the steering wheel, you take a deep breath and close your eyes. You begin to have some negative thoughts. You're a disorganized mess. What were you thinking? Then you pause and correct your thoughts, shifting to more compassionate self-talk. Wait a minute, that's kinda harsh. Would I speak to a friend that way if she called me for support? No. I shouldn't be so hard on myself. I'm not the most organized person, but this was unexpected and hard. I pushed grocery shopping today so close to naptime. Next time, I need to go out earlier and work around lunch and naptime. This is one of those moments in motherhood where I can learn from what went wrong and improve it next time. I feel so embarrassed having to leave the market without paying, and I can only imagine what people thought. But I know that if they have kids, they've probably gone through something like this. I need to learn from it and move on. This moment doesn't define me—it's just one of those days.*

The second scenario demonstrates that being aware of how our thoughts can intensify our feelings can improve how we respond to a moment of defeat.

TIP #4: GO FOR A WALK OR EXERCISE.
Shadow moments of feeling defeated can negatively impact your mood and how you feel for the rest of the day. While it may not be easy to find the time, even taking fifteen minutes to do some

kind of physical activity can boost your mood and reduce tension. Exercise gives us a boost of endorphins, which increase creativity and decrease stress, and is a great self-care skill to manage emotions. When you're in the moment of feeling defeated or shortly thereafter, go for a walk or do some yoga poses—try any activity that gets you moving. You may notice a little physical activity releases the stress you've been holding from the situation and allows you to take a new perspective and approach on how to work through this problem.

TIP #5: FIND THE LESSON IN EVERY DEFEAT.

Every moment of defeat creates an opportunity to learn something. Have you heard the phrase *Monday morning quarterbacking*? This phrase describes a person who analyzes and reviews the mistakes made in the previous day's football game. When you feel defeat, after you have spent some time in self-care and have calmed down, I want you to do a little mothering review: What went wrong, and what could you have done differently?

Ask yourself the following questions:

- What can I learn from this?
- Is there something I could have done differently?
- Knowing what I know now, what would I do differently?
- Do I need to be more consistent?
- Can I be more disciplined with follow-through?
- Do I need to change something in our family's schedule or routine?
- Do I need to learn more about a specific topic to help the situation (e.g., read a parenting book on child development

or on teenagers)?

If you truly can't see or find something you could have done differently, I want you to do two things: First, share the difficult scenario with a *supportive* person. (The most important word here is *supportive*. Tell someone who is truly understanding and who won't criticize you.) Ask this person for their perspective. Ask them what they would do. Second, if you can't see the lesson in this defeat or know what could have been different or improved, then I want you to move on from what has happened, and perhaps at another time, you'll understand this situation differently.

TIP #6: MAKE A PLAN.

After you've reflected on the situation, make note of what you could've done differently. In the supermarket example, maybe the plan would be as simple as going to the market first thing in the morning (double-checking to make sure you have your wallet) and arriving home forty-five minutes before naptime. Learning from tough situations and creating a plan to do something different is a great way to move forward. Remember, give yourself grace. Even if you didn't necessarily plan the best the first time around, it's okay. You now have some data to use to help you plan better for next time.

Thriving Mama Reflection

Motherhood can be a minefield of mini battles. Some can be anticipated, and others, despite our best efforts or intentions, result in outcomes that we'd rather avoid. Feeling the shadow emotions of ineffectiveness, defeat, and helplessness is part of the landscape of mothering. In these moments, don't judge yourself harshly. Take responsibility for your part and try to understand another person's perspective and contribution to the situation. Hold off on blaming yourself or others as it takes away a chance to learn from the situation and how things could be improved.

Mothers, just like children (or anyone else for that matter), are works in progress. Remember that in these shadow moments, you have strengths, even if you feel down. Take a few minutes and write down five of your strengths. Make five copies of the list. Then, think of the five places you go most frequently in a day. Start with the first place you go every morning and tape one copy there. Perhaps it's the bathroom mirror or the nightstand in your bedroom. Then place one copy in four more places where you go multiple times a day—maybe the visor or dashboard of your car, the fridge, or your computer. Highlighting your strengths is a self-care act of compassion.

running on empty

how feeling exhausted and burned-out creates opportunities to grow

Maybe we feel empty because we leave pieces of ourselves in all the things we used to love.
—R. M. Drake

The shadow emotions of emptiness, exhaustion, and burnout all have in common the emotional, physical, mental, and spiritual depletion of resources and energy. Of course, it's understandable why these emotional reactions happen in motherhood; mothers rarely get a day off! Regardless of feeling awful from migraines, period cramps or postpartum recovery, headaches, cold and flu, injuries, sleep deprivation, or overwhelm, a mama will still do what it takes to care for her family, even with the obstacles. Maybe not at full capacity, but somehow she'll find a way.

Exhaustion, whether physical or emotional, is part of the landscape of motherhood. What mom isn't *exhausted?* Exhaustion in mothering happens as a result of the amount of time and energy needed to care for and raise a child, not having enough support, not making time for self-care, dealing with stressful life events, overfocusing on productivity without a lot of fun, and going through a tough parenting phase with your child.

However, prolonged physical and emotional exhaustion creates distress and, without intervention, this type of stress becomes detrimental to your health, making you as a mother vulnerable to burnout, depression, and anxiety (not to mention weakening your immune system and creating vulnerability for illness).

As I've supported moms for over two decades, I've found that knowing the signs, symptoms, and severity of these shadow emotions and then creating a plan of support and intervention is a relief and comfort to mothers. So many moms suffer in silence, believing something is wrong with them or that they're not good at mothering when in fact none of this is true! Instead, these mothers' symptoms are in response to *real* and valid physical and emotional issues—intervention, support, and solutions for these issues are not only available, but they are also needed to get moms back on the path to thriving and enjoying their lives and children.

Signs and Symptoms of Physical Exhaustion

- Feeling tired, regardless of getting sleep
- Craving high-fat, sugary, processed foods for energy or comfort
- Clenching teeth
- Reduced productivity
- Changes in appetite
- Headaches
- Upset stomach
- Fatigue
- Reduced stamina and endurance

Signs and Symptoms of Mental Exhaustion

- Feeling nervous and/or irritable
- Feeling mentally foggy
- Problems concentrating
- Tearfulness
- Lack of energy
- Difficulty making decisions

Signs and Symptoms of Burnout

- Irritability
- Exhaustion
- Low productivity (not being able to complete responsibilities and tasks, such as caring for yourself, your children, your partner/spouse, and volunteer and/or work responsibilities)
- Problems sleeping
- Reduced enjoyment of your children
- Teeth grinding or jaw clenching and/or jaw pain
- Negative attitudes (about oneself and/or others)
- Lack of motivation
- Decline in job performance
- Sense of detachment and feeling disconnected to those you are caring for
- Cynical or sarcastic interactions with your child, family, and others
- Lack of interest in activities you once enjoyed

If these symptoms persist and are paired with tearfulness, appetite changes, sadness, hopelessness, and passive thoughts of escaping your life (e.g., wanting to go to sleep and never wake up or wishing something harmful would happen to you to take away what you're experiencing), or more active thoughts of self-harm (e.g., wanting to end your life), then you need to reach out to a medical or mental health professional for support and evaluation, as these additional symptoms indicate a mental health issue that requires intervention.

If you'd like to find out whether you're a burned-out mom and learn skills and strategies to reduce burnout, you can go to MomsWellBeing.com and take the quiz entitled "Are You a Burned Out Mom?"

These shadow emotions are not always in reaction to physically feeling awful and depleted; they can be reactions to emotional and psychological stress as well as changes and transitions in motherhood. Many mothers experience feelings of emptiness, loss of purpose and meaning, or sadness with role changes and changes in the intensity and strenuous pace of mothering; for example, when moms return to work after maternity leave, when a child goes to daycare or school all day, or when a child goes to college and transitions to independent living. Feelings of emptiness can also occur without an identifiable reason or situation (this often indicates a mental health issue such as depression).

Feelings of emptiness, exhaustion, and burnout at any level in motherhood can be challenging. The good news here is that you're not alone—many mothers face these shadow emotions throughout their motherhood journey. Sometimes just being able to understand what you're going through and knowing you're not alone helps increase self-compassion.

At the Heart of Feeling Empty, Exhausted, and Burned-Out

At the heart of these shadow emotions is a need to feel better—whether in your body, mind, or soul—and a desire to get back to a place of thriving. But often beneath the surface of these feelings are beliefs and behaviors supporting a productivity mindset, such as a propensity for doing everything for everyone without adequate support, difficulty setting limits and drawing boundaries, and pursuing limited self-care. At the heart of this pattern can be a belief that giving to others all the time is what a mother "should" do, which may lead to the belief that mothering is akin to being a martyr. A mom may believe that she *must* place everyone and everything ahead of her well-being.

There's no denying that motherhood takes an enormous amount of energy. However, what we mothers can do is create awareness and be responsive when these shadow emotions show up. We can take steps to intervene when symptoms are moving from the expected exhaustion and depletion (e.g., the exhaustion we feel after caring for a feverish child all night) to detrimental depletion (e.g., the compassion fatigue we may feel after months of caring for our child), which could lead to impairment (e.g., the inability to properly care for ourselves and our families).

At the heart of feeling emptiness due to a loss or change (say, in a particular phase of mothering or life transition) is sadness, fear, and uncertainty of the unknown. Embracing change is not always easy to do; recognizing that endings open to new beginnings can be difficult. New opportunities after loss can introduce both excitement *and* uncertainty. If we think of the future through the lens of what has been lost, an opportunity to grow is blocked. But if we can see feelings of emptiness as a call

79

You Are Not Alone: Sydney's Story

The first thing Sydney did when she woke up in the morning was reach for a pain reliever. She had been grinding her teeth again, a habit that came out during times of stress. I began working with Sydney when her primary care physician referred her to me for stress management. Sydney worked part-time and had three children, ages eight, five, and three. She was feeling overwhelmed with the amount of responsibility she carried: caring for her children, completing the chores, cooking the meals, driving in the carpool, and seeing to the kids' bedtime routine on top of working. She had a belief that because she wasn't working full-time, it was her "job" to do everything, which was sending her exhaustion off the charts, not to mention creating resentment toward her husband for not doing more to help with these responsibilities.

My work with Sydney started with increasing her self-care, which came in the form of setting boundaries (e.g., not saying yes to everyone, especially when she didn't have time), delegating evening routines to her husband, and taking at least two hours on the weekends to do something not related to chores, kids, or taking care of someone. Sydney filled this time with walking on the beach, reading a book in a coffee shop, or meeting up with friends.

After a few months, Sydney's teeth grinding subsided. Sydney used her jaw pain and teeth grinding as a sign to stop, pay attention to her stress levels, and examine where in her life she had been giving too much, which helped cue a realization that she needed to set limits, delegate responsibility, and increase the joy and fun in her life.

to action, if we can become aware of what needs to change or be redefined, a shift occurs. We can see the change as two separate adventures: the closing of one phase and the beginning of another. Each experience stands on its own but can be understood as being influenced and impacted by the other—in other words, a new beginning isn't possible without an ending. We can enjoy a sense of hope in the possibilities that lie before us instead of focusing solely on the loss. Shifting into this mindset opens us up to appreciating past experiences while opening our arms to welcome the adventures and personal growth—uncertain though they may be—that are possible in the future.

Reframe Your Mantra

Thoughts are powerful. Your self-talk (the things you say to yourself) has a deep impact on what you feel and how you respond. Keep this principle in mind and reframe problematic thoughts that increase your shadow emotions.

SHADOW MANTRA If you're saying this . . .	THRIVING MANTRA Positively reframe to say this . . .
I feel awful. I don't see how this will ever change.	Believing I'm powerless will keep me stuck and make me feel worse. If a friend came to me and was feeling this way, what advice would I recommend? What's the one thing I can do now to feel better?
I really want to feel better.	Wishing that I felt better won't make a change. What are the action steps I can take to feel better?

(continued)

SHADOW MANTRA If you're saying this . . .	THRIVING MANTRA Positively reframe to say this . . .
I have nothing left to give.	I've been giving so much to everyone and everything that I feel empty and depleted. I need to pause and take care of myself. What is the one action I can take that would make me feel better?
I need a break from everything, but I can't take a break.	When I have these thoughts, I need to make a plan to rest. I'm not able to take a break from everything, but thinking this way shows me I've been doing too much at the expense of my health and well-being. If I keep going like this, I'll feel worse and I could get sick.
I don't know what my purpose is anymore. I feel so uncertain.	I'm feeling sadness and loss. There is some uncertainty about what my purpose will be. Transitions and changes are hard. I'm uncertain about the future. If a loved one was experiencing this, what would I say to them? Perhaps the advice I would give a friend is what I myself need to know right now.
I'm so exhausted, I could sleep for days. It's exhausting taking care of everyone. I can't think straight, I'm so tired.	Being a mother is exhausting. I'm not alone in this—many mothers feel this exact way. Reaching out to a caring mom friend and getting some support would really help me.

Moving Beyond the Shadows

TIP #1: KNOW YOUR BASELINE.

In motherhood, you likely have an emotional baseline and a range of what feels most like the "normal" you compare to when you are stressed or ill. Knowing your emotional baseline is important. On a scale of one to ten—ten feeling the best and one feeling horrible—

what is the range where you can function and feel most comfortable, content, productive, and connected to others—in other words, most like you? Is your baseline between four and seven? Knowing your range is important, because when you begin to dip below your range, it means your stress levels are increasing and subsequently taking you away from a state of well-being. The more self-care skills and strategies you can learn and the more you can set limits, delegate responsibilities, and reach out for support when you notice this dip, the more you will be able to skillfully manage stress, reset, and move back into your thriving baseline range.

Smartphones are a great metaphor for motherhood: Smartphones have automatic pop-up reminders to notify you when the battery is getting low and you need to recharge. Feeling empty, exhausted, and burned-out is our emotional pop-up notification. These shadow emotions tell us that it's time to pay attention, that our energy is getting low, and that we need to rest and recharge.

TIP #2: ASK QUESTIONS TO CREATE SELF-AWARENESS.
When you use phrases like, *I feel awful, I'm exhausted and am going through the motions*, or *I'm so burned-out*, let this be a signal that it's time to figure out why you're feeling this way. Be specific about what's making you feel physically, emotionally, or mentally depleted.

- What have I been doing, or not doing, to take care of my physical health? Am I getting enough sleep? Have I been eating healthy and drinking enough water? Have I been getting enough exercise and activity?

- Am I feeling a need to be alone? When was the last time I was alone? How does not having time alone impact my mood, my energy, and how I interact with my family or other people?

- What is contributing to my emotional exhaustion? Have I been critical, angry, or judgmental toward myself and others? Have I been feeling sad, overwhelmed, and stressed? Have I been managing my feelings? Would starting (or resuming) counseling help me right now?

- Is there a reason why I'm feeling mentally depleted? Am I distracted? Worried? Disorganized and not thinking clearly? Am I taking care of my physical health by getting enough rest, sleep, and nutrition? Is my mental fogginess, impaired judgment, impulsivity, or disorganization because of stress, lack of sleep, drinking too much alcohol or using substances, or not taking prescription medication as directed?

- What is contributing to my feeling burned-out with mothering? Am I feeling emotionally and physically exhausted from caregiving? How long has this been going on? What do I need to feel better?

- Am I feeling empty and sad due to a life transition? What change can I identify in my life or in my mothering? Is there something I can look forward to and embrace as I face this new beginning and phase?

TIP #3: SET SOME GOALS.

Now that you've created some awareness about what's contributing to the shadow emotions you're dealing with, it's time to move back into thriving.

Start by writing down the three to five triggers or situations contributing to your physical, emotional, or mental exhaustion and depletion.

Next, rank the triggers and situations in order of stress and disruption to your life. What is the number one stressor on this list?

Then, write down a couple of solutions for each of these situations. Goals need to be specific and the steps to achieve the goal need to be clear and measurable. What are the actions you can take to feel better and work toward your goal? What is missing that needs to be added to your routine? What may need to be taken out of your routine that has been toxic or stressful and has been contributing to your exhaustion? Do you need to create stronger boundaries and limits (especially regarding what people ask of you)? Do you need more support or to delegate some of your responsibilities to feel better? Write down as much as you can about what you need.

Looking at your list, identify the area in which you are able to make changes and improvements first. Pick one issue and work on the solutions for the next week to see if you can reduce your level of exhaustion. If you're stuck and can't seem to think of goals, reach out to a supportive person in your life or a therapist and brainstorm some ideas.

Let's look at an example of a goal and some action steps. When you're managing exhaustion and burnout, a good initial goal to set is to intentionally set aside alone time every week to regroup and restore.

Step 1: Specify what I need. Is it to go to the market alone? Take a spin class once a week? Sleep in late and have my sweetie be in charge? I will write down three to five things I'd love to do to take care of myself on a weekly basis.

Step 2: Share with my sweetie what I'm feeling—fatigue, overwhelm, and irritability. Be specific about what they can do. Ask for what I need: more time alone and sharing the childcare and chores. I will share my goal for both of us to be caring and supportive of time alone for self-care.

Step 3: Schedule these self-care activities. I will make time alone a weekly priority and schedule it in my planner.

TIP #4: INCREASE SELF-CARE, EVEN IN SMALL WAYS.

A critical action step to thriving in motherhood is to increase our self-care. I often hear parents say there is no time in their busy life of caring for their children to make time for self-care. A mindset like this is problematic. If we wait to take care of ourselves until we are forced to, we can set up a cycle in which we run ourselves into the ground, only stopping when we are forced (such as when we get sick, suffer an injury, or experience severe emotional distress).

Set a small goal of taking fifteen to thirty minutes a day for the self-care practices that are meaningful to you. Limit sedentary and inactive coping strategies you may use to avoid or escape, such as sleeping too much, spending time watching TV or other screens, and scrolling through social media or playing games as well as excessive eating, shopping, or drinking. Engaging in these behaviors may alleviate stress *briefly* but will not sustain balance, joy, and well-being. Avoiding shadow emotions delays you from taking care of your emotional health; eventually, you'll be forced to deal with these feelings. Exercise is one of the best forms of self-care, which even in small amounts can shift your mood and increase your energy by boosting endorphins, improving circulation, revving up your metabolism, and releasing tension.

TIP #5: REDISCOVER INTERESTS THAT YOU ENJOY.

One way to transition out of feeling these shadow emotions is to add behaviors and activities that bring positive emotions such as joy, confidence, and calm. Take a few minutes to reflect on what you used to enjoy doing but haven't had the time to do lately. Then list all of the activities and interests you enjoy or would like to try, taking into account your time, resources, and capability. Start with one of your ideas and schedule a time to make it happen. Even small steps can add up to make a noticeable difference.

TIP #6: LEARN TO SAY NO AND ASK FOR SUPPORT.

If you notice a pattern of exhaustion and depletion in your life, please—*please*—learn to say no to a few things. When you're run-down, adding more responsibilities to your to-do list is a recipe for disaster. Take a break from what you can and say no to overcommitting yourself. Respite from commitments doesn't mean you have to stop saying *yes* forever. It just means now is a good time to care for yourself. And be sure to tell others what you need. Don't be afraid to delegate and let go of your high standards—done is better than perfect, and we all know perfect is impossible!

TIP #7: STILL CAN'T PINPOINT YOUR EXHAUSTION?

If you're unable to pinpoint why you're experiencing the shadow emotions of emptiness, exhaustion, and burnout, visit with your doctor. For example, if you've been feeling exhausted *and* have been taking care of yourself, it's time to make an appointment for medical evaluation. Your exhaustion may stem from a physical issue or condition. In my practice, I work mostly with women, and I've discovered that some common physical reasons for exhaustion include thyroid disease, iron deficiency, vitamin D deficiency, and depression. So make an appointment with your primary care physician or OB/GYN for evaluation and support.

Thriving Mama Reflection

Feeling empty, exhausted, and burned-out is the ultimate call to action to take care of ourselves—to pause, assess, rest, and restore. While this can be challenging as a mom, here's what I want you to consider:

- If you can't take a break from your duties and responsibilities, pause at least once every hour and regulate your breathing.

- If you don't have anyone to help you, lower your standards a bit. Remember, *done* is better than *perfect*. And some things that you think need to be done now (such as cleaning or laundry) can really wait until later, when you have more time or support.

- If you have to keep going, then reduce multitasking. It only creates more stress, increasing the chances of making errors and feeling worse.

- If you talk to yourself in a critical voice, change your tone and reframe to be more compassionate.

Give yourself permission to take care of yourself. You're human, and your sole purpose is not to constantly be productive and "doing" for others. Feeling the shadow emotions of emptiness, exhaustion, and burnout is a call to pay attention and replenish yourself for the unbelievable acts of love you give to your family by giving small gestures of love and care to yourself.

chapter 6

you can't undo the past

a guide to managing guilt and developing more self-compassion

There are two kinds of guilt: the kind that drowns you until you're useless, and the kind that fires your soul to purpose.
—Sabaa Tahir

Moms feel *guilty*—a lot. Guilty for not doing enough, not being enough, for doing too much of something and too little of another thing. If you've never experienced guilt in mothering, please share your secrets!

For years in the therapy room, I've heard moms talk about feeling guilty. Seldom do they discuss the guilt with other moms, for fear of being judged and losing the social perception of being "perfect" and "having it all together." But once the therapy door closes, the guilt comes pouring out. And what a relief it is when moms do talk about it, because once they do, they learn they can do something about it.

Guilt comes in many forms. Following are some of the types of guilt moms have shared with me.

Guilt for Not Doing Something

Guilt for not doing something can arise in a few ways. First, guilt can occur due to an act of omission; for example, forgetting to do something, not being able to do something, or not even knowing what to do. Second, guilt can show up when we unnecessarily take on responsibility for a situation beyond our control. To be human means to make mistakes—and we *all* make mistakes! The right way to respond to a mistake is to take responsibility, learn from it, correct it going forward, and apologize to those you hurt. Sounds pretty healthy, right? Well, the *unhealthy way* to respond to guilt is to overfunction, which means taking responsibility for things or situations or others' actions beyond our control.

Guilt for Doing Something

Guilt can crop up when we do something, or fail to do something, and believe our actions are harmful or hurtful to family members or others. Moms often feel guilty, whether the guilt is rational or not. Moms have told me they feel guilty for:

- yelling at their children;
- having limited finances;
- saying hurtful things;
- separating or divorcing;
- working;
- not spending enough time with their kids;
- taking time for self-care;
- not being able to or choosing not to breastfeed;
- feeding a baby formula; and
- drinking too much.

Guilt for Not Being Enough

More often than not, moms share with me in our therapy

You Are Not Alone: Erin's Story

Sitting at her son's parent-teacher conference, Erin felt her face flush as the teacher inquired about what home life was like after school for Gabe, who was in fourth grade. Looking directly at Erin, the teacher shared her concern: Gabe had missed homework, sometimes did not have a snack, and did not always wear his winter coat on cold days. Erin had recently been promoted at work, and her travel schedule had increased since the beginning of the year. Her husband, who worked from home a few days a week, was in charge of the afternoon schedules when he didn't have meetings, and a high school sitter came on days Erin was traveling.

Riddled with guilt, Erin felt horrible, attributing these issues to her working and not being able to "do it all." She wondered how she did not know any of this was happening. Our work together focused on learning from this parent-teacher conference and using the guilt in a productive way, to make a plan and move forward. We also explored how guilt showed up in Erin's life when she was growing up, which contributed to how she felt in the present.

Erin was able to see that Gabe needed structure, a more solid plan and routine after school, and instead of figuring out childcare on a week-to-week basis, Erin realized she needed to find a more regular sitter. Erin and her husband came up with a detailed plan to have support five days a week, regardless of her travel or his meetings. In addition, they created a schedule not only for the sitter but also Gabe and each of them to follow. I encouraged Erin to keep her guilt in perspective, limit her negative self-talk, and commit to making changes, as well as to be more compassionate to herself.

sessions that they don't feel good enough. They doubt themselves in so many ways—as people and as mothers—while they question their parenting skills or life choices and fear that they're failing at raising their children. Sometimes the "not enough" feelings are relatively minor because they made a mistake or because their child was struggling academically or socially and they felt guilty, making the association that their child's challenges were their fault as mothers because they worked, or had another child, or went through marital difficulties. Other times, moms share that the guilt of *not being enough* was deeply rooted in their childhood or family of origin—they may struggle with feelings of inadequacy because of childhood trauma, abuse, and neglect. Becoming a parent can open unresolved childhood wounds, which creates a current of insecurity and doubt in their mothering. A mother may feel she is not a *good enough* mother to her children.

Guilt for Not Knowing Better

Maya Angelou has been attributed as saying, "When you know better, you do better." Genius, don't you think? Many mothers, knowingly or unknowingly, are trying to be perfect. But not only is perfection unattainable, it's unrealistic. In motherhood, we're in process, we're learning, we're developing skills. And there's no measure of perfection in these moments. Mothering is the great classroom of experience. There are times when we let people down: our kids, our friends, our partner, our family, or ourselves. In these moments, when you feel guilt for not knowing better, forgive yourself and hold in your heart Maya Angelou's wisdom.

Guilt is a feeling that is important to understand and manage. Unmanaged guilt often develops into regret. Regret is the desire to go back in time and change a behavior, a choice, or a situation.

Regret is the worry that time was wasted and opportunities were passed over for reasons that often we cannot recall or that don't seem to matter in the present moment. Regret is the wish to redo a moment in time to create a different outcome.

When the shadow emotions of guilt and regret are managed with internalized negative self-talk that we believe to be true (e.g., *I'm a bad mother* or *I'm a failure*), the shadow emotion of shame develops. If you notice this emotional experience in motherhood, be sure to review chapter 17, and please reach out to a supportive counselor to work through the shadow emotion of shame.

At the Heart of Guilt and Regret

At the heart of guilt is sadness, worry, and fear that words, actions, and behaviors have negatively impacted what is most important to us. Underneath guilt is varying degrees of regret, our desire to take wisdom from the present moment and apply that understanding to a time, place, or situation in the past in an attempt to repair a loss. Guilt and regret can come in many forms: wanting a second chance, wanting to do more or less of something, wanting to have an opportunity again that was not taken, or to have an experience that may not be possible in the present moment. At the heart of regret is a desire to connect. Perhaps this connection involves spending time with another person and expressing remorse or sharing perspective in a genuine way needed for healing, growth, and closure. Regret represents a desire and a need to finalize and heal unresolved situations and experiences.

Reframe Your Mantra

Thoughts are powerful. Your self-talk has a deep impact on what you feel and how you respond. Keep this principle in mind and reframe problematic thoughts that increase your shadow emotions.

SHADOW MANTRA If you're saying this . . .	THRIVING MANTRA Positively reframe to say this . . .
If only I had done something different.	If I could have done something different in the moment, I'm sure I would have. All I can do is apologize, move forward, and use this as an opportunity to grow as a person.
I wanted to do more. I don't know why I didn't do more.	I wish I could have done more. But that time is gone—what I have is right now and the future. What can I do to make things better?
If only I had done something, this wouldn't have happened. It's all my fault.	Blaming myself and taking on too much responsibility is not productive, nor is it healthy. I can be responsible for my words and actions only, and other people have to take responsibility for theirs.
I feel guilty when I'm out with my friends, or at work, or otherwise away from my child. I shouldn't go out or spend time away from them.	Spending time with friends helps me manage stress and is self-care. I have to figure out what amount of time feels like the right amount to be away. When I take care of myself, I show up for my family with more energy and am able to connect more.

SHADOW MANTRA If you're saying this . . .	THRIVING MANTRA Positively reframe to say this . . .
I can't believe I reacted that way to my child. I feel horrible. I'm an awful mother.[1]	All I can do is learn from my mistake, take care of myself, and make healthier choices with my words and actions. My child is still learning about the world and how to be, and reading up on child development would be a great way to understand what they're capable of and what they're not. I need to rebuild the trust between us and apologize. I'm not an awful mother—I had an awful moment.

Moving Beyond the Shadows

TIP #1: IDENTIFY AND LABEL YOUR GUILT.

When you experience guilt, identifying which type of guilt you're feeling creates awareness and understanding. Begin by asking yourself these questions:

- **Do I feel guilty for not doing something?** Is there something I forgot to do? Or wanted to do but didn't have enough time to accomplish? Or didn't do because of a lack of skill or organization? Am I able to identify exactly what went wrong?

- **Do I feel guilt for doing something?** Did I do or say something that negatively impacted a situation, person, or myself? What were the actions or words that influenced what happened? And what is my role here?

- **Am I experiencing guilt because I believe I'm "not good enough" in some way?** Do I struggle with low self-esteem? Or perfectionistic standards? Or unrealistic expectations on

---

1 If you say this, please know this self-talk is also the shadow emotion of shame. See chapter 17 for more on shame.

how I should be? Is there some unresolved issue or pain from my childhood experiences or from what I learned growing up in my family of origin that is contributing to this feeling of not being enough?

- **Do I feel guilty for not knowing better?** Am I holding myself to high expectations and standards? Do I expect that I should never make a mistake? Did I do something that hurt or harmed someone unintentionally? If so, how can I make amends and learn from this mistake? Is there a skill I need to learn or something I need to do in my life that I'm not doing (but that this situation has made apparent I need to do)? If so, how can I use this as a learning experience to grow and move forward?

TIP #2: KEEP PERSPECTIVE.

To think we will never make a mistake as a parent is unrealistic. I can't think of one mother—not my clients, not my friends, not myself—who hasn't made a mistake or felt some guilt at some point in mothering. So find comfort in the fact that if you're a mom, you will feel guilty at some point for something. The key is not to let guilt become consuming or overwhelming. If you did something or forgot to do something, then take the necessary steps to apologize and make amends. Keep guilt in perspective by knowing it's a universal mothering experience. Knowing this can help reduce isolation.

TIP #3: LIMIT NEGATIVE SELF-TALK.

Feeling guilty can be all-consuming and take up a lot of space in our minds, like a constant running dialogue. You need to turn down (and, ideally, turn off) the negative self-talk. The way to do this is to recognize what you're thinking and saying to yourself.

First, it can be helpful to write down the thoughts you're having. Writing out your thoughts forces you to push the pause button and pay attention to what you're actually saying or thinking rather than repeating it endlessly in your mind. Next, I want you to look at the thoughts you've written and ask yourself the following questions:

- What part of this belief is true?
- Am I taking blame for something I have no control over?
- Am I labeling this situation accurately, or am I being harsh or generalizing this experience too broadly to other parts of my life?
- If a friend were coming to me with this same thought or situation, what would I say? And what perspective would I share?
- Is there something I can do right now to turn down the volume of this thought and not make it so prominent in my mind?

TIP #4: IF NECESSARY, APOLOGIZE.

When we feel guilty, it is often because we've made a mistake; we've done something or not done something. When we've done something wrong, it is important to take responsibility and apologize. We need to work to heal the wound, reestablish connection, and acknowledge that we need to do something different. I know that women are more prone to over-apologizing compared to men. So I don't want you to apologize when it comes to feeling like you're not enough. Be cautious to not over-apologize and rather apologize for actual actions or lack of actions.

Let's say you've yelled at your child. An apology would look like this:

I'm sorry I yelled and raised my voice. I was frustrated for having to repeat myself so many times. That is no excuse or reason to yell. I can see yelling made you feel scared. I'm sorry. If this happens again, when I feel frustrated, I'm going to take a break and take care of my feelings so I don't yell. Yelling is scary and doesn't help.

The following is a sample apology that you can rephrase in your own words when you want to express remorse in order to repair a relationship and reconnect with someone:

I'm sorry I _____(label the actions, words, or behavior). I can see my _____(specify the actions, words, or behaviors) caused you to feel _____(label the feeling the person was experiencing). I'm going to learn from this and be sure to _____ (name the goal for a healthier outcome next time).

TIP #5: LEARN FROM GUILT AND REGRET AND COMMIT TO MAKING CHANGES.

One of my core principles in life is to learn from situations. After going through a tough situation or experience, I often say, "What can I learn from this? What could I do differently going forward?" Staying stuck in the mental worry and process of guilt will keep you stuck. When you feel guilt, the only way to move forward is to work through it, which means gaining insight about why you're feeling this way, making an apology if needed, and having a plan to do something different in the future.

As mothers, we grow and learn from our experiences. And guilt, well, it's a great opportunity to learn. In order to learn from your mistakes, you need to start by asking yourself: *If I were presented with this same situation in the future, what would I do differently?* While we can't change what happened, we can ask and reflect upon these questions:

- What has guilt and regret taught me?
- How can I allow this experience to change me for the better? How can I allow regret to shape me and help me evolve as a person and a mother?

TIP #6: WRITE A LETTER.

A powerful therapeutic tool is letter writing. In a world of texts, Snapchat, and social media visuals with snippets of words and phrases, asking you to write a letter may seem bizarre—but trust me, there's therapeutic value here! If you find yourself mentally and emotionally focused on guilt and regret, carve out ten to twenty minutes in your day and write a letter about your regret.

Perhaps the regret is for something you've done or didn't do to another person (or yourself). Before you start writing, understand this: *You do not need to send the letter anywhere.* The goal is to write the letter for the benefit of expressing yourself through catharsis and, hopefully, closure. For example, you can write a letter addressed to your younger or future self, a person who hurt you, or a person who you hurt (this can include a shadow moment you had with your child). However the regret came to be, you can write a letter as a way to work through the emotions and thoughts associated with it and address what likely needs to be expressed but is living inside of you as regret.

TIP #7: REACH OUT TO A PROFESSIONAL.

If you find any of these suggestions or solutions overwhelming, or trying one of them has a detrimental impact on your ability to function, please reach out to a mental health professional for support in working through these powerful reactions. Sometimes, guilt and regret are buried so deep in our hearts that once we express ourselves, the feelings can be intense and overwhelming. Please seek the support of a mental health professional to help you through this process. We're trained in just this type of tender and delicate work and can give you the help you need to work through deep-rooted guilt and regret.

Thriving Mama Reflection

Guilt and regret are feelings that steal time, energy, and happiness. These feelings are powerful emotional responses centered on loss: a lost opportunity, lost time, or a lost connection with another person or yourself. The most challenging part of carrying guilt and regret is that what happened in the *past* is felt in the *present*. When you feel this way, open your heart and learn from your mistakes or absences or lack of caring for someone or something. For a moment, imagine that what you're experiencing with guilt or regret is exactly what your child is going through. What would you say to be of comfort and support to them? What suggestions would you offer? What perspectives would you share? How would you help them move past this regret? Take the compassion and unconditional love you have for your child and extend those same bundles of understanding to yourself. You are human, and on this journey, you are learning. If you allow them, guilt and regret can be your greatest teachers in helping you live more fully in the present.

reducing loneliness in motherhood

skills and strategies to find connection and bring in fun

Motherhood can feel like a lonely journey for someone who is rarely alone.
—Anonymous

When a baby is born or a child is welcomed into your home, there's so much focus on them, what they need, and how they're doing. It's as if a mother slowly begins to fade into the background, unnoticed and forgotten by others and herself. All of a mother's attention and energy is focused on the outer world of her child's needs—it's easy for her to unintentionally ignore her inner world and create many shadow emotions, which leaves her feeling alone, isolated, lonely, and excluded.

At first glance, feeling alone, isolated, lonely, and excluded may seem as if they are variations on the same emotional response. And while there are some commonalities to these feelings, there are significant differences. All of these emotional responses have social relationships in common. The differences between these shadow emotions are as follows:

- **Alone:** A physical state of being alone or feeling alone in what you're feeling, thinking, or experiencing.

- **Isolated:** Being separate physically, socially, or emotionally from others.

- **Lonely:** The state of being alone, isolated, or abandoned and feeling sad about it.

- **Excluded:** The experience of being socially left out, either rejected or ignored.

Now let's look at how these variations of emotions happen in motherhood.

Alone

Feeling alone is different than *being alone*. Aloneness in motherhood is a type of emotional isolation created when a mother goes through something friends or family may not have experienced, which creates a sense of separateness on her motherhood journey.

The first time I felt emotionally isolated in motherhood was when my first children, fraternal twin girls, were born six weeks premature and stayed two weeks in the neonatal intensive care unit (NICU) for medical care and support. At the time, I didn't have any friends who had twins, nor did I have any friends whose babies had been in the NICU. I will never forget having delivered my babies, only to experience the waves of helplessness and aloneness that came with my entrance into motherhood.

While I was recovering in the hospital, the daytime was busy, filled with visitors, my sweetie, and my family. Hardly was I *alone* during the day. But by nighttime, those feelings of aloneness in my *experience* would hit me fiercely, amplified as my twins were down the hall, hooked up to monitors and in isolettes with a team of nurses tending to their needs. When I heard newborns' cries echoing in the hall, I was reminded that other babies were rooming-in with their mothers, and I felt separated from what having a newborn "should" and "could" be like. I felt alone in my experience, wishing I had someone to commiserate with, someone who could understand what I was going through in this unfamiliar experience.

Isolation

Isolation is a more intense form of aloneness. Isolation can be in the form of *physical isolation* (a physical separateness from others), *social isolation* (not having enough friends or a desire to increase your social connections), and *emotional isolation* (feeling alone with an experience or situation or not wanting to share emotional experiences with others). Perhaps you've never considered all the different ways to experience isolation! Knowing these differences and understanding how these feelings can present in different ways and situations is the first step in helping manage these emotions.

Examples of physical isolation can include:

- moving to a new place and having to reestablish your life and social connections;

- perceiving that you are unable to leave home after the birth of a new baby because of the sleep deprivation and constant feeding;

- working (from home or in a workplace) or being a homemaker, which can make it feel as though you rarely see anyone besides your coworkers and your child (with the exception of the cashier at the grocery store);

- going through a stretch of time when everyone in the family has been sick, as sickness creates physical isolation from friends and extended family as well as your normal routines and activities; and

- shouldering the majority of the parental load and childcare duties, which can create barriers to social connections.

Examples of emotional isolation can include:

- enduring a life event such as infidelity, the loss of a job, relationship conflict, separation, divorce, or chronic illness and not receiving social and emotional support; and

- struggling with mental health issues (such as social anxiety, depression, or undisclosed substance abuse and dependence).

Examples of social isolation can include:

- withdrawing from your social relationships due to mental health issues, such as anxiety or depression;

- feeling a lack of confidence or insecurity regarding your social skills;

- feeling socially limited due to financial constraints;

- not sharing common values, beliefs, or parenting styles and philosophies with your friends; and

- having children in multiple stages and of different ages, which can make social connection challenging.

Loneliness

One of the most unexpected shadow emotions a mom can experience is loneliness. New mothers are most vulnerable to this shadow emotion. Loneliness is a combination of feeling sad and disheartened from social isolation; loneliness is the chasm between what a person wants or expects in a relationship and what a person actually experiences in a relationship. To complicate matters, this chasm is often filled with anxiety about being rejected in one's attempts to connect with others.

Over my two-plus decades of providing support to clients who experience loneliness, here are the five categories of loneliness I've seen in my practice:

1. **Loneliness from transitions in life.** In life, there are many planned (and unplanned) transitions that create changes at home, work, in our social lives, and in how we identify with a certain role or responsibility. Some examples of transitions in motherhood include moving or relocating, changing jobs or pausing our career to stay at home, going back to school, or having a partner who travels often or is deployed. Loneliness can also show up as the result of life transitions for our children that impact us as mothers; for instance, a child going to school, learning to drive, or leaving for college.

2. **Loneliness from loss.** *Loss* is a broad term that can refer to a literal loss, such as when we lose someone or something. The term can also refer to a lack of support or the need to let go of someone or something because of the negative impact the person or thing has on your mental health and well-being. Some examples of this kind of loss in motherhood include raising a family far away from supportive extended family or friends, making the decision to limit or end a toxic relationship with an unhealthy friend or family member, sensing the loss of your personal identity from not working outside the home, or going through separation and divorce.

You Are Not Alone: Eve's Story

Eve sat on the bench at the playground, scrolling on her phone as her six-year-old daughter, Paige, played. She used her phone as a distraction, a way to avoid awkward small talk with the other moms at the playground. Eve had moved to the area six months ago with her husband and Paige. She found it nearly impossible to make new friends—she had tried joining a book club and inviting a few of Paige's classmates' moms over, but nothing seemed to blossom into a friendship. She felt isolated and lonely. Eve came to me after being referred by her primary care physician for support.

Since Eve and her family had moved, the challenges in making friends came from Eve working full-time, her husband traveling during the week, and the weekend often being focused on family time. Eve also had mild social anxiety, which contributed to her feeling awkward about making conversations and small talk. I asked Eve to reflect on what she'd like her social life to look like in specific detail as well as the types of activities and outings that had worked for her in the past. I also encouraged Eve to plan one night during the week to call a friend or family member who lived out of state and connect with them to decrease her loneliness. We also worked on social skills to help Eve navigate the stress of small talk by reading the *Social Skills Guidebook: Manage Shyness, Improve Your Conversations, and Make Friends, Without Giving Up Who You Are.*

Refocusing her efforts and being mindful to choose activities as well as looking for qualities and values in others similar to hers, Eve was successful over the next few months at beginning a friendship with a mom she met at a school event and joining a walking group.

3.   **Loneliness after growth.** As positive as change and self-growth can be, it can also be challenging and tough. I've seen in the therapy hour how self-growth and becoming a more authentic version of ourselves can have an unexpected outcome: *We can outgrow relationships.* Common reactions to outgrowing a relationship include these thoughts: *Where do I fit in now? How can I be myself with relationships that don't embrace who I am?* The most painful and difficult growth is outgrowing a partner, parents, siblings, a friend group, or a group you were once affiliated with.

4.   **Loneliness from caregiving.** Loneliness can be the result of giving too much to others in a caregiving role. Examples of caregiving stress in motherhood include constantly caring for your child and family, caring for aging parents, being in a profession focused on caregiving (e.g., if you are a nurse, teacher, first responder, therapist, or doctor). And for mothers who have a child with special emotional, mental, or physical needs, health issues, or developmental delays, their stress as caregivers will be high and can increase their feelings of loneliness.

5.   **Loneliness from an experience.** Loneliness can be a response to going through a disruptive experience (such as a health issue, change in health status, or chronic illness) or a stressful life event (such as infidelity, separation, divorce, job loss, pregnancy loss and miscarriage, being the first one in your friend group to become a mother, or not being able to have the birth or nursing experience you had hoped and planned for).

Excluded

Have you ever heard the saying, "Motherhood is the new high school"? It's so true! Over the years, I've worked with many clients who are smart, capable, and strong mothers who collectively have felt at times as if they've been put in a time machine and transported back to the cliques of high school. They feel insecure, want to fit in, and want to be included in a mom group. Motherhood is more complicated than high school; the stakes are higher and far more complex with the addition of children. Women can handle being rejected or excluded—it is part of life. But when it happens to their *child*? Well, that can plunge mamas into a whole new depth of pain and anger, opening up old high school social wounds once forgotten but currently relived.

The shadow emotions of feeling excluded can be very painful and result in multilayered reactions ranging in intensity from isolation to loneliness. I've been with countless moms in session who have been brought to tears because they were left out, or because there was an interaction with another mom characterized as bullying, or because their child was bullied, excluded, or treated in an unkind way. The negative dynamics happen in playgroups, neighborhoods, children's sports teams, parent-teacher organizations, and workplaces.

While there are endless possibilities for moms to feel excluded, nothing hurts more than when your child is excluded. The pain and anger are intense. And children *will* be excluded—from birthday parties, sleepovers, playdates, sports teams, you name it. Unfortunately, being excluded is part of life. And what makes feeling excluded more painful is when we perceive that our (or our children's) being left out is *intentional.*

I imagine your head may be spinning after reading this section, as you've never considered the variations of, differences among, and reasons for these shadow emotions! Take a deep breath in on this one. You're learning, and the first step to managing emotions is to understand the situations creating emotional responses in your life.

At the Heart of Feeling Alone, Isolated, Lonely, and Excluded

At the heart of these shadow emotions is the longing to be connected to others, to be part of a group, and to be accepted, appreciated, and liked. While there are varying degrees and individual differences regarding how much social interaction and activity we as individuals may want, at the core, we're social beings living in community. And when there's a loss of connection via isolation, loneliness, or exclusion, it hurts and is upsetting, which is understandable. When we are rejected by or isolated from those we care about, it can create debilitating suffering. The consequence is often our questioning our self-worth, importance, and value. Understanding these shadow emotions is important because you already have value, because you matter, and because these shadow feelings can block you from knowing that truth.

Reframe Your Mantra

Thoughts are powerful. Your self-talk has a deep impact on what you feel and how you respond. Keep this principle in mind and reframe problematic thoughts that increase your shadow emotions.

SHADOW MANTRA If you're saying this . . .	THRIVING MANTRA Positively reframe to say this . . .
I wish someone could understand what I'm going through as a mom.	One way to feel more connected is to reach out to a supportive person and share what I'm experiencing. While I may feel alone with this experience, I can reach out for support to feel less alone in my life.
I wish I had more friends.	If my child came to me with this exact phrase and they were in a similar situation, how would I respond? Wishing for something is passive. What action steps can I take?
No one has reached out to see how I'm doing—my friends must not care.	Where is the evidence no one cares about me? I'm thinking through the lens of my feelings and making a lot of assumptions. My friends do care. We all are super busy and while that's not an excuse, it makes it easier to understand why I haven't heard from them. I can reach out and initiate and let them know what's going on with me and what kind of support I'm needing right now, and I can also ask how they are.
I can't be around anyone, I'm so stressed, and no one wants to hear my problems.	I'm jumping to conclusions and making assumptions that my loved ones and friends won't want to support me. They care about me, and reaching out for support is what I need right now. I can also go to therapy to get more support and take care of myself. Isolating myself right now is making me feel worse.

SHADOW MANTRA If you're saying this . . .	THRIVING MANTRA Positively reframe to say this . . .
Why was I left out? It must be something I did. They must not like me or my kid.	Assuming I did something wrong is not accurate. Chances are that it has nothing to do with me. Reaching out to a friend would be a good way to talk this out. Where is the evidence they don't like me or my child?
I didn't think I'd feel this lonely as a mom.	Instead of judging myself or dismissing my feelings, I can be more compassionate with myself and acknowledge what I'm experiencing. Loneliness happens to many moms. Right now, I'm feeling lonely. Responding to myself with kindness and understanding is important—I can decide the steps to take to move through this feeling.

Moving Beyond the Shadows

TIP #1: ASK QUESTIONS TO CREATE SELF-AWARENESS.

Take a moment to identify the specific feeling you're experiencing.

Alone or Isolated

- Am I feeling alone or isolated?

- Is my isolation physical, emotional, or social?

- **Physical Isolation:** Am I separated from the supportive people in my life because of geography? Do I have difficulty spending time with friends or family because of the phase of life I'm in, or because of our busy schedules? If I feel isolated from supportive people in my life, is there a way we can be together more often?

- **Emotional Isolation:** Do I feel alone because of an experience or situation I'm in right now? Is there a mental health issue contributing to this isolation? For example, am I dealing with depression or social anxiety? Am I struggling with substance or alcohol abuse or dependence? Am I working on sobriety? Do I share my emotions and open up to others, or do I keep my emotions and experiences to myself?

- **Social Isolation:** Is it possible I've isolated myself by pulling away from a group of friends, my sweetie, or my family? If so, am I able to see this behavior and understand the reason why?

Lonely

Am I able to notice a pattern or trend with feeling lonely? For example, does this happen after I spend time with certain people or after I am in certain situations (for example, when I've lost sleep or had a long workweek)? If I'm not able to find a trigger that started this feeling, can I identify when I first noticed feeling this way? How do I cope with loneliness?

Excluded

What are some of the fears, worries, or beliefs I have about being excluded? Does this feeling or situation remind me of something? If yes, what does it remind me of from a previous experience? How does this situation inform me about my friends or social group? Do they have the qualities and values I consider important in friendships?

TIP #2: DEVELOP AN ACTION PLAN AND SET GOALS.

As you've learned, at the heart of these shadow emotions is a desire for more connection, for more companionship, and for feeling understood. The good news? There are choices and ways to bring more connection into your life. Let's take a look at a few examples.

Scenario #1

Problem: You are feeling isolated and haven't connected with friends in a long while.

Goal: Reduce your feelings of isolation.

- **Step 1:** Look at your calendar and find three possible times to get together with or call friends or family within the next week.
- **Step 2:** Reach out to your friends or family via a text or phone call and make plans to chat or get together.
- **Step 3:** During your outing or phone call, share briefly what's been going on and express positive emotion about talking and spending time with your friends or family.
- **Step 4:** Look at your calendar and make appointments to reach out and call, text, or see important people in your life. Set reminders on your phone to encourage you to take these small steps (for example, *Reach out to my friend every Monday* or *Call my parents and sibling on Sunday*).

Busy modern life, which has us rushing from one thing to the next, makes it hard to remember to reach out, and often when we do remember, it's late at night. Using modern technology can help remind us to make the goal of connection happen.

Scenario #2

Problem: You don't feel your friends or sweetie understand the stress in your life and you don't want to burden them with your issues.

Goal: Learn to share more about your feelings and stress with your friends and loved ones; give yourself permission to share what you're going through as an important act of self-care that can ultimately strengthen the relationship.

- **Step 1:** Start with your most trusted and supportive person. Share what you appreciate and enjoy about the relationship. Then share what you're feeling; use *I* statements, such as, *"I feel lonely and I miss you. I enjoyed having fun together and that hasn't happened in a while."* Ask for what you need; for example, *"I want you to know and understand how I'm feeling. I feel alone a lot. It would mean so much if we spent more time together and if you could ask how I'm doing from time to time."*

- **Step 2:** Schedule regular times to touch base and connect. If you want to connect with your sweetie, find times every day when you can be focused on each other. If you want to connect with a friend, schedule time to get together or chat.

- **Step 3:** Be mindful to balance conversation topics by taking turns sharing and connecting. If one person dominates the conversation all the time, the interaction is unbalanced. Sharing is mutually supportive and healthy.

Scenario #3

Problem: You are feeling lonely and isolated because you want to make more friends and do not know how, or you have a group of friends but feel that you've outgrown the friendships or don't have much in common anymore.

Goal: Make friends and increase the number of social outings you participate in.[1]

- **Step 1:** Make a list of all the activities and hobbies you enjoy (e.g., painting, running, practicing yoga, hiking, cooking, reading, traveling, watching movies, listening to live music, volunteering, or writing).

- **Step 2:** Look in your community for organizations or groups that host events related to things you are interested in

---

1 Remember that making friends in the absence of an activity can put a lot of pressure on people. Finding social groups or activities in which there's a common interest is a great place to start; connecting with people who have similar interests, values, or passions and participating in a focused social activity takes the pressure off when it comes to deciding what to talk about.

doing. Some examples may include: book clubs, parent-teacher organizations, playgroups, meet-ups, fitness groups, or nonprofit organizations that rely on volunteers. Find three activities that you could do.

- **Step 3:** Schedule one of the three activities (or more if you like) in your calendar for the month.

- **Step 4:** Attend the activity with an open mind and heart and be curious about how it unfolds. Give yourself credit for trying something new!

TIP #3: STRENGTHEN YOUR SOCIAL SKILLS.

Research has shown that people who experience loneliness can have underlying anxiety about social interactions. This is why planning a social outing around an activity (such as walking, painting, playing board games, watching movies) helps take the pressure off of having to talk the whole time and focuses on a shared interest.

If you're feeling lonely, I suggest strengthening your social skills to boost your confidence and decrease some anxiety. Three skills you can focus on include:

1. **Creating meaningful conversations:** Pick up a book or do some research online and write down five to ten conversation starters. Asking, *"How are you?"* will likely get a vague or general response. To create meaningful conversations, try asking more specific questions, such as, *"What was the best part of your weekend?"* or, *"What is the one thing that surprised you most as a mom?"* Exhibiting curiosity without being too intrusive is a great social skill to have.

2. **Initiating activities and get-togethers:** A common theme I hear from clients who are lonely is that they're waiting for a social invitation. It's not uncommon for people who feel lonely to also feel insecure, anxious, and fearful of rejection. So asking someone to do something can feel overwhelming. Learning the skill of initiating activities and get-togethers will help you move past loneliness. The more times you initiate, the better you'll feel. And remember, at times your invitations will be turned down—for every invitation you make that is accepted, you may make several more that aren't. While that can be hard, just keep asking and practicing. People are often busy, and you never know what's going on in someone's life.

3. **Avoiding taking things personally.** Initiating social interaction is risky and requires vulnerability and courage. When you get a no, don't jump to conclusions or make assumptions—you never know what someone else may be going through. It can be easy to slip into a pattern, thinking that the person's rejection of your invitation is about you, but more often than not, the decline has nothing to do with you; rather, it is more about the circumstances in a person's life that you may not be aware of unless they share or you ask. And if you ask, well, that could feel intrusive and perhaps too intense. If you want to reissue an invitation without seeming intrusive, you could say something like, *"Hey, I've really missed seeing you. We've had some plans and they've fallen through—I know we both have a lot going on. If you're able to, let's get together next week. I can meet on this day or this day. Do those work for you?"*

TIP #4: LIMIT SOCIAL MEDIA.

Experiencing these shadow emotions of aloneness, loneliness, isolation, and exclusion is a call to action to limit the amount of time we spend scrolling through social media. The irony of social media is that the ease of reaching out to anyone at any time can make us more connected and accessible, but we've never been so disconnected as a society. Instead of mindlessly scrolling, comparing your life to the images and stories on social media, which can fuel loneliness, limit your time on these platforms and pursue activities you enjoy and that make you feel energized, confident, and content.

TIP #5: BEGIN COUNSELING.

Reaching out to a mental health professional to learn more about yourself, your relationships, and how they're impacting you is an act of self-care. One myth surrounding counseling and therapy is that a person has to be in crisis, going through a disruptive life event, or have a mental health disorder in order to go to therapy. And while those are indeed reasons why some people pursue counseling, you can begin counseling simply to learn more about yourself and learn skills and strategies to help you on your motherhood journey. This kind of therapy falls into a "self-growth" model of therapy and could be effective at helping you deal with feelings of loneliness.

TIP #6: REALIZE THAT LONELINESS COULD BE DEPRESSION.

Feeling lonely doesn't mean you are depressed. What's important is to be aware of how often you feel lonely, how long you feel lonely, and the intensity of the loneliness you experience. When loneliness is disruptive to your daily life and gets in the way of completing your responsibilities, taking care of yourself (e.g., bathing, dressing, exercising, eating, being productive at home or work), spending time with your family and friends, and experiencing joy and meaning in life, it can signal a mental health issue like depression. If you notice any of these symptoms lasting two weeks or longer, it's critical to reach out to a mental health or medical professional and share your experiences to receive support, evaluation, and treatment.

TIP #7: PRACTICE SELF-COMPASSION.

When you or your child has been excluded, the pain is made worse when you believe that the exclusion is proof of something missing in you or your child. Of course it hurts. Of course it's upsetting. Of course you're angry. But right now, the last thing you need is to pile on the self-criticism and tear yourself down with blame or harsh words; doing so keeps the pain of being excluded alive long past the event. In moments like this, self-compassion goes a long way. Start by acknowledging how crummy it feels to be excluded. It is not easy being excluded, whatever the reason. Relationships and connection are essential for people, especially mothers. And while as adults we can understand we won't be included in every gathering or event, nonetheless it can sting when we are on the outside of any circle.

Let yourself feel what you are feeling without judging the emotion. Instead of saying, "*It is silly to feel this way*" or, "*I should just get over it*," allow yourself to feel what you are experiencing. Then give yourself a dose of self-compassion by reflecting on what you're feeling and acknowledging your suffering. Then you can take a moment and reflect on an act of self-kindness, asking yourself what you need right now from yourself to feel better. And if you can't think of what to do to take care of yourself, imagine what you'd say to your child to comfort and help them. Then do the same for yourself.

TIP #8: OWN YOUR PART.

When we've been excluded, our thoughts can haunt us, and we may wonder: *What did I do wrong? Was it something I said or did?* Maybe, and if you made a mistake or hurt someone, I'd recommend apologizing. If you have a friendship with the person with shared trust and history, then reach out and talk about what may have happened. But, if the person in question is an acquaintance or someone you are just getting to know, you may want to let it go and move on. Not every person you spend time with will develop into a friend. Friendships and relationships grow, evolve, and sometimes end for a variety of reasons that are often out of our control.

TIP #9 DON'T JUMP TO CONCLUSIONS.

When we've been excluded, we often make the assumption it must have been something to do with us. But the reality is that it may have nothing to do with us. More often than not, social relationships in motherhood develop because of four things: (1) shared values and interests, (2) proximity (how close you live or work to someone), (3) frequency (how often you see one another), and (4) having children of similar ages and genders. If these factors aren't in place, it can be difficult for friendships to blossom. So keep this perspective in mind—the exclusion likely has nothing to do with you or your child.

TIP #10: DON'T CREATE MAMA DRAMA.

Being excluded can light a match of anger, which starts a fire of retaliation. One of the sharpest weapons we have is our tongue. When we're hurt and angry, our tongue can become more powerful than a sword. And once words of contempt and hurt are out, we can't take them back. Confronting someone when our emotions are intense only creates more drama and chaos. In moments when you've been excluded, hold off on expressing your anger, saying hurtful things, or starting gossip about another person or a group. You'll thank me on this one.

Put a little pause and perspective on the angry moment. If you need to vent, do so to trustworthy, supportive people. Whatever the reason you or your child were excluded, try not to focus on whether it was intentional or an oversight.

TIP #11: EMBRACE BEING EXCLUDED AS A TEACHABLE MOMENT.

Feeling excluded hurts, no matter your age. And when your child is excluded, well, that's a whole different layer of pain and anger. As a mom of four daughters, I've seen my girls experience the joy of inclusion and, unfortunately, the pain of exclusion. After comforting them with phrases like, *"I'm sorry you found out that way—that must have been tough being at school all day and hearing them talk about the party (or get together),"* I ask some questions and do a lot of listening. Some helpful questions I ask include the following:

- How are you feeling?
- When you first heard about it, do you remember where you felt it in your body?
- Can you describe the feeling?

- How did you take care of those feelings?
- What did you do?
- How are you feeling now that you are talking about it with me?
- Is there something I can do right now to help you?

Then I embrace the teachable moment: I share with my daughters that often it's not intentional that they are left out. Sometimes we get together with friends and another friend wasn't invited. Sometimes friends are on a sports team or take art class while we dance and take piano, so the other people may see each other more and do things spontaneously. And other times, we think someone is a friend, but we may not get along or have the same interests or want to play the same thing, so they're more of a "sometimes" friend.

The most important message I give to my girls is this: *Don't take someone else's behavior personally, even if it hurts. Not being included is not a measure of your self-worth. Take this feeling you have right now of being excluded and remember how it feels, so when you see someone not being included, you can be the one to reach out and include them.*

All of this applies to us mothers as well! When you've been excluded, for whatever reason, you can use this perspective for yourself and your child.

TIP #12: REACH OUT TO SUPPORTIVE PEOPLE IN YOUR LIFE.
After feeling excluded, reach out to supportive people in your life. Let them know what happened, express yourself, and, if you want, ask for suggestions on what they would do if they were in a similar situation. I would also encourage you to

initiate an outing or activity with friends to help remind you of the friendships you do have in your life. There's nothing more rewarding than spending time with the friends and family who lift you up and help you refocus on the important parts of life.

Thriving Mama Reflection

Follow me in the following exercise: Take your hand and place it on your heart. Feel your heart beat against your chest. Close your eyes and take a deep breath in while counting to five. Hold your breath while counting to three, and exhale your breath while counting to five. Repeat this cycle for five minutes, just breathing, holding, and releasing. As you do, you'll notice that your heart rate slows down, your muscles release tension, and you feel a sense of calmness compared to before this exercise. In just a few minutes, without spending money or going to great lengths, you've changed your experience. If I had started this reflection with a command—*"Relax! Bring your heart rate down! Let go of tension!"*—this suggestion would have had the opposite effect. You'd likely feel confused, annoyed, and even more tense.

The shadow emotions related to social relationships you're experiencing right now will not be changed through a harsh command or a demand to just get rid of your feelings. These shadow emotions are living in your body right now, in your heart, and in the energy of every breath. With compassion and care, you can shift these shadow responses in a gentle and loving way, just as you brought your heart rate down and relaxed your body by changing your breathing. You have everything in you needed to connect and create meaningful relationships. You matter. You can change how you're feeling, with one small step and gesture each day, beginning with self-love and compassion.

time goes slow and children grow fast

how to honor your feelings and stay present in the midst of missing and longing

This longing, too large for heaven and earth,
fits easily in my heart.
—Rumi

In the beginning, motherhood is all-encompassing, defining every minute and detail of your life. Then slowly over time, bit by bit, there's a new phase to embrace, a new milestone is reached, a new rite of passage is slowly moving your child toward independence. As soon as you settle in to one developmental phase with your child, you're back to the beginning, embracing a new phase, age, and stage. As a mother, you are in a constant state of adaptation as you nurture and provide support for this sweet little human on their journey. The old saying is true: "The days are long, but the years are short." And the fast pace of motherhood can leave us missing, longing for, or yearning for a certain time.

Each of these feelings—missing, longing, and yearning— are emotional reactions to loss or the desire to go back in time or to spend time with someone. The feelings are different only in the intensity of the emotion. Let's examine them more closely:

- **Missing** is an expression of sadness in the absence of someone or something we love.
- **Longing** is the feeling of wanting something that is difficult to have or challenging to obtain.
- **Yearning** is a deep, painful emotional and physical longing for someone or something. The word *yearning*, when we look at it on the page or when we say it out loud, seems to convey physical characteristics—twisting and heaviness—things that are often felt when we experience this shadow emotion.

Missing, longing, and yearning are emotions I like to frame as being on the same channel but at different volumes. The feeling of missing starts out mild, almost like you're craving something. But if you ignore this craving, chances are that the feeling will get louder and more disruptive, breaking its way into your thoughts and feelings, asking and then forcing you to pay attention.

Missing, longing, and yearning in motherhood show up in many ways: when we endure the loss of a pregnancy, when we experience the longing to be a mother, when we desire to have another baby but face the struggle of infertility, when our toddlers throw a tantrum with wild, irrational abandon and we long for the days when we could leave the house or get through a meal without a battle. We can also experience missing, longing, and yearning as our children mature. For example, we may miss those toddler days and long for our children to sit on our laps for storytime and snuggles. But as school-age children, they are focused on independence, and their friends begin to take priority. When our children are teenagers, we long for them to let us into their world; instead, they communicate through grunts, one-word responses, or eye rolls. And as mothers of college students, young adults, and grown adult children who have launched into a new phase of independence and autonomy, we long for the days when they slept under our roof and we had moments to connect by living together.

Motherhood has many moments of longing, moments in which we wish that we could recapture the joyous parts of raising children. Being able to acknowledge these shadow moments creates an opportunity for you to connect deeply with what you're feeling. Perhaps what you need to do is cry in order to release the tension you're holding. Some things you can do to connect with what you're feeling include reaching out to your child or loved one and sharing a meaningful story that's been on your mind, looking through photos from the past that make you happy, and making a favorite meal from your or your child's youth. While we can never go back in time, we can honor our shadow emotions by giving ourselves permission to feel and to be compassionate with ourselves.

At the Heart of Missing, Longing, and Yearning

At the heart of the shadow emotions of missing, longing, and yearning is the intense desire for a sense of comfort, security, and connection and the ability to go back to a time, person, or place that represents a peaceful, calm, enjoyable, soothing, and happy time. When we experience these emotions, we are stuck between points of time: the past (we wish we could go backward in time) and the future (we want something to look forward to, a hopeful sign that things will be different and what we have lost will be made whole again). At the core of these shadow emotions is a desire to be connected and to honor what is most important, meaningful, and valued in your life.

Reframing Your Mantra

Thoughts are powerful. Your self-talk has a deep impact on what you feel and how you respond. Keep this principle in mind and reframe problematic thoughts that increase your shadow emotions.

SHADOW MANTRA If you're saying this . . .	THRIVING MANTRA Positively reframe to say this . . .
I wish it was like it used to be.	I'm missing a time or person in the past. I know I can't go back, but I'm longing for that time or person because _____. Finding things to do to help me feel connected to this time or person would be helpful.
I want it to be different, more than words can describe.	I'm suffering so much, and I wish it was different, but I have to accept what's happened, even if I don't know what to do next. Reaching out to supportive friends and family to help me through this time is so important.
My heartache is so intense right now, I feel it in my body.	The heaviness I'm feeling can't be expressed through words. This is part of the grieving process. While I can't change what happened, I can be compassionate to what I'm feeling and going through. Taking care of my body by getting rest, making sure I'm hydrated, avoiding alcohol, and reaching out to supportive people are acts of self-care I can do right now.

SHADOW MANTRA If you're saying this . . .	THRIVING MANTRA Positively reframe to say this . . .
I just want to _____, then everything will be all right again.	I'm feeling so sad right now. What I'm feeling is a form of grief; I may be feeling shock with what's happened and need to be gentle and supportive with myself. Longing for things to be different is a sign that I'm grieving. All I can do right now is take care of myself, be compassionate, and reach out for support from caring people.

Moving Beyond the Shadows

TIP #1: ASK QUESTIONS TO CREATE SELF-AWARENESS.

The shadow emotions of missing, longing, and yearning can catch us off guard. Pay attention to how these shadow emotions show up in how you think, in how you focus on past events or times, and in what you find yourself sharing and talking about with others. And be sure to ask yourself the following:

- Which feeling am I experiencing: missing, longing, or yearning?

- Can I identify when this feeling started? Can I pinpoint the situation that created this emotional reaction? Is there a time in my life I want to go back to? If so, what does this time represent to me?

- What's going on in my current life right now that is stressful? How does this relate to my feelings of missing, longing, or yearning?

- Is what I'm longing for really what I'm missing, or is there something else going on that I may not be giving my attention to or dealing with?

- Have I experienced a loss? If so, have I been taking the time to acknowledge my feelings and take care of myself?

- Am I grieving a loss right now? If so, what is it I need right now to take care of myself?

TIP #2: JOURNAL AND EXPRESS YOURSELF.

Missing, longing, and yearning are powerful emotional responses. Expressing your thoughts and feelings by writing about the reasons you're feeling this way will help release the emotions. When you journal, write without editing, revising, rereading, or judging what you are expressing. Write for the sake of purging your thoughts and feelings onto paper in order to heal and understand yourself.

TIP #3: SPEND TIME CONNECTING WITH CARING FRIENDS AND FAMILY.

Experiencing these feelings can create emotional isolation. When you're feeling this way, reach out to supportive and caring people in your life. Let them know how you are feeling and what you need. Perhaps talking to them for a short time, scheduling a get-together with them, or letting them know you need support right now would be helpful.

TIP #4: REACH OUT TO A PROFESSIONAL.

If you find yourself experiencing intense feelings of loss that are disruptive and preventing you from living or enjoying your life fully, then please reach out to a medical or mental health professional for evaluation and support. Disruptive or debilitating feelings from loss could be the symptom of another mental health issue related to grief or a mood disorder.

Thriving Mama Reflection

When we have a longing or a yearning—a physical ache that words can't fully describe—tuning into what you're feeling is important. When you have any variation of the shadow emotions discussed in this chapter, acknowledge what you're feeling. Then find some time where you can sit alone in the quiet and, closing your eyes, allow yourself to feel. As you do, what images, words, or experiences come into your mind? If you could record this moment on video, what scene would unfold? Allow yourself to feel and daydream this feeling into motion. What is it that you need in this moment? Do you need to just be and acknowledge this scene or moment? Are you longing for a deeper connection with this time or person?

As you open your eyes, take a deep breath and find a concrete way to connect with what you're feeling. Perhaps it's looking through photos that have positive memories associated with this person or time, preparing a recipe that reminds you of this person or time, doing an activity you used to do with this person, or writing a letter expressing all that you're feeling with the goal of expressing yourself without ever having to send it. Allow yourself to feel, ask yourself what you need, and take one concrete step to connect to yourself, a moment in time, or a person you're missing.

chapter 9

transforming suffering

the steps to take to turn despair into hope, meaning, and purpose

Despair is suffering without meaning.
—Viktor Frankl

Despair, devastation, and hopelessness are very intense shadow emotions in response to unimaginable loss—either personal loss or loss as a mother. Despair in milder forms may appear when our children are in a stressful, unhealthy, or worrisome situation, which creates a sense of hopelessness and powerlessness for us mothers. In the work I've done supporting parents, mothers have felt despair when their child is sexually abused or traumatized, when their child receives a medical diagnosis or suffers an accident, and when their child struggles with substance abuse, dependence, or overdose. Nothing makes a mom feel more helpless than not being able to protect her child from stressful and harmful circumstances. And on the extreme level, unimaginable despair happens after a miscarriage or the loss of an infant or child, leaving an indelible impact on a mother for the rest of her life.

These shadow emotions can also arise out of profound loss

in other areas of your life. Following are some examples of profound loss:

- Losing your job
- Dealing with infidelity
- Struggling with addiction
- Enduring family-of-origin conflict
- Suffering an illness or the loss of your physical health
- Having your living environment damaged by a fire or natural disaster
- Experiencing domestic violence
- Experiencing violent crime
- Enduring separation and/or divorce
- Facing financial stress or bankruptcy
- Suffering chronic stress in your workplace (e.g., harassment)

These situations are not only personally disruptive, but they also often impact and impair your ability to show up and take care of your children. This creates additional shadow emotions of loss and guilt for not being able to parent the way you want to.

Despair can make it feel impossible to decide what to do next or how to be; it's as if your life becomes overwhelming. Even the smallest and simplest tasks seem like too much. Hopelessness like this is felt not only emotionally but physically, impacting your body in ways words can't fully express. You may experience a physical ache, a heaviness in your body centered in your heart that weighs down your movement, energy, and hope in the future.

Despair is the absence of hope. Hope is the feeling of optimism, belief, and resolve to move forward and survive after the stress of a situation or life event. When you feel despair, please remember there is hope. Even if you cannot hold the hope yourself, know and trust there are other people who can hold the hope for you. Feeling despair lessens when we reach out to supportive people. If you don't have supportive people in your life, then it's time to seek a counselor, medical doctor, or religious guide to help carry and hold the despair you are feeling.

At the Heart of Despair, Devastation, and Hopelessness

At the heart of the shadow emotions of despair, devastation, and hopelessness is incredible suffering, profound loss, fear, and uncertainty about how to rebuild and accept a new way of living.

At the heart of devastation is never being able to go back to the way life was, always defining your life as pre-trauma or post-trauma or loss. However we experience loss and trauma, it's as if there is the ending of one familiar world and the beginning of a new one that requires energy, patience, and compassion in order to rebuild and heal (a process that can feel uncertain and overwhelming at times).

At the heart of hopelessness is a belief, which is rooted in fear, that suffering will always be as it is in the current moment. Hopelessness removes any meaning or purpose or assurance that life in the future could be anything other than it is now. But the truth is that *hope* is the path forward after these shadow emotions; it is the anchor in the darkness, grounding us and exhorting us to be still and rest, so that we may emerge into the light restored and transformed. When we feel optimistic about the future, we hold a belief that things will improve, circumstances will change, and happier days are ahead.

Reframe Your Mantra

Thoughts are powerful. Your self-talk has a deep impact on what you feel and how you respond. Keep this principle in mind and reframe problematic thoughts that increase your shadow emotions.

SHADOW MANTRA If you're saying this . . .	THRIVING MANTRA Positively reframe to say this . . .
This feels so hopeless.	I'm having negative thoughts about the future and what to do next. All I can do is take care of myself and reach out for support so I don't feel so alone. If a friend was going through the exact same thing I am right now, what would I say to them?
No one can understand how this feels. I feel so alone.	My feelings are so big right now that I don't feel like anyone can understand me. And that feeling is partly true—no one can fully understand what I'm going through. Reaching out to a supportive person and sharing what I'm feeling is one way to reduce my feelings of isolation.

(continued)

SHADOW MANTRA If you're saying this . . .	THRIVING MANTRA Positively reframe to say this . . .
Life will never be the same. I'm heartbroken.	It is true that life is different and this feels overwhelming. While many things have changed, there are things and people in my life that will be constant, such as _____. It's important to focus on the strengths I have, such as _____ and _____. I've faced challenges before, and using those past experiences could be helpful now.
I have no purpose or meaning anymore.	While I may have the thought that I have no purpose, I must challenge that thought. I do have purpose. I'm important to _____ and _____. I can't change what happened, but I can decide how I'm going to respond and manage this experience. Perhaps at one point, I can turn this suffering into something meaningful to help other people.
How am I ever going to recover from this?	I'm feeling so many emotions right now, it's hard to imagine how I can ever recover. I don't need to have all the answers today. But what I can do is focus on what I need right now and the immediate future.
I can't even begin to think about the future and what it's going to be like.	I may need to take a very short-term approach to what I do. For example, maybe I need to decide what to do for the next hour, then the next. Focusing on the future right now is contributing to my overwhelm. If a friend were going through something similar, I'd probably tell them to be extra compassionate and understanding right now.

Moving Beyond the Shadows

TIP #1: BEGIN MENTAL HEALTH COUNSELING.

The profound loss accompanying the shadow emotions of despair, devastation, and hopelessness is a process of moving through grief, crisis, and the loss of hope and shifting into healing and finding meaning in your life, redefined though it may be after the loss. Healing takes time. And devastation creates a complicated range of emotions; it's a journey from darkness to healing that you have to travel over a period of time. If ever there was a time to reach out and get support and guidance from a mental health professional, it is now. You may wonder, *How can talking to someone help? How can they begin to understand what I've gone through? I don't have the energy to share my story and relive the pain.* What I want you to know is this: A trained mental health professional is not only going to support you, they're going to be an ally in understanding you, providing you with skills and strategies to help you cope and work through your suffering.

Therapy and counseling are transformative, powerful, and healing. There are some things you can say to a therapist that you just can't say to a friend. Having been on both sides of the couch, so to speak, I can honestly say that therapy is a real gift in facilitating change and healing. And consider this: Therapy is the one space where you can say whatever you need to say. You do not need to censor yourself or worry if your feelings are too much or your thoughts too overwhelming. Sometimes with family and friends, we hold back and we don't say what we need to, fearing we're a burden or that we will hurt a loved one. Working with a mental health professional is one of the most important self-care skills and acts you can give yourself after a trauma, loss, or crisis.

TIP #2: COMMIT TO RADICAL SELF-CARE.

Do not make self-care optional. Committing to radical self-care is a top priority. The first goal is to take care of your body by getting enough sleep, nutrition, hydration, and exercise. Taking care of your physical health will improve your mental and emotional health and help you move through the feelings of despair. Trust me on this one. While this tip may sound overly simple, it isn't. Your physical self-care is equally as important as your mental and emotional self-care.

TIP #3: DO NOT USE ALCOHOL.

When you've experienced loss and have shadow feelings like despair, devastation, and hopelessness, please refrain from drinking alcohol. Alcohol is a depressant, which means it can worsen and intensify your mood state. Abstain from drinking until you are in a stable emotional place that you've been able to sustain for some time. I feel strongly about this recommendation, because alcohol is too often used as a coping mechanism that can bring about adverse, detrimental, and impulsive choices and behaviors, and blocks, delays, and complicates healing.

TIP #4: ALLOW YOURSELF TO TAKE A BREAK FROM RESPONSIBILITIES.

After a devastating event, you will be feeling so many emotions and likely not have the stamina to complete all of your tasks and responsibilities as usual. The particularly stressful part of going through loss as a mom is that you still have the responsibility of caring for your family. And when it comes to caring for children, you may find you don't have the reserves or patience to deal with unexpected and ongoing demands. Sometimes it's not possible to take a break from caring for your children or going to work. But if you can, let others help you and take a break from your responsibilities at work and home.

In the world we live in, we place value on productivity and being strong, pushing through any obstacle. But now is the time to say no to extra things, to simplify and limit what you don't have the energy to do, and to prioritize the nonnegotiable responsibilities of your day-to-day life. Being strong doesn't mean sacrificing your mental and physical health when you've experienced devastation. That is what sick days are for! And while moms never get sick days, at the very least, let go of the things you don't have to do.

TIP #5: TAKE THE HELP AND KNOW WHAT YOU NEED.

When something devastating happens, hopefully you have caring people in your life who ask, *"How can I help? Is there anything you need?"* What I've observed is when people say this, they really mean it—they want to help and support you. However, accepting help and support is not always easy. When people ask you how can they help, be honest and direct about what you need. Perhaps you need them to take your child for a playdate, or make a meal, or call or text to check in every few days. Or maybe what you need is to talk about something other than what you're going through because you need the distraction. Think through what you need, be specific, and don't be afraid to accept help. When friends and family ask how they can help, they truly do want to ease your burden.

TIP #6: FOCUS ON THE SHORT TERM.

When something devastating happens, we crave normalcy and the life we had before the trauma. Accept that after something devastating, "normal" has to be redefined and transformed. While it's an understandable response to want life to go back to how it once was, understand that part of loss is acknowledging and accepting change. This means that something new has to be created after a devastation. And this creation will take time. Allow yourself to take time and space to recover.

What I encourage clients to do is to stay focused not on the long term but the immediate future. This can be a tricky balance. Part of healing is to look ahead to the future while also working through grief. I encourage clients to stay in the short term by focusing on small, achievable action steps each day to heal and rebuild. Put your efforts into tasks you can measure and accomplish today, tomorrow, and this week. Progressing through problems in manageable steps will help you stay grounded and give you momentum for progress. Focus on the here and now, allow your feelings to come and go, and to realize that how you feel at this moment will likely be different a week from now, a month from now, and three months from now.

Thriving Mama Reflection

Hopelessness is a dark place. Hope is the flicker from the smallest of flames in the darkest of nights, serving as a reminder that there is always a way and there is always a choice on how to respond. In moments of hopelessness, finding light can seem impossible. Perhaps you're looking outside of yourself for the light of hope. And while this is one way to anchor yourself in dark times, have you ever considered that the light is within you? Your state of being right now is challenging, and the suffering you feel permeates every part of you, dimming the light in you to the tiniest ember. When moments of darkness in the external world seep into your internal world, filling your heart and mind, taking action to protect the light within you is the greatest act of self-preservation you can perform. As you experience these feelings, take a tea light candle, place it in a small glass or candleholder, and light it. As you focus on your breath, let this external light be a concrete reminder to nurture and protect the hope in your heart and mind. Know that you don't have to have everything figured out for the next day or the next week or the next month. All you have is this moment. Ask yourself, *"What do I need to keep the light of hope burning and inspiring me to move forward and change the conditions I'm experiencing? How can I take one step forward today to feel better and protect the light of hope?"*

PART III

conquering fear and anxiety to cultivate calm

Sometimes I don't think I can do it, there's so much
to worry about.

I can't stop thinking of all the what-ifs.
I feel so anxious all the time, it makes it hard to focus on my
kids. I wish I could do more with them.

I feel so insecure around other moms—I never knew how
hard it would be to make friends.

What are you afraid of and what do you worry about as a
mother? Probably a lot of things you never anticipated!
The shadow emotions of fear and anxiety happen often in
motherhood. From the moment a baby is placed in a mother's
arms, there is worry: *Are they eating enough? Gaining weight?*
Pooping enough? Is it gas or colic or something more? Is my
baby growing, meeting developmental milestones, and thriving?

Few of us receive direct training on how to care for our baby.
Combine this lack of knowledge with sleep deprivation and the
stress of getting to know our child, and conditions are perfect
for the shadow emotion of insecurity to pop up. Even if you feel
confident as a mother, the temperament and personality of your
child can be a wild card; you never know if you'll have a baby
with a calm or more challenging temperament. Meeting and
getting to know your child is the great unknown, which is both
anxiety producing and incredibly exciting!

Feeling the shadow emotions of fear and anxiety continue
in motherhood long past the baby phase; every developmental

stage of childhood, adolescence, and even adulthood brings its own worries.

In a way, all this fear and anxiety makes sense by nature's standards: These shadow emotions ensure that helpless babies and children will be protected by their mothers. But the problem is in modern motherhood, we don't need the level of anxiety and fear that has been hardwired in our amygdala, the part of our brain that scans our environment looking for dangerous things and encourages us to protect ourselves and our children from them.

In modern motherhood, stress, worry, and anxiety happen when we interpret things as dangerous when in reality, they're not—we're just uncomfortable with our thoughts, which we believe as true, accurate forecasts of the future. The shadow emotions of fear and anxiety are driven by the thoughts we have, and a few things happen in response: Our body releases stress hormones and adrenaline to respond to the danger. Our body creates physical symptoms (such as increased heart rate, higher blood pressure, faster breathing, heavy sweating, dilated pupils, and shaking and trembling) telling us that the perceived danger is real and that we must get ready to respond. And when we perceive this danger to be directed at our child, watch out, because mama bear is coming out in full force!

Knowing how our body is predisposed to perceive danger, we have to override what we think about by managing our thoughts and being aware of ways to calm our body when we start to feel the physical symptoms of these shadow emotions. Discerning what is real danger and what is perceived danger can be super challenging!

I truly believe, and have seen in my years of mothering, that mothers are given the gift of mother's intuition. A mother will know in her heart, or she'll have a sense, that something isn't right, to check on her child, to ask a certain question, to make a decision, or to avoid something—and she can't really tell anyone why. Mother's intuition is real. But the problem is, if you are an anxious mom, you may have trouble figuring out the difference between the shadow emotions of fear and anxiety and your mother's intuition.

I do see a difference between a mother's intuition and fear and anxiety, whether the threat is real or perceived. I frame the differences this way: A mother's intuition is applicable in the present moment. It's mother's intuition when you feel something in your gut, and you haven't been feeling anxious or worried. You feel a little "nudge," or something comes into your awareness, a sense that you listen to and act on. Nervous or anxious thoughts, on the other hand, tend to stick around a while longer. Or perhaps the same fearful thoughts show up over and over again over the course of days or weeks.

Adding to this complexity are the shadow emotions of fear and anxiety in response to *actual* threats and danger that are not imagined or created, that fall into the category of true potential risk and harm. There are safety standards and guidelines that are simply not a matter of opinion but are in place to ensure parents do instinctively what they want to do: keep their child safe, healthy, and happy. Great examples of this in motherhood are baby-proofing your home, transporting your child in a safe child carrier or seat when you're in a car, being mindful of choking hazards (including food), and teaching your children about what items are safe to touch.[3]

Sometimes, though, we experience the shadow emotions of

fear and anxiety in response to *perceived* threat and danger when in actuality, there is no danger. The shadow emotions covered in the following chapters will explore how worry, nervousness, and anxiety, including feeling afraid and frightened, show up and impact how we take care of our child and ourselves in motherhood. We will also focus on the shadow emotion of insecurity in motherhood, whether about ourselves in a social context or about our skills and abilities in motherhood.

These shadow emotions will happen at some point in varied intensity in motherhood. Similar to sadness, when these shadow emotions create distress or disruption in your life through persistent worry or unwanted thoughts and physical symptoms (e.g., a racing heart or palpitations, agitation, digestive issues, difficulty getting through the daily responsibilities of caring for your child or going to work), then please reach out to a mental health or medical professional for evaluation and support, as these symptoms can signal a mental health issue. If you experience these symptoms along with intense feelings of irritability that can flare into anger and rage after the birth of your baby, then this could be postpartum anxiety, and support and treatment will help you feel better so you can enjoy your life and thrive in motherhood.

overcoming anxiety

how to manage worry and anxious thoughts to create joy and connect with others

Worrying is like sitting in a rocking chair. It gives you something
to do, but it doesn't get you anywhere.
—English proverb

Long before a mother holds her child in her arms for the first
time, she's spent a lot of time worrying, preparing to care for her
baby, whom she hasn't even met. Worry is nature's way of getting
a mother ready to nurture, protect, and care for a baby—a job
she has no training or experience in. Everything a mother does
to care for her baby starts with a concern: *What does my baby
need? Am I doing this right? Is there something else I need to do?*
But worry is only beginning when a baby is born. Every age and
stage of development in raising a child brings new experiences,
challenges, and things to worry about!

Being a mother is getting used to the shadow emotions of worry,
nervousness, and anxiety. Like some of the other shadow emotions,
I frame these as feelings on the same channel, just with different

volumes. The "channel" that all of these feelings run on is fearful negative thoughts, which then impact how a mom responds—what she does or doesn't do. It's almost as if these shadow emotions are the background noise in motherhood; some days you can't hear the sound, and other days, you want it to stop and crave the quiet. Let's break down the differences between these shadow emotions.

Worry

Worry is thinking about the "what-ifs" that could happen; we ruminate on fearful possibilities about future situations or scenarios, whether they are real or imagined. Worry is all about control—when we worry, we are trying to control outcomes with our thoughts by thinking through every possible situation or potential outcome as a way of being prepared. Worry in motherhood shows up in many ways and is not limited to, but can include:

- Worry about whether your child is eating, sleeping, growing, making friends, healthy, happy, confident, and learning.

- Worry about something happening to your child (e.g., your child contracting a cold, flu, or illness or your child being safe around the water, in a car, or with other caregivers and family who may be watching them).

- Worry about the amount of money it takes to raise a child (e.g., the cost of childcare, education, enrichment activities, and college).

- Worry at night about all the things you have to do the next day (e.g., worry about how you'll get it all done and what you may be forgetting).

Worry in motherhood never really goes away, no matter what age and stage your child is in—even when the kids are adults with children of their own, many mothers still worry. For some mothers, worry can be an expression of love and a gesture of caring; for example, we often say, *"I was worried about you,"* as a way of saying, *"I'm thinking of you and you're important to me."* However worry shows up in motherhood, the key is paying attention to when worry is stressful, taking away your health and well-being.

There are two kinds of worry: *productive* and *unproductive* worry. Unproductive worry is focusing on something that is without solid information, probability, or possibility paired with the absence of taking steps to productively manage your worry. For example, let's say your child's classmate had a choking incident at lunch when they swallowed a piece of fruit the wrong way. Thankfully, teachers intervened and got the fruit out, but it was scary for all involved. After hearing this, your concern and relief for this classmate turns to unproductive worry about your child. Your worry thoughts include a cycle of wondering, *What if that happened to my child? What if no one saw? What if the teachers were talking and didn't see? What if I hadn't cut the fruit that day? What kind of fruit was it the classmate choked on? Maybe that's a fruit I can no longer give to my child. What if this happened at home and I wasn't around?* Unproductive worry is thinking about all of the "what-if" scenarios that could happen or may be possible. It is fueled by negative thoughts and feelings that we often perceive as accurate and true.

In contrast, productive worry can be seen as "good" worry. Consider the same scenario: Your child's classmate chokes on a piece of fruit at lunch, teachers intervene, and all is well. This time, though, after learning about this incident, you chat with your child about what they saw at lunch and how they felt. You then remind them of the safety rules around eating: "Chew your food all the way. Don't take too big bites. Take a bite, chew, then swallow, then talk with friends." Concerned about what happened, you ask your child what they would do if they were to have trouble swallowing or choke. You show them the sign for choking and how to get someone's attention by grabbing another person's arm or making noise with their own hands. Then you take your worry and move it into an action plan by being sure to cut up foods that are choking hazards for your child's age (e.g., hot dogs, grapes, super cheesy pizza) and remind any caregivers to do the same. In this example, you have prevented the shadow emotion of worry from spiraling and intensifying to the shadow emotions of nervousness and anxiety.

Nervousness

Nervousness is a combination of thinking about what might happen paired with fear. Nervousness involves small moments of fear, an emotion more intense than worry but less intense than anxiety. Nervousness can be the small waves of fear that ripple through your body and mind, disrupting harmony. Nervousness also has an element of anticipation (i.e., waiting for something you want and being anxious or fearful should the desired outcome not work out). Nervousness in motherhood can happen when you are:

- waiting to see if the lines on the pregnancy test will turn the desired color or waiting on a call from the fertility specialist;

- driving to a doctor's appointment during pregnancy;

- thinking about becoming a mother, going through childbirth, or caring for a baby;

- waiting and watching your child perform in a play, on a sports team, or in a competition; and

- thinking about being separated from your child (e.g., for travel or work, because of divorce, or simply as part of the day-to-day routine).

You Are Not Alone: Maria's Story

It was a Tuesday night. Maria tossed and turned in her bed, wondering if this would be another sleepless night. She was unable to fall asleep, even though she'd had an exhausting day at home with her daughter, Parker, who was eighteen months old, and her son, Joshua, who was four years old. She couldn't stop the racing thoughts about Parker—Maria was worried about her growth, development, and speaking delays. Her pediatrician said not to worry, that they'd keep an eye on it and make decisions if intervention was needed at Parker's next checkup. But this only increased Maria's anxiety. Would Parker need to go to a private school to get the support she needed as she started kindergarten? Maria wondered if she should cut back to part-time work and spend more time with Parker.

Joshua was thriving, and Maria couldn't help wondering if, because of her overwhelm with work and two kids, she hadn't seen the issues in time or if she had done something wrong. I counseled Maria on ways to increase her self-care skills—not consuming caffeine after 1:00 p.m., making it a priority to exercise at least fifteen minutes a day, and journaling out her worry thoughts earlier in the day. Maria also worked on not comparing her two children, as each child grows and develops in unique ways, and to let go of her self-blame and guilt. There was no evidence Maria had done something wrong or had been negligent as a mom. I encouraged her to not search the internet for possible diagnoses or worst-case scenarios.

All of these self-care methods helped reduce her anxiety, worry, and sleeplessness. When Maria had a setback, a sleepless night with spiraling worry, she used the skills she learned and reached out for support.

Anxious

Anxiety happens when nervous feelings are not managed and they become more intense. Like any emotion, anxiety can range from mild to severe. Anxiety comes with a sense of fear, danger, and apprehension that creates issues concentrating, sleeping, eating, and focusing at work or home and disrupts your everyday living and relationships. Some triggers of anxiety in motherhood include:

- going back to work after maternity leave;
- your child being sick or ill with symptoms that heighten your anxiety (e.g., a rash or high fever) or your child suffering an injury and requiring tests, scans, X-rays, or specialized medical treatment;
- comparing your child and their development to their peers (e.g., your child is not sleeping through the night or is experiencing delays in talking, crawling, walking, or other developmental milestones), even though your child is within what is considered "normal" development;
- your child having difficulty learning, trouble in school, or problems with making friends or is being bullied;
- facing specific fears or phobias you have (e.g., a fear or phobia of driving over bridges, flying in planes, or driving on the highway) that trigger your anxiety and limit the range of activities you feel comfortable doing with your child or friends; and
- experiencing social anxiety, which can create dread and lead to the avoidance of meeting up and connecting with other moms at child-centered activities, birthday parties, and other events.

Anxiety becomes a mental health issue when you experience excessive worry or anxiety most of the time that causes you problems functioning at home, at work, or in relationships or that disrupts sleep, appetite, and gets in the way of enjoying your daily life. If this describes the kind of anxiety or worry you're experiencing, then I recommend reaching out to a medical or mental health professional for support and evaluation.

At the Heart of Worry, Nervousness, and Anxiety

At the heart of worry, nervousness, and anxiety is fear, uncertainty, discomfort, and preoccupying thoughts about something happening in the moment or in the future. These shadow emotions impact motherhood by taking away the joy of raising a child. While a substantial part of motherhood is about being prepared and anticipating what your children need, at the heart of these shadow emotions is an irrational expectation to rarely (if ever) experience uncertainty or discomfort in motherhood, the desire to anticipate every possible risk, and the urge to receive reassurance that things will be okay. The problem is that these shadow emotions can become so out of control that no amount of reassurance or avoidance will reduce the distress—only by learning skills and strategies to tolerate the uncertainty in motherhood can we manage our shadow emotions of worry, nervousness, and anxiety.

Reframe Your Mantra

Thoughts are powerful. Your self-talk has a deep impact on what you feel and how you respond. Keep this principle in mind and reframe problematic thoughts that increase your shadow emotions.

SHADOW MANTRA If you're saying this...	THRIVING MANTRA Positively reframe to say this...
I'm so worried about what could happen. It's difficult not knowing.	Uncertainty is tough, but focusing on all the possible outcomes is increasing my anxiety. What productive strategies can I employ to manage this worry?
I wish there was a guarantee that everything will be okay.	I'm feeling anxious and I'd love a guarantee. However, I know there are no guarantees in life, so what would be helpful in managing my anxiety is focusing on what I can do right now. Distracting myself and going for a walk (or exercising) can release some stress.
What if this happens, then that?	What steps can I take to reduce my worry in a productive way? If I can't think of any, then I need to be compassionate with myself and respond to myself in the same way I would respond to my child if they came to me with this exact concern. What would I say to them?
I'm nervous I'm not a good mom.	So many mothers wonder if they're a good mom, and today, I'm wondering that too. If a friend came to me and said this, what would I say to her? The same applies to me. I'm a good mom, and I'm doing my best. Highlighting what I feel confident about as a mom is going to help me.
I am so anxious about what could happen.	Right now I'm filled with so much anxiety in my body, it's hard to calm down and release stress. Grounding techniques and practicing 5-4-3-2-1 skills (page 154) would be a great thing to do right now.

SHADOW MANTRA If you're saying this . . .	THRIVING MANTRA Positively reframe to say this . . .
I'm worried I won't be there to protect my child or stop them from getting hurt.	Some days, being a mom is overwhelming as I think about the responsibility of keeping my child safe. I can't protect them from everything, but I can take steps to put safety measures in place and respond the best I can. And I can comfort them when they are hurt.
I need to avoid uncomfortable situations.	Being uncomfortable is not easy. There are times I'll have to do things I don't want to do. What are the ways I can manage my discomfort? Focusing on what I can do besides avoiding will be more comforting than avoiding.

Moving Beyond the Shadows

TIP #1: ASK QUESTIONS TO CREATE SELF-AWARENESS.

Ask yourself the following questions to help you navigate the shadow emotions of worry, nervousness, and anxiety:

- Which feeling—worry, nervousness, or anxiety—do I experience most often?

- Is there a situation or event that triggered my feelings of worry, nervousness, or anxiety? Did these feelings come out of the blue, or have they been building for some time?

- How have these shadow emotions impacted my life?

- Have I experienced these shadow emotions in the past? If so, what helped me manage these symptoms and how did I help myself feel better?

- Am I able to identify what I need to feel better? If so, what do I need?

TIP #2: PRACTICE GROUNDING TECHNIQUES.

Grounding techniques take your overactive mind, focused on negative thoughts or upsetting scenarios, and soothe it by taking you out of your mind and into the moment happening right now. Using grounding techniques, you focus on your senses and your breathing, which creates a sense of calm. Try the following techniques for each of your senses and your breath:

- **Sight:** Pick up a stone, crystal, geode, or another item and focus on the object. Examine all of its details. Look at the object as if you've never seen it before, taking in each detail.

- **Sound:** Download an app on your phone that has soothing sounds like the ocean, birds, rain, or peaceful music. When you feel stressed, listen to the sound. Alternatively, go outdoors and listen to the sounds of nature.

- **Touch:** Massage scented lotion into the skin of your arms and hands to release tension.

- **Taste:** Keep a few peppermints, pieces of chocolate, or sticks of gum within reach. Savor each bite.

- **Smell:** Inhale the scent of a piece of citrus fruit or an essential oil (try lavender or vanilla).

- **Breath:** After trying a few or all of the preceding grounding techniques, focus on your breathing, inhaling as you count to five, holding your breath as you count to three, and exhaling your breath as you count to five. Repeat this process for five minutes.

TIP #3: PRACTICE SOOTHING MANTRAS AND MUSCLE RELAXATION.

At this point in the book, you're well aware of the powerful impact thoughts have on how we feel, act, and interact with our child and the larger world. One way to override the effects of these shadow emotions on our mind and body is to actively practice skills that challenge our thoughts and help our body reduce physical symptoms by creating calm.

First, when you feel anxious, repeat a soothing statement. For example, when you feel anxious or fearful, say to yourself, *"Just because I think I'm in danger doesn't mean that I am. I am uncomfortable, I'm experiencing physical discomfort, and I am safe. I'm uncomfortable, but I'm not in danger."*

An important skill to practice in conjunction with saying this mantra is to regulate your breathing as we learned in the preceding tip. You can then build on your mantra and your breathing by adding a skill you can do anywhere when you feel the shadow emotions of worry, nervousness, or anxiety escalating: *muscle relaxation.*

To start this exercise, sit in a chair with your feet flat on the ground and your shoulders relaxed. Take in a few breaths. Then begin tensing your muscles in your head and neck. Hold the tension for ten seconds, then release it for ten. Make your way down to your arms, tensing this large muscle group for ten seconds, then releasing for ten seconds. Do the same for each muscle group, individually tensing and releasing your chest, abdomen, bottom, thighs, calves, feet, and toes. You can repeat the cycle as often as you like. What I love about this calming technique is that you can do it anywhere and no one notices.

TIP #4: LOOK FOR THE GOOD.

Focusing on negative events or circumstances creates a perception, which then becomes a reality, of hopelessness for the future. Of course, there are sad, unjust, horrible things happening in the world, and at times they feel overwhelming. When you are worried, afraid, or anxious, the distress you are experiencing may be a signal to take a break and detox from social media, the news, and anything that feeds your cycle of anxiety. It doesn't mean you forgo these things forever, but just for right now. For example, watch the news to be informed but limit how much time you spend so as not to be overwhelmed—there is a difference between being informed and being overwhelmed, hopeless, and filled with anxiety regarding the world you're raising a child in. During this detox, shift your attention and focus on the acts of love, kindness, and service you see or can do in your community. Read and share stories that give you hope and notice how, even after a few days, focusing on the positive things happening all around you likely reduces the shadow emotions you've been struggling with. And no matter your child's age, one way to focus on the good is to raise your child to be kind, generous, and thoughtful through helping others and performing acts of service in your community and the larger world.

TIP #5: EXPRESS GRATITUDE.

When we are in a negative place, it's hard to think of what is going well in our lives. Expressing gratitude helps reduce anxiety and improves our mood, creating positive emotions and reactions. Before you get out of bed each day, think of three things you appreciate and are grateful for. And at the end of the day, do the same: Reflect on three things or situations that happened during the day that you appreciate. You can be thankful for something as simple as an easy bedtime with your toddler, a dinner you made that everyone enjoyed, or your sweetie cleaning up the dishes and folding the laundry. Often, shifting our perspective to gratitude can move us from feeling stressed to feeling calmer and more appreciative.

Thriving Mama Reflection

The shadow emotions of worry, nervousness, and anxiety can create a lot of mental chatter in a mother's mind. When we're in constant motion and our mind is always active, our outer *and* inner worlds become very noisy. So much so that we crave *stillness*. But for many of us moms, the only moments of stillness we get are at night when our heads hit the pillow, just as our noisy, worry-filled thoughts turn on, preventing or delaying our much-needed sleep. If the only time you have stillness is when your head is on the pillow, then what you may need most is to find time to be still. Create in your routine small moments of time for enjoying stillness, quieting your mind, focusing on your breathing, and just being—even if it's for five minutes.

In the stillness, focus on your senses instead of your thoughts. Take some lotion and massage your hands, look around the room you are in and label what you see, take a moment to eat something and savor it without rushing, listen to sounds in nature or inspiring music, or seek out a soothing smell, the peel from an orange or flowers nearby, taking a few breaths in. Finding moments to slow down and create stillness is an act of self-care.

chapter 11

finding your strengths

how to transform moments of insecurity into sources of confidence

Comparison is the thief of joy.
—Theodore Roosevelt

Rooted in anxiety and fear, insecurity in motherhood is a shadow emotion fueled by mental chatter in a mother's mind as she wonders if she's a good mother, fearing that somehow she may be failing her children. This shadow emotion is more than the waves of uncertainty all mothers experience from time to time; it is persistent anxiety stemming from a lack of confidence in your skills and abilities, as well as feeling inferior in your mothering. It often shows up in two ways: *feeling inadequate* and *comparing yourself to others.*

Feeling inadequate shows up in the form of lack: you may believe you lack skills, accomplishments, talents, likability, intelligence, or anything else of value. This type of insecurity has you thinking and believing other people hold more worth and value than you do. There are a few reasons we may experience insecurity:

- **Situations or events:** Certain situations or life events can create insecurity and anxiety. Stressful life events can include infidelity, separation, or divorce; a physical or mental health issue; or a substance dependence issue. Any stressful life event for you, your sweetie, or your child can create feelings of anxiety and insecurity—you may fear that others will find out, what they will think of you, and how the stressful life event will impact your and your child's life.

- **Social anxiety:** Insecurity shows up with anxiety in social situations due to the fears of being evaluated or rejected, doing and saying the right things, and being accepted, appreciated, and liked. For example, many moms struggle with making friends as adults, and playdates, mom groups, and activities where kids and parents gather create anxiety about how to connect, fit in, and manage their insecurities.

- **Perfectionism:** Insecurity flourishes when we hold overly high expectations and perfectionistic standards for ourselves, our sweetie, and our child. You may be struggling with perfectionism if you find yourself trying to be the "perfect mom." For example, you may believe that you should always know or anticipate what your child needs (to the point that your baby should never cry or that your child should never be uncomfortable, unhappy, or bored), that you and your child should always look good when you're in public, that your child should always behave well, and that mothering should come easily and be rewarding and enjoyable most of the time.

The reasons you may feel inadequate in motherhood are varied. Perhaps you had a difficult childhood or you're estranged from your family of origin, which creates feelings of insecurity and sadness around the holidays, birthdays, celebrations, or milestones for your child. Perhaps you wish you had grown up in a healthy family system and that your child had relationships with extended family. Or maybe you're going through marital difficulties and possibly considering separation—if so, you may be feeling inadequate and anxious that you're creating distress in your child's life.

Comparison, as a form of insecurity, comes in the form of not feeling "good enough" compared to other moms, especially when you form a pattern or habit of it. We can make comparisons in appearance (*She looks so put together; I'm always a mess; I feel like such a failure*), happiness (*She always looks happy and radiant with her baby; I'm so jealous*), or abilities (*How is it that she always knows what to do? I constantly feel lost; my child would be better off with a different mom*).

Insecurity happens to every mom at some point. But if insecurity is a frequent emotional response, disrupting your everyday living and taking away from your overall happiness, an act of self-care to improve well-being is to manage this shadow emotion. I recommend working with a counselor to understand and reduce these feelings.

At the Heart of Feeling Insecure

Insecurity is a vulnerable feeling. At the heart of insecurity is the longing to be accepted, appreciated, understood, and valued as a person. Insecurity can be most prominent during times of transition, stress, overwhelm, and taking on new roles and responsibilities. At the heart of feeling insecure is also a fear of rejection.

Insecurity is often created through trauma, rejection, and suffering from any point in the past. It may start somewhere in childhood with messages about us from significant adults (e.g., parents, teachers, coaches), friends and family, or impactful situations or experiences in our development. Insecurities can also develop later in life for similar reasons, or they can begin in a relationship with a critical partner, friend, or colleague. When this suffering has not been properly healed, it can play

You Are Not Alone: Caroline's Story

Caroline struggled with body image throughout high school. With a more athletic build, she thrived being part of the crew team in high school and college. Focusing on athletics and not weighing herself helped her and highlighted her feelings of strength. After the birth of her first child, Caroline had complications from delivery, making exercise and physical activity nearly impossible for an extended period. Her baby wasn't sleeping through the night and was newly diagnosed with allergies, making it difficult for Caroline to feel comfortable leaving her baby to work out.

Caroline came to me seven months postpartum for support on how to cope with the transition to motherhood, her physical pain from delivery, and her feelings of being irritable and anxious. A lot of Caroline's anxiety was rooted in thinking her life as it was right now would never be different, that it was always going to be this uncomfortable, and in feeling insecure from not being able to exercise and accept the changes in her body postpartum. One of the things I asked her to do was to limit comparisons, focus on her strengths, and manage her thoughts. While life was challenging right now, it would not be like this forever. And while she was limited in what she was able to do right now, this was a good time to be curious and explore what she was able to do for exercise comfortably.

We also came up with a plan to reduce her fears about leaving her baby by taking practice times in which her partner would be in charge and she could do something in the house, gradually increasing the amount of time she could leave the baby. Caroline worked on productive ways to reduce her anxiety with success.

out in the present as insecurity if we hold unhealthy inner beliefs about ourselves that we project onto our mothering, relationships with others (including our child and sweetie), and social situations.

Reframe Your Mantra

Thoughts are powerful. Your self-talk has a deep impact on what you feel and how you respond. Keep this principle in mind and reframe problematic thoughts that increase your shadow emotions.

SHADOW MANTRA If you're saying this . . .	THRIVING MANTRA Positively reframe to say this . . .
I don't think I'm a good mother.	Where is the evidence for this? I'm feeling insecure. Just because I think I'm not a good mom doesn't mean it is true. I can challenge this negative thought by listing five things I'm good at. If one of my mom friends said this to me, what would I say?
It's so hard making mom friends. They probably didn't want me to go—I bet they just invited me because my child and I were standing there.	Is it possible they invited me because they wanted to spend time with me? I'm focusing on the negative instead of looking at the positive: They included us.
I feel so insecure around other moms, and I just don't know what to talk about.	Many moms feel this way. I'm not alone. Maybe I could read up on how to make conversation. And talking to a counselor would help me feel better. I can learn the skills to feel more comfortable in social situations.

SHADOW MANTRA If you're saying this . . .	THRIVING MANTRA Positively reframe to say this . . .
Compared to other moms, I don't measure up; they have it all together.	Comparing myself to others is only keeping insecurity alive. I have no idea what goes on in another mom's life—what I see is a small moment in time. No mom is perfect, and all moms have tough times. Instead of comparing myself, I can spend time highlighting my strengths and what I do well, which is an act of self-care.

Moving Beyond the Shadows

TIP #1: ASK QUESTIONS TO CREATE SELF-AWARENESS.

Feeling insecure can be an internal struggle that presents in outward ways. Creating a deeper awareness about what you're feeling and why you're feeling this way is a great place to start. Ask yourself the following questions:

- What am I insecure about?

- How would I describe what's going on underneath my insecurity? Is it self-doubt? Fear of rejection? Regret over failures? Fear of being judged, criticized, or evaluated? An unresolved trauma?

- When I have these feelings, do my thoughts increase or decrease my negative feelings? What behaviors do I do that increase or decrease these feelings?

- What would I need to take away my insecurity?

- What would a friend tell me I need to do to address these insecurities?

- How has this insecurity I'm dealing with today been influenced by a past event or experience?

163

- Did my insecurity start in childhood? If so, how does this impact me today?

- How does insecurity show up in my life? Are my thoughts critical? Do I compare myself to others? Do I limit the activities and social situations I participate in? Do I gossip about others?

- What did I do then to make myself feel better and increase my confidence?

TIP #2: GET TO KNOW YOURSELF AND HIGHLIGHT YOUR STRENGTHS.

Changing the way you think and talk about yourself can increase your confidence and reduce your anxiety. Instead of focusing on what's missing, think about your strengths. Take a minute and list ten strengths you have. If you get stuck, reach out to a supportive person and ask them to help by highlighting what they observe in you. Write your strengths down, make a few copies of the list, and place them where you will see them often. If you've been going through a particularly challenging time and feel like you're not living up to your expectations, give yourself a pep talk. Write it in a letter to yourself—or share with a friend or family member—everything that you are working to manage right now. I bet the list is pretty long! Remember that perfection is impossible, and focus on the most important things that you are doing well instead of focusing on the little things you may not be doing perfectly.

Next, reflect on what it is you enjoy doing and how you like to spend your time. Is there an activity or hobby you used to enjoy doing but don't have the time to do? Is there an activity or hobby you'd love to try but have been nervous to pursue? If you knew you wouldn't fail, what would you like to do or try? Often, answering these questions and getting to know yourself more deeply can lead you down the path of healing and authenticity. The more you can focus on the activities and interests that bring you joy, happiness, and contentment regularly, the more you can increase your confidence, which can help you let go of insecurities.

TIP #3: DON'T COMPARE YOURSELF.

Much like a fire needs certain conditions to burn, so does insecurity. Comparing yourself to other moms keeps insecurity burning brightly. When you compare yourself to another mom, you're not seeing the situation accurately; you're viewing only a moment in time and making lots of assumptions about her and her life. What you see at school pickup or a playdate is only one part of her day. You have no idea what happened before or what she may be going through. Comparison is toxic—nothing good comes from it, and it breaks the connections between people and relationships.

When you compare yourself to another mom, catch yourself, and ask: *What about this mom inspires me? Is there a quality or trait I'm seeing in her life that I'd like to develop in mine?* And remind yourself that what you see is a small part of her day; you can never really know what another mom goes through unless you ask her and she tells you.

Another way to manage insecurity is to be aware of the situations that trigger this feeling. For example, many clients I work with inadvertently trigger their insecurity by scrolling on social media; the more time they spend on social media, the more they compare their lives to the feeds and stories they see and the more insecure they feel. One way to manage these feelings is to pay attention to the situations you find yourself in or the people you spend time with. Does spending time in these situations or with these people correlate with the shadow emotion of insecurity? Once you can identify the triggering situation, you can then take steps to limit how often you do these activities or spend time with certain people as an act of self-care when you're feeling stressed or vulnerable.

TIP #4: PRACTICE MAKING DECISIONS.

Lack of confidence and insecurity can create a dynamic of being overly accommodating in relationships. You may agree to most anything without voicing your opinions or preferences, believing your view doesn't matter or count. Underneath indecision can also be a fear of upsetting someone; you may perceive that saying no or voicing an opinion will create conflict. Some individuals hate making decisions, especially when others are involved, because they believe that if things don't go well, then they'll be held responsible for the negative outcome. One way to address insecurity is to develop the skill of verbally expressing your ideas, making decisions, and planning outings. Practice expressing your thoughts and ideas as often as you can with supportive people, and be ok if/when things don't go exactly as planned. You're practicing using your voice, so be sure to focus on this accomplishment!

Thriving Mama Reflection

When we look in the mirror, why is the first thought often a negative one—*What's wrong?*—instead of, *What's true?* When we look in the mirror, we often scan for imperfections and wish we could change. Looking at our reflection, our mind is active, but our body is still. Is this a true representation of ourselves, or just a motionless one? Standing in front of a person who you know will criticize you creates tension, anxiety, and discomfort. Perhaps what is being reflected in the mirror when you see your flaws instead of your strengths and beauty is how you feel in the presence of a critical person. Conversely, if you were to move in front of a mirror, dancing, smiling, and laughing with your child, what would you see? Likely you'd experience the energy of joy and beauty in this moment between you and your child. It is the same mirror and the same *you* being reflected, but what's changed is how you relate to the mirror. However insecurity presents in your life, think about this example of the mirror. Try this exercise: Every day for a week, whenever you look in the mirror, highlight one strength you have that has nothing to do with your appearance.

Whenever you feel insecure, remember how you feel when you're standing in front of a critic. Encouraging yourself with love, kindness, and compassion will allow you and others to experience the most authentic and truest parts of yourself.

fear is a great teacher

how embracing what you are afraid of helps you to develop trust and calm

Being a mother is learning about strengths you didn't know you had, and dealing with fears you didn't know existed.
—Linda Wooten

Motherhood is filled with many moments of uncertainty, from the first night at home with your child, to the first fever and the cries that you can't seem to soothe. Over time we adjust to the uncertainty of motherhood, finding a new rhythm and confidence and knowing what our child needs by going through a decision tree to problem-solve until they are safe, content, and calm. Then there are the shadow emotions that take anxiety and fear to a whole new level, catching us as moms off guard. We experience these shadow emotions on a continuum of intensity, from being afraid, on the mild end of the continuum, to becoming scared and frightened, in the middle of the continuum, to feeling terrified, on the severe end of the continuum.

In motherhood, being afraid is feeling fear in the form of apprehension regarding something that hasn't happened yet (such as being afraid the first time your child rides the bus to school). An example of being scared—a state of nervousness, fear, anxiety, or panic—is when your child is riding a bike and falls, and you just know their cries mean they're really hurt. Until you can get to them to help, you're feeling scared. Feeling frightened is a fearful response to something sudden that happens. For example, the first time you go to your child's room in the morning, only to find they're not in the crib, they've learned to crawl, but much to your surprise, looking into an empty crib creates an incredible fear response! When frightened, your adrenaline surges until you realize your baby has just learned how to climb out of the crib! Feeling terrified is an intense fearful response to a situation or imagined scenario or thought; for every parent, terror is losing your child in a store (even for a minute) or seeing something horrible in the news about a child.

Moms I've supported have shared some of the reasons for feeling these shadow emotions:

- They are afraid harm could happen to their child (or them).
- They are scared of being separated from their child.
- They are frightened by the intensity of love and responsibility that comes with being a mom.
- They are afraid of turning into their mothers.
- They are frightened when their baby sleeps through the night for the first time.
- They are scared of their child growing up and blaming them for something they did or didn't do.
- They are afraid of a situation, person, or event.
- They are scared of making mistakes or "messing up" as parents.
- They are terrified of getting a disease or illness that has

afflicted other family members (e.g., Alzheimer's disease, multiple sclerosis, or cancer).

- They are afraid of losing themselves and who they once were now that they are mothers.
- They are scared that something will happen to them and they won't be able to raise their child.
- They are afraid or frightened of the unknown.

All of these situations have one thing in common: They started with a thought, whether true or not, which creates a response in the body. Thoughts are incredibly powerful and believable! Remember from our earlier discussions of fear and anxiety—it's as if our body turns on a light switch. It immediately begins to show physical symptoms (increased heart rate, higher blood pressure, faster breathing, sweating, dilated pupils, shaking, and trembling), all trying to tell you this situation is dangerous for you and your child. But remember, just because you may feel the physical symptoms of fear or anxiety doesn't mean you or your child are truly in danger.

As an example of how our thoughts influence our feelings, let's imagine you're at the market with your toddler and they insist on walking with you instead of sitting in the cart. As you head to the parking lot, holding your toddler's hand, they bolt from your grip, distracted by an object they see, and run into the parking lot. Likely, your first reaction is panic, which comes out as yelling your child's name and running to them. As you get hold of your child, you say in a loud voice, "*Why did you do that? That was dangerous, and you could have been hurt! You always hold Mommy's hand in the parking lot!*" Your reaction likely came across to your child as anger, perhaps fear.

Later that night, when you are trying to sleep, you begin having a lot of thoughts about the scene earlier in the day: *What if I had been on the phone and had been slow to run after my child? What if my child is with another adult and does this? Maybe I can't take my child anywhere, because they could bolt. If I'm not there to protect my child, will someone else be able to? What if this happens again?* As you go through all of the "what-if" scenarios, you begin to feel panic and anxiety yet again, similar to what you felt earlier in the day. Your thoughts convince you these things are true: Your child is not safe with any adult, you can never go to the store with your child, and your child bolting in the parking lot will happen every time you go out, making going anywhere with your child dangerous.

Sometimes our worries and fears are based in real-life events, not just our thoughts. Personal trauma can impact a mother profoundly. Trauma is an undercurrent that runs beneath these shadow emotions of fear. Trauma is an emotional response to a threatening or horrible experience, such as a threat to your safety (e.g., a car accident or house fire, violent crime, sexual assault, or domestic abuse) as well as trauma you witnessed in childhood or adolescence (e.g., parental substance abuse and dependence, untreated mental health issues, domestic violence). There are other forms of traumatic experiences, such as parental divorce with one parent abandoning the family, or living in poverty without adequate food, shelter, or stability, and personal trauma from loss (such as having a sibling with a chronic illness or losing a sibling in childhood). And many women have traumatic losses from miscarriage, stillbirth, or infant loss that continue to impact their mothering. Traumatic life experiences may have happened in the past, but they often continue to impact a mother in the form of what she worries about—she is afraid something awful could happen again to either her or her child.

Understanding the layers to these fear-based shadow emotions is an important aspect of managing these feelings.

At the Heart of Feeling Afraid, Scared, Frightened, and Terrified

These shadow emotions are emotional responses to fearful moments or situations that we worry about happening in the moment or sometime in the future. (Or we fear that these moments or situations are a possibility or have the potential to happen.) At the heart of these variations of emotional responses is a need for control, a need to make sure we are prepared for a situation or outcome. Another layer beneath these emotions is our desire to be safe, secure, comfortable, and pain-free. If we are uncomfortable, feel unsafe, or are in physical or emotional pain, we may have fears rooted in uncertainty. We may believe that things will never get better, that they will always be like they are now. Also, a core instinct and drive in motherhood is to protect, and when a mama perceives threat or harm, her emotional drive is to move through the fear and do what it takes to protect her child or herself. The challenging aspect of fear is that sometimes a mama can't distinguish actual danger from something that's not dangerous at all.

Reframe Your Mantra

Thoughts are powerful. Your self-talk has a deep impact on what you feel and how you respond. Keep this principle in mind and reframe problematic thoughts that increase your shadow emotions.

SHADOW MANTRA If you're saying this . . .	THRIVING MANTRA Positively reframe to say this . . .
What if this happens, or what if it doesn't happen?	My mind is jumping ahead to all the worst-case scenarios, which is increasing my fears. I'd love to have certainty right now, and that's not possible. The best thing I can do is deal with the facts and prepare for actual risk. If a friend came to me worried about this exact concern, what would I say?
I wouldn't feel this way if I knew everything was going to turn out okay.	I'm uncomfortable and scared. I can't predict an outcome, but I can manage my fears by focusing on what I can do; for example, I can reach out for support to help me through this.
I'm scared something bad will happen.	Feelings are not always accurate, so I have to challenge the thoughts that fuel the feeling. Where is the evidence that something bad will happen? Focusing on my strengths and the actions I can take to care for my child and myself in a productive way is what I need to focus on.
I'm afraid to think about it or talk about it.	Paying attention to what I'm feeling is an act of self-care. Ignoring or avoiding my feelings will create more stress, and the feelings will get more intense. Reaching out to a supportive person and sharing what I'm going through is an act of self-care.

(continued)

SHADOW MANTRA If you're saying this . . .	THRIVING MANTRA Positively reframe to say this . . .
I'm terrified that an awful event could happen again.	That event was really traumatic, and I hope I never feel that type of emotion again. What do I need right now to take care of myself? I learned so much from that experience that I have to trust my intentions and actions. I have to trust that I will not be in a situation like that ever again.
I'm afraid of it, so I avoid it. It's too scary to talk about.	Facing my fears can feel terrifying. But to thrive I need to look at my fears. I don't have to go this alone; reaching out to a mental health professional is an act of self-care.

Moving Beyond the Shadows

TIP #1: ASK QUESTIONS TO CREATE SELF-AWARENESS.

When you have a fearful emotional response, it is important to label and identify the feeling. Ask yourself these questions:

- What am I feeling right now? Am I afraid, scared, frightened, or terrified?

- What was the situation, event, or conversation that started this emotional reaction?

- How would I categorize my shadow emotion: as a real threat or danger or as a perceived threat or danger?

- What are the physical symptoms in my body? Does my heart race? Do I breathe fast? Do I perspire? Does my stomach become upset? Do I feel light-headed? Do my muscles become tense? Do I clench my jaw?

- When I have felt this way in the past, what has helped me? What has made me feel worse? What do I need to do to take care of myself?

TIP #2: INCREASE YOUR SELF-CARE.

When you're in a space or stretch of time when fear is becoming disruptive to your life, self-care is a must. Not getting enough sleep, consuming too much caffeine, drinking alcohol, and enduring chronic stress can increase your fear-based emotional responses and thoughts. The self-care skill of getting enough sleep helps restore your body, and feeling rested makes it easier to use healthy coping skills (e.g., it provides you with enough energy to go for a walk and challenge irrational or fear-based thoughts).

One of the most consistent recommendations I share with clients who are anxious or have fearful thoughts is to increase water intake and keep caffeine intake below 400 mg per day; consuming more than 400 mg of caffeine can increase heart rate, anxiety, and agitation.

Find three ways you can improve your self-care. Perhaps you need to make your sleep a top priority, take a day off from work, or begin counseling to talk about the persistent fearful thoughts that are disrupting your life. And self-care can also be as simple as starting your day with a few minutes of quiet time, turning off the car radio and driving in silence when your day feels loud and noisy, or taking a break from social media and the news for a few days until you feel better.

TIP #3: PRACTICE GROUNDING TECHNIQUES.

Feeling afraid or scared can propel thoughts of low-probability things becoming a high possibility or reality. One way to work through these feelings is to stay in the here and now by practicing grounding techniques. This skill involves focusing on your five senses (sight, sound, touch, smell, and taste) to reduce anxiety and increase a sense of calm.

5-4-3-2-1 Grounding Technique

Option #1: This technique was originally created for people who are anxious about traveling by plane, car, or other form of transportation.[4] But it is effective far beyond those specific situations. Whenever you're in a stressful situation and need to move into a calmer state, this is a great grounding technique to use.

Start by naming the following things in the environment or situation you're currently in:

- Name five things you *see* (look around your environment and name what you see).

- Name five things you *hear* (listen for sounds in your environment or outside).

- Name five things you *feel* (focus on the pressure of touch, whether you are standing or sitting, and notice what you feel).

- Name four things you *see*, four things you *hear*, and four things you *feel*.

- Repeat the preceding steps to name three things, then two things, and then one thing in each category. After completing one 5-4-3-2-1 cycle, check in with how you're feeling and repeat the whole cycle once more if needed to continue to create calm and release tension.

Option #2: Here is an alternative way to practice this grounding skill:

- Look and say out loud five things you *see*.
- Touch and notice four things you *feel*.
- Listen and notice three things you *hear*.
- Sniff and notice two things you *smell*.

- Eat or drink and identify one thing you can *taste*.
- Repeat the cycle once more if needed.

Thriving Mama Reflection

Feeling any of these fearful emotional responses can be upsetting and uncomfortable. I want you to think of this feeling differently by acknowledging this word: *scared*. When you feel scared, you perceive danger and respond accordingly to protect what is important to you. However, sometimes danger can be misperceived, and the misperceptions trick your mind into believing that danger is inevitable, even when there is no proof of a potential threat.

If you take the word *scared* and reorganize it, another word is created: *sacred*. What is sacred to you are the things you cherish, respect, and hold at the center of your heart. And nothing is more sacred than your child, your life, and your family. When you feel any variation of this feeling of being scared, your internal drive is to protect. However, when there is no imminent danger or threat, shifting your perception can help you think more rationally. Moving the letters around in *scared* to form *sacred* is a perfect illustration of how shifting your perception can create a different experience. When you have these fear-filled moments, be compassionate toward yourself, allow yourself to feel, and remember that what you are *scared* for inside is often what is most *sacred* to you.

PART IV

using anger as a teacher for growth and joy

I yell at my children all the time—I feel so guilty for losing control.

I'm so frustrated. I just need some help and someone to listen to me.

I'm afraid one day I'm going to snap and really hurt my child. I'm afraid of what I could do or say.

I wish I didn't have to work so much, like some of my friends, so I could spend more time with my child.

I'm going to be bold and make a declarative statement: Mothers get angry. Whether they share it or not, whether they express it or hide it, all moms experience the shadow emotion of anger.

Anger is the broadest of the shadow emotions. It can be felt on its own or as a buildup of other unmanaged shadow emotions like sadness, fear, disgust, and embarrassment. Anger is the shadow emotion with a goal to protect you against threat and to prepare you for self-defense. But it's also the shadow emotion that protects you from *previous* pain and suffering. Spend time with anyone who is angry, and when you hear their story, it will be apparent that somewhere along the way, they felt sad, experienced a loss, and now harbor regret for something they can't go back and change (although they wish they could).

Experiencing the shadow emotion of anger often seems like a natural choice, as dealing with suffering and pain takes energy, strength, and vulnerability. It can be scary to feel pain, to cry, to put words to feelings and experiences, so anger is the better choice. Or so it seems. Anger is energizing and keeps people moving. And for moms who are under pressure, overwhelmed, and exhausted, often there is not enough time to deal with what's underneath their anger.

Anger can feel comfortable for many moms; it's what they know and what they're used to. Generally speaking, the average mom doesn't intend to or want to feel angry. She starts her day feeling exhausted, or maybe pretty good—nothing a little coffee or tea can't help. And as she goes throughout her day, she coaches herself with statements like, *Today's going to be different. You're not going to lose it, you're not going to yell.* But as small frustrations escalate into battles with her children ("Don't argue with me; you have to sit in the car seat.") and internal disappointments with her sweetie (*They promised to do the dishes and laundry. Why can't I ever get any help around the house? Do I have to be responsible for everything?*), her optimism about not yelling fades away as tension rises through her neck and shoulders.

With her child finally in the car seat, she slams the car door, letting out a sigh, then climbs into the driver's seat and grips the steering wheel tightly. As they head to daycare, her child talks nonstop. Mom asks for a couple minutes of quiet. But as she accelerates onto the highway, her child says, "Mommy." She yells in response, "WHAT IS IT?! I just need a minute of quiet! Why can't you give me a minute?" Her child begins to cry, and she asks angrily, "WHAT? What was so important?" Through their tears, her child says, "I just wanted to say I love you, Mommy."

And you know as well as I do what this mother instantly feels: guilt, regret, sadness, resentment toward her sweetie or others in her life (she wouldn't be so angry if she had more help), and shame.

Mothers who express their anger in words or actions as the mom did in this example can spiral into a deep hole of guilt, sadness, regret, shame, and more anger. Which is why understanding the shadow emotion of anger and learning the skills outlined in this section and throughout this book (and putting them into practice) will help a mother heal the suffering she's been pushing down, the suffering she manages to express only through angry words, actions, and interactions. Anger in motherhood comes out in many ways and variations, and in the chapters that follow, we will explore this shadow emotion in detail.

chapter 13

the red flags of anger

how paying attention to irritability, frustration, and anger is the path of self-care & joy

If you are patient in one moment of anger, you will escape a
hundred days of sorrow.
—Chinese proverb

I have no doubt that as a mother, you experience some form of
anger—perhaps when you are running late for school or practices
or doctor's appointments, or when you are stuck in traffic with
a fussing child in the back seat, or when your child refuses to
cooperate and throws a tantrum over the simplest things. Anger
is often the emotional response we experience when things don't
go as we've planned, when there's a glitch, delay, or outcome that
we're unable to prevent.

Sometimes feeling angry has little to do with our children and
more to do with something else: an upsetting conversation with
a friend or family member, a rough day at work, or our feelings
of exhaustion, hunger, or being unappreciated or unsupported.
Many roads can lead to feeling the shadow emotion of anger in
motherhood. Anger is an emotion expressed on a continuum, as it

has different intensities. Like many of the other shadow emotions, anger is a feeling on *one channel* with *different volumes*; how loud the volume becomes is the intensity of the anger we experience.

In motherhood, low levels of anger start out as annoyances and increase to irritability throughout the day; for example, forgetting to restock the diaper bag with wipes, being the only one in the house who seems to know how to replace the toilet paper roll, or leaving for work with no time to spare only to realize the car needs gas. Then there are the more frustrating things: cleaning the floor only to have our sweetie and kids walk in minutes later, tracking mud across the freshly mopped floor; our kids complaining about the dinner we've made; and constantly repeating the simplest requests (*"Make your bed," "Brush your teeth," "Put your toys away and your laundry in the hamper"*).

These small moments of the shadow emotion of anger build up throughout the day. The volume that started out low as annoyance and irritability is beginning to get louder and louder, developing into feelings of frustration and tension because things aren't going as we'd planned despite our good intentions. The volume reaches moderate anger with the lack of cooperation and support from our sweetie and children. This buildup of pressure can eventually explode as fury and rage, the most intense forms of anger, when we have reached our breaking point.

The shadow emotion of anger can also be felt in any intensity without a prolonged buildup, in response to situations posing perceived or actual threat, harm, or hurt to us, our child, or anyone or anything of value to us. Regardless of how this shadow emotion is created, left unmanaged or untreated, chronic anger can become problematic, disrupting our health and well-being and signaling a mental health issue such as depression or anxiety.

Anger is often created by our perceptions and appraisals of a situation. When we have a fixed belief of how things *should* be or how things *should* go, we create an expectation; if this expectation isn't met, we end up feeling frustrated, upset, and angry. Anytime we have a fixed position or expectancy in the outcome of a situation, we become vulnerable to feeling frustrated, disappointed, annoyed, or sad.

Years ago, before I was a mother, I was working at a community mental health center treating adolescents and their families who were struggling with substance abuse and mental health issues. I'll never forget a conversation I had with my supervisor as we were discussing a very challenging family I was working with. Both parents had a lot of anger issues, expressing verbal rage and at times physical abuse. I remember thinking, *How could they be so angry with their child?* My supervisor chuckled and said, "Oh just wait—you don't have kids, but when you do, you'll understand. You get angry as a parent, but taking it out on your child is never okay." I thought of this conversation years later when, as a new mom, I was exhausted, sleep deprived, incredibly overwhelmed, and feeling angry because all I wanted to do was sleep.

Since then, almost two decades later, I've experienced and continue to experience many moments of anger, frustration, irritability, and upset. A few times I have felt anger that is close to rage, although these moments have been related to other stressors in my life, not mothering. It can be a very uncomfortable and scary feeling to experience anger. But once you learn the skills to identify and manage anger, you can experience the emotion and *not act on it.*

When interacting with an angry person (or when you feel this way), it's not uncommon to label this person (or yourself) as rude, nasty, mean, manipulative, or unhappy. But looking a little deeper than the surface of labeling and judging, you will find valuable information. What I've observed in my years of practice is that anger may be the *expressed* emotion, but prior to someone feeling anger, they felt various shadow emotions of fear, sadness, embarrassment, or disgust. The reality is that most angry people have experienced hurt, pain, rejection, injustice, frustration, loneliness, depression, anxiety, and suffering in some form. This *doesn't* give the person permission to treat someone aggressively through their words or actions, but it allows understanding as to what may be going on beneath the surface.

In the moment, anger can be experienced as a powerful, energizing, and organizing response to defend and protect. That kind of response is helpful when there is actual threat, but what happens when the *perceived threat* is our child not listening or doing something we expect of them? Or our child throwing a tantrum at bedtime? Or our frustrated attempts to leave the house in the morning to get to school on time? Or when we make a mistake or forget something and we have a disproportionately negative appraisal of ourselves, turning the anger inward and defining ourselves as a *bad mother*? Or when there's a buildup of pain or suffering with other emotions that comes out as an outburst of rage in an unexpected way, like yelling at our child for asking the same question for the tenth time that day? Then anger can be detrimental to a child and a parent.

Regardless of which shadow emotion is being felt (frustration, anger, or rage), we can use similar tips, skills, and strategies to decrease the feeling and move into thriving.

Examples of the Anger Continuum in Motherhood

- **Rage:** feeling violent, uncontrollable anger

- **Furious:** feeling extremely angry

- **Angry:** experiencing strong feelings of annoyance, displeasure, hostility

- **Mad:** feeling intensely angry or displeased

- **Upset:** feeling troubled mentally or emotionally or feeling a sense of disorder

- **Frustrated:** feeling prevented from achieving a goal, feeling a lack of courage and confidence

- **Annoyed, Aggravated, and Irritable:** feeling or showing irritation

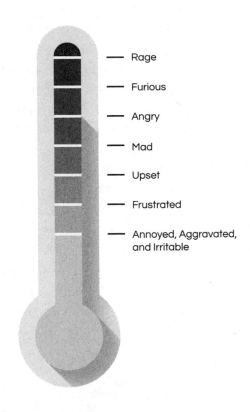

— Rage

— Furious

— Angry

— Mad

— Upset

— Frustrated

— Annoyed, Aggravated, and Irritable

Annoyed, Aggravated, and Irritable

- When a situation goes a certain way that is unexpected and disappointing.

- Feeling aggravated when you repeatedly ask your children to do something and they do not, forcing you to repeat yourself multiple times.

- Not having free time by yourself.

- Having to change plans because of a sick child or another demand that is needed of you from your family.

- Finally getting children to sleep, the only alone and quiet time of the day for you, only to have them wake up and not be able to go back to sleep, and quiet time doesn't happen.

Frustrated and Upset

- Annoyance builds to frustration and upset as you continue to repeat yourself over and over again, requesting that your child or sweetie do something, perhaps complete a chore or stop fighting with a sibling, only to have your requests ignored.

- Despite your best efforts in planning to get out of the house for work, school, or an appointment, something comes up; for example, your child throws a tantrum because they don't want to wear shoes to school, sabotaging your well-planned intentions, and you're late.

- Being touched, pulled on, or bumped into constantly, all day long.

- Giving to others most of the day, whether at home, work, or volunteering with no time alone or to restore yourself (that is, not being able to replenish what you are giving away).

- Being short on sleep and high on demands and responsibilities.

- Lack of time to do what you want.

- Too many competing demands and roles to fill (that is, work is never done, and there is always something more to do).

Mad and Angry

- Frustration and upset escalate until you're feeling mad and angry about repeating yourself over and over and over again to your sweetie and children.

- When someone leaves your child out of a party and they heard about it at school and come home crying because they weren't invited.

- Anger when you find out your child has created a secret social media account and isn't making great choices.

- Anger that you're always or almost always the one to get up in the middle of the night with the kids, instead of your sweetie.

- Feeling the burden of the mental load and wanting things to change at home.

- Not having enough support, whether emotional or physical, to help with the demands placed on you.

Furious and Enraged

- Chronic exhaustion paired with unresolved anger from your child talking back, the lack of support from your sweetie, no personal freedom or time to reset, and challenges with bedtime can send you over the edge.

- Anger is felt intensely when a child lies or refuses to do something, and there is potential for name-calling and verbal abuse in an attempt to get your child to listen and follow through with your requests, only to feel horrible and guilty afterward.

- Anger that is rageful can potentially breed aggression in the form of physical altercations, throwing objects, slamming doors, road-raging, or committing physical and emotional abuse.

- Frustration builds with constant battles with your children to do the most reasonable requests that you lose your temper, raise your voice, and use your physical size and presence to intimidate your child into doing the requested behavior.

Now that you have an overview of the continuum of anger and can see how the many levels may manifest, pay attention to where your "temperature" is throughout the day. As with any shadow emotion, having awareness is the first step to thriving. When you feel anger, check in with yourself, but don't ask, "How angry am I?" Instead, create some distance between you and your feeling and ask yourself, "What is my temperature?" and, "How can I bring this temperature down if I need to?" The next section is filled with great ideas and skills to help you bring down and keep your shadow emotion of anger at a comfortable temperature.

Suppressing Anger

Suppressing anger comes in the form of denying it, ignoring it, or not allowing yourself to admit this shadow emotion. Some examples of suppressing anger can include:

- being impatient about small things in day-to-day activities;
- being reluctant to open up and share personal concerns and issues with others;
- denying or being unwilling to share or admit to feeling angry when asked directly about your feelings;
- avoiding expressing your feelings;
- avoiding addressing and talking about hurt feelings;
- ignoring or having difficulty directly addressing or working through conflict or disagreements;
- being described by others as moody, edgy, or unpredictable;
- responding to others when asked how you're feeling with, "Fine," when things are not;
- stomach and GI upset;
- tense muscles; and
- clenching teeth/jaw.

Pushing down and ignoring anger can create physical symptoms such as: headaches, upset stomach and gastrointestinal issues, sleep difficulties, problems eating or with your appetite, shoulder, back, and neck tension, and teeth grinding or jaw clenching.

Passive-Aggressive Anger

When anger is not directly acknowledged or when it is ignored, pushed down (suppressed), or not managed, this shadow emotion can be acted out and expressed through words, voice tone, and behaviors. Some examples include:

- sighing;
- talking under your breath;
- agreeing to help someone or do something, only to forget or intentionally delay completing others' requests or your personal responsibilities;
- being defensive and argumentative;
- blaming others instead of taking personal responsibility;
- making fun of or mocking someone;
- being stubborn;
- expressing nonverbal anger, such as rolling your eyes, shaking your head, using threatening hand gestures, and so on;
- not cooperating;
- complaining;
- acting sullen, pouting, or giving someone the silent treatment;
- being unwilling to hear another's perspective;
- photographing or videotaping an upset child;
- being upset but responding with curt, short answers, or saying, "I'm fine"; and
- ignoring someone or shutting down (also called stonewalling).

Aggressive Anger

When the shadow emotion of anger is not managed, anger can be expressed through words or behaviors meant to intimidate or harm. Unmanaged anger can also result in direct physical or emotional abuse and violence. Some examples can include:

- gossiping or spreading rumors;
- criticizing others directly or to other people;
- ignoring or leaving others out of a group (e.g., family members, friends, and so on);
- being defensive and argumentative;
- blaming others instead of taking personal responsibility;
- intentionally giving someone you're upset with the silent treatment;
- calling another person names;
- making fun of or mocking someone;
- bullying someone;
- slamming doors;
- intimidating others through your voice, tone, body language, size, and behaviors;
- throwing objects either directly at someone or indirectly, creating intimidation and a fear response; and
- physical aggression, such as pushing/shoving and hitting.

Heathy and Assertive Ways to Express Anger

The shadow emotion of anger can be expressed in healthy ways as an effort to increase self-care and coping within yourself, as well as within your role as a mother, partner, friend, daughter, colleague, volunteer, and so on. Some examples include:

- expressing feelings in a direct way without intimidating or blaming others;

- sharing your feelings without being threatening;

- taking responsibility for your words, behaviors, and actions;

- showing a willingness to resolve conflict;

- demonstrating a willingness to hear another's point of view and perspective without defensiveness;

- accepting responsibility for your mistakes when you've hurt another's feelings or had upsetting interactions;

- using caring, calm, and thoughtful behaviors, words, and tones of voice;

- using respectful ways of communicating;

- confronting conflict and disagreements in a gentle, calm, and loving way; and

- practicing nondefensive listening (e.g., not interrupting or showing contempt through your facial responses or gestures).

At the Heart of Anger

Anger is a shadow emotion that can be threatening, scary, and uncontrollable. Of course anger can be an emotion felt on its own, but usually before we feel anger we felt other feelings. Often beneath the surface of anger are many emotional reactions: exhaustion, fear, sadness, anxiety, worry, jealousy, loss, depression, embarrassment, disgust, rejection, and so many more feelings.

Sometimes it's easier to express anger than it is to share what's really going on. Many of us mothers experience incredible exhaustion in motherhood, making it feel overwhelming at times to practice self-care or identify what we're stressed about, because all we can think about is moving through our list of obligations in order to get to the end of our day so we can rest. So we put off what we're really feeling, pushing it down, ignoring it. Anger can seem easier than dealing with what's going on beneath the surface when we are exhausted.

Because anger has energy, it can seem powerful and useful for motivating, invigorating, and protecting us and keeping us moving forward. However, at the heart of anger is suffering, and we need to embrace this shadow emotion with compassion and curiosity to find a way to heal what is hurting inside. Instead of judging this feeling by saying, *"It's wrong to feel this,"* or *"I'm out of control,"* or *"I'm not a good mother for feeling this way,"* we need to simply see the emotion of anger as something neither good nor bad. It just *is.* At the heart of anger is something else, a type of suffering that needs to be taken care of, managed, and worked through with compassion.

Reframe Your Mantra

Thoughts are powerful. Your self-talk has a deep impact on what you feel and how you respond. Keep this principle in mind and reframe problematic thoughts that increase your shadow emotions.

The thoughts in the following table are some examples of thoughts of anger, beginning with milder forms (such as undertones of frustration and annoyance), then moving to more moderate feelings (such as anger), then progressing to more severe forms (such as fury and rage).

SHADOW MANTRA If you're saying this . . .	THRIVING MANTRA Positively reframe to say this . . .
I need a moment to myself, okay?	Letting others know what I need when I start to feel irritation or overwhelm is a good thing. Making sure to say this in a kind way, without directing it at anyone to feel punishing or scary or hurtful, is important. Asking for what I need to reset and take care of myself is an important skill to learn.

(continued)

SHADOW MANTRA If you're saying this . . .	THRIVING MANTRA Positively reframe to say this . . .
I'm so angry repeating myself! If only they'd listen.	Repeating myself is super frustrating and leads to anger because I'm not getting the cooperation I need. I do not like how my children are behaving and responding to me, but they're kids and I have to understand their development. What is it that I want to teach them about listening to me? Yelling or expressing anger will show them these behaviors are okay. I need a minute or more to regroup so I can approach this with curious problem-solving instead of an angry, blaming reaction.
I'm tense and can feel it in my shoulders and neck.	Knowing the first signs of anger in my body is important. When I feel tension in my neck and shoulders and feel frustrated, I need to stop and do something to take care of myself. What is the one thing I can do in this moment to help me manage this feeling so the tension doesn't escalate?
I'm not sure I can do this anymore.	I've been so stressed, my anger is creating hopelessness. I know I can keep going, but not the way I am right now. Thinking this way is a sign I need a break and more support and cooperation. What is the one step I can take to feel better?
I'm so annoyed. Why did it have to go this way? I just wish it would go the way I planned.	I'm upset and disappointed with how things turned out. Believing things should go a certain way, especially with kids, can set me up to feel this emotion. Can I focus on what I could do differently next time? How can I manage my disappointment and anger right now? What act of self-care would help me release this tension and anger?

SHADOW MANTRA If you're saying this . . .	THRIVING MANTRA Positively reframe to say this . . .
Please, I just want to be left alone. Is that too much to ask?	Motherhood involves losing a lot of personal freedoms, and some days that is so hard to deal with! When I notice myself thinking this way, it can be a signal that my energy is depleted and I need to recharge and have some time away from my responsibilities. Which supportive person in my life can help me with this?
Stop that! You don't want to think about what can happen if you don't listen!	I'm so angry right now, and threatening others is not managing my emotions—it's taking my emotions out on them. I'm being threatening as well, and that destroys trust in relationships. How can I take care of myself and manage my frustration differently right now? Calling a supportive person to talk this through and getting some physical activity would be helpful.
I'm so angry, I could hit something or say something I regret.	Sometimes my standards and expectations are unrealistic and perfectionistic. Sometimes I just have one of those days. Expecting that things should go exactly as I want or that others should do it exactly my way is a setup for conflict and frustration. If a friend came to me with this exact situation, what advice would I share?

Moving Beyond the Shadows

TIP #1: ASK QUESTIONS TO CREATE SELF-AWARENESS.

Creating awareness about what you're feeling and experiencing is the first step to managing your emotional responses. As you read through the following questions, remember to be curious about what you learn about your anger. Let go of judgment and have an open heart to identify the ways you react—having this information will help you make healthier choices going forward.

- Imagining the thermometer we discussed on page 186, think of your emotional baseline, a range of what you most often feel in a given week. Using this scale from one to ten, what is your emotional baseline of one of the anger shadow emotions? Now, what are the triggers, situations, or issues that arise and move this number up the scale? How often does this happen (e.g., in a given week or month, around the holidays or family visits, or when your child is sick and you've lost sleep)?

- What are some of the other shadow emotions present when you feel anger (e.g., sad, lonely, afraid, worried, embarrassed)?

- What physical symptoms do you experience when you're angry?

- How do you express anger in your behaviors? Are you passive-aggressive when you are angry? Are you aggressive? Do you suppress, ignore, or avoid? Do you work it out through talking and self-care?

TIP #2: REMEMBER THAT YOU'RE A WORK IN PROCESS.
We're all *works in process*. Before we can make change, we need to have awareness, and awareness is about *observing* and *processing* what is happening inside your mind, body, and spirit. When you can understand this, you can move into problem-solving mode and decide what you'd like to modify and respond to.

One way to understand how anger impacts you is to reflect on up to five recent episodes when you were angry. Remember, hold off on judging yourself. Shift your fears regarding how this anger sounds or what it looks like or what it can mean into a place of curiosity and compassion to understand what you experience when you feel angry. Creating this awareness is the first step to making change. Take a minute to process a few recent episodes. I've created some example charts to help you see what this exercise might look like (see chart on pages 200–201). Use a notebook to recreate the chart or go to MomsWellBeing.com to download a copy and fill it in according to one episode from your life.

- Identify the situation or stressful interaction or episode.

- Rate your anger in the moment on a scale of one to ten, with one being calm and ten being enraged and furious.

- When you were angry, where did you hold this anger in your body? For example, did you experience a tense jaw, back pain, headaches, facial tension, high blood pressure, or a racing heart?

- Write down any self-talk you had or other thoughts you observed.

- Sometimes anger is an emotional reaction that happens on its own. Often there are other shadow emotions contributing to and residing under the surface of anger. Try to identify and label other emotions you may have felt before or in addition to the anger.

- Jot down how you reacted in this incident or situation.

- Processing this event, how would you like to respond in the future in a similar situation?

When you finish filling out your own chart, take a minute and ask yourself these questions:

- What is the one thing that stood out most for me while reviewing these episodes?

- What are the steps I can take to reduce the intensity of what I'm feeling or to intervene sooner with a skill or strategy so I don't get to level-ten rage?

- How can I be more compassionate and caring to myself in these moments?

Understand + Manage Your Anger

Situation or Stress	Level of Anger (1–10)	Where Did You Feel Tension in Your Body?	Thoughts You Observed	
Phone call with sweetie about in-law visit.	5	Felt it in my neck and stomach.	I don't want to be judged or hurt.	
Daughter isn't listening to me.	8	Clenched jaw and racing heart.	I'm so angry—she never listens to me. I'm tired of repeating myself.	
Not enough support from family/sweetie with chores.	4	Feeling exhausted in my whole body.	I need help. Why do I have to keep asking people to do their part? Why am I the one to see what has to be done? I'm always on repeat or yelling to get everyone to help.	
Son getting bullied at school.	9	Heart racing, tension all over. I want to punch someone.	What is wrong with this kid? What is wrong with the parents? I'm going to lose control.	

Identify a Feeling That Came before the Anger	How You Reacted	How You'd Like to Respond
Sadness.	Assertive but raised my voice a few times.	Maybe a bit calmer. Didn't expect to talk about the in-law visit; was taken off guard. Maybe delay planning until we have more time to chat instead of having a rushed call.
Frustration and worry: What am I doing wrong that she doesn't listen?	Yelled, slammed the door, threatened her.	Walk away or ask for a moment to compose myself. Talk to her with the goal of problem-solving, not with anger and threats.
Frustration, exhaustion, aloneness, annoyance.	Yelled, slammed the door, threatened them.	Walk away or ask for a moment to compose myself. Talk to them with the goal of problem solving, not with anger and threats. I don't want to scare my family by slamming things anymore.
Rage, sadness, worry for my son.	Helping my son, keeping my emotions in check, focusing on him. Left a message with the kid's mom that was intense but direct; saw the bully at school pickup and glared at him, mumbled under my breath.	Leaving a message of anger only made things worse. The bully told his mom I was threatening and scary, which was not totally true (but what I did was probably not helpful). React with reason instead of rage and revenge.

TIP #3: CONFLICT IS NOT BAD OR NEGATIVE.

Conflict happens in every relationship, even in the strongest, healthiest relationships with those we love and adore most— our children. How we respond to and deal with conflict is what is most important. Being direct and clear when sharing your perspective is being self-assertive, not getting angry. There is a big difference between being self-assertive and getting angry. But when we are not skilled at using healthy self-assertiveness, we can have underlying anxiety or overwhelm and be perceived by others, even our children, as angry, when in fact we're learning a new skill that may come off awkward or intense when we're first practicing it.

When you feel angry, focus on being assertive by letting others know what you need, specifying what is upsetting you, or asking for time to process what you're feeling and then taking time to feel calmer. Resist the urge to engage in *passive-aggressive* or *aggressive behaviors* (see pages 191–192 for some examples). Being assertive is a skill you practice over time. The more you use self-assertive skills, the more comfortable you will become using them. Use the following fill-in-the-blanks to help you practice:

- I feel _____.
- I need to _____.
- I can do _____ to help myself.

Or you can say something like the following directly to another person when conflict arises:

I can see we're having conflict right now, and I'd love

to be able to work this out. However, I'm feeling a bit overwhelmed and I'm feeling a lot of things. I don't want to make things worse by saying or doing something that would create more tension or escalate this situation. So I'm going to go for a walk or take a shower. Let's circle back and work this out after I've taken care of myself.

These are some examples and ways to use self-assertive skills even if underneath you're feeling anger. Just because you feel an emotion doesn't mean you have to act on it or express it.

TIP #4: TAKE A MOMENT.
Here is a simple skill you can practice right now if you're feeling angry: Take a moment or two. Literally, when you recognize the tension in your body or have negative thoughts or feelings that start to escalate, you can say to yourself: *"I need a moment." And then take it.* Not every feeling has to be acted on, not every thought has to be believed, and not every impulse to act is the right one in the moment. *Pausing* is a simple yet vital skill to learn. The key is to pay attention to the signs your thoughts and body give you. Think of your anger like a switch or button— *taking a moment* is the gesture of turning that switch or button off and reflecting on how you'd like to respond instead of react. Remember, *reacting is more impulsive,* whereas *responding uses thought, reason, and perspective.*

TIP #5: DON'T TAKE YOUR CHILD'S BEHAVIOR PERSONALLY.
Nothing can incite a shadow moment in motherhood more than a toddler or child who is uncooperative, emotional (i.e., screaming, crying, or inconsolable), and refusing to comply with reasonable

requests. And nothing can rouse your anger like a school-age child, tween, or teen being defiant, disrespectful, contemptuous, or hurtful. I've been there, and I'm sure you have too! Here is the gem I want you to hold in your heart: *Do not take how your child behaves as a reflection of how they feel about you. Their behavior is not personal.* Children, tweens, and teens express what they're feeling, thinking, or experiencing through behavior. So yes, it's upsetting and feels *incredibly personal* in the moment. But this is where I want you to repeat this mantra: *My child's behavior is not personal to me; their behavior is a reflection of their inner world.*

I use this mantra all the time, and it helps me stay in an objective place of curiosity, a place of wanting to know what's going on with my child so I can then give support for what they need. Of course there are consequences and limits in my home, but staying grounded in a calmer emotional state allows me to connect with my child rather than escalate a situation between us or harm our relationship.

And when things are chaotic, remember that kids love routines, schedules, and knowing what to expect. Which is why structure and being consistent is so important with kids. You can't be lax and easy-breezy for a few days and then become super strict as a way to get your kids to listen. This is confusing from their perspective and is just not effective.

TIP #6: ASK YOURSELF, WHAT IS THE COST OF ANGER?

Expressing anger through negative self-talk or behavior, whether to yourself or others, has an impact emotionally, socially, mentally, physically, and spiritually, which equates to a measurable cost. This cost can be lost wages, time, and money as well as the toll anger takes on relationships, as it breaks trust and creates isolation. Ask yourself the following:

204

- What has my anger cost me?
- How has anger impacted my relationships?
- How has anger impacted my social support and social life?
- How has anger impacted my physical health?
- How has anger impacted my family?
- What is the cost of anger at my work or in my volunteering duties?
- How has my anger impacted my sense of self?

These questions are important to ask because your answers will help guide you on how to repair, set goals, and change behavior for the future. Understanding that anger has a cost to it—time, energy, the breaking of trust, and efforts to repair damage—is one step toward finding healthy ways to manage anger.

TIP #7: TRY PERSPECTIVE-TAKING.

We all know that there is limited time in motherhood. So when you're presented with a frustrating and upsetting situation, important questions to ask yourself are these: *What is the bigger picture here? Will this matter in an hour, tomorrow, next week, or next year? What is the amount of energy I want to put into this? How have I gotten through situations like this before? My feelings are valid, but am I responding in proportion to what happened—or are other things that were upsetting me amplifying this situation?*

Keeping perspective is one way to create a path to awareness and understanding of how you'd like to respond instead of reacting without thoughtfulness. And when I'm angry, I ask myself before I speak: *Is it kind? Is it true? Is it necessary?* This mantra has been a life-saver, because it generates a pause between a thought and how I express and manage my anger.

TIP #8: CREATE SOLID BOUNDARIES.

In motherhood, the most valuable resources are often time and energy! Many mamas overextend themselves, saying *yes* to things they *don't really want* to do and placing themselves last on the priority list. Of course, part of motherhood is built around putting children first so they can be cared for and nurtured. What I'm referring to is the ongoing pattern of self-sacrifice at the cost of your personal health and well-being. Chronically not caring for yourself creates conditions for angry emotions. One strategy to manage anger is to create solid boundaries, which is also an act of self-care. Frustration and irritability, the beginning of the path to more intense anger, often happens when mamas are tired, overextended, and lack support or help. Solid boundaries can be set in several ways:

- **Learn to say no.** It's okay to say no to appropriate things you don't want to do, can't do, or don't have time to do.

- **Learn to set limits.** Not managing your time, or giving to the point of stress, is not healthy. Set a time limit to what you can give and stop when you need to stop.

- **Don't try to please everyone.** You can never make everyone happy—it's impossible. Focus on doing your best, taking into consideration the needs of most, but then make decisions based on what feels right for you.

- **Let go of *should*.** Let the word *should* be a code word for taking in the thoughts and beliefs of another person, or unrealistic standard, or perfectionistic mindset that you may not fully agree with, but feel guilt to do. *Should*s are a sure way to create frustration and stress. When you hear or use the word *should*, let it be a warning that you may not be doing something because you want to; rather you may be doing it because you feel guilt or an obligation to do so. For example, *should* often shows up in self-talk: *I really should do this* (e.g., volunteer for the book fair, host a playdate, clean up the house instead of taking a nap).

- **Let go of unattainable expectations.** Having high and perfectionistic standards of how things should go is not only a setup for anger but it's also unrealistic. Nothing is perfect, and having unattainable expectations creates a narrow path of what is acceptable and what can be seen as a failure. Instead, flexibility is the key—do the best you can and respond in healthy ways when tension arises.

TIP #9: INCREASE YOUR SELF-CARE AND CREATE ALONE TIME.

Recognize that feeling the shadow emotion of anger can be a signal you may not be taking care of your basic needs: sleep, nourishment, hydration, physical movement, and enjoyable and restorative activities. Anger in motherhood often happens when demands and responsibilities are high and time is short, when help is scarce and you are carrying a chronic sense of overload, when you haven't recharged and are in need of rest. Setting aside time every day for self-care is one way to manage anger. While this may seem overly simple, it's not. Starting with the basics is a great place to begin. Sleeping, eating a healthy diet, exercising, and doing activities you enjoy all add up to help you manage stress and frustration. And when you feel anger starting to increase, add more self-care skills and strategies to help you manage your emotions.

Spend fifteen minutes alone every day and an additional sixty minutes alone once a week. This time is not meant for sleeping or watching television or other screens. Find quiet, grounding time when you can get in touch with yourself and anchor and tether yourself to *you*, so you can continue to care for your family and other demands. And ask yourself, *How am I doing? What is working and what needs some improvement? What is it that I need today?*

And know that it is always possible (and wise) to seek support in counseling to help you work through any emotion or stressful situation you're experiencing. Pursuing counseling is an incredible act of self-care. If you notice a pattern of anger that is disrupting your life and relationships, then working with a counselor for anger management would be an excellent way to learn more about yourself and gain skills to help you thrive.

TIP #10: GET SUPPORT AND COUNSELING.

After reading this chapter, you may have come to an awareness that your anger is holding you back from fully enjoying motherhood. Anger, and all of the shadow emotions, are part of what mothers naturally feel in motherhood. But we have a choice in how we respond to our children when we feel shadow emotions. Reacting angrily to our children through verbal attacks, put-downs, teasing, or mocking is never okay. Using anger as a way to justify physically acting out (e.g., pushing, shoving, hitting, throwing objects) or intimidating our child when frustration, anger, and overwhelm creates rage is a form of emotional, verbal, and physical abuse. Actions like those are never acceptable or justifiable—they leave permanent emotional scars on children and break the loving, trusting bond between a parent and child. If you have reacted in anger this way, I need you to make a commitment to yourself and your child to never do it again. You need to reach out to a mental health professional to learn the skills to manage your anger and heal the suffering inside of you that so desperately needs compassion. You also need to learn how to create a peaceful environment in which to parent your child. I know admitting this is not easy, but neither is the suffering your child has endured. And it hasn't been easy for you, holding on to your suffering and feeling the aftereffects of guilt, shame, and remorse for losing control. Getting support is a priceless gift for you and your child.

Thriving Mama Reflection

Anger is an emotion many of us can be uncomfortable experiencing, let alone acknowledging! As with any emotion, remember there is nothing "bad" or "wrong" about feeling anger. What is important is how you manage and express the feeling. When you feel anger, instead of judging yourself or pushing the emotion down or away, I want you to embrace and understand what your anger is trying to tell you: Perhaps it is trying to show you something about yourself that you may not be aware of. Imagine yourself as a child. What do you look like and what age are you? What are your main feelings? What is your world like, and what do you like to do? What are the things you're most afraid of? What causes you the most pain? Are you worried? If so, what are you worried about? Keeping all this information in mind, imagine this younger version of yourself in a safe space that brought you joy (perhaps that space was school, your home, your childhood neighborhood, or nature). Imagine for a moment yourself as an adult walking into the scene and sharing that space with the younger version of yourself. Imagine that the child you is feeling the anger you're feeling right now as an adult. With your heart full of compassion, wanting to help the younger version of you, what would you say and do? How would you comfort your younger self? Perhaps you'd give yourself a hug and offer support, reassurance, and comfort and just be. Right now inside of you is the same child; the only thing that separates the two of you is time, space, and experience. Often beneath anger is suffering and unresolved pain that are getting louder. When you feel anger, slow down, pause for a moment, close your eyes, and picture yourself as this child. Greet your adult self with the same care and compassion as you would the child version of yourself feeling this anger—because care and compassion can help you heal.

healing the roots of pain

how to transform bitter and resentful feelings into peacefulness, acceptance and connection

Hanging onto resentment is letting someone you despise live rent-free in your head.
—Ann Landers

Motherhood is bittersweet and the saying "The days are long, but the years are short" captures the essence of the shadow emotions of bitterness and resentment. The days of motherhood can be all-consuming, stressful, and very long. Many mothers see themselves coming and going, day after day, month after month—days and months that eventually turn into years. And then there will be a day when she's knocked over by a wave of sadness as her child matures to independence. She fears she missed so much in those early years of being exhausted and overwhelmed, and she begins to feel the shadow emotions of guilt and regret. All of these feelings add to the shadow emotion of bitterness.

The shadow emotions of bitterness and resentment are emotional reactions that are closely related, but they do have some differences. Bitterness is anger that has built up over time for a variety of reasons: unmanaged anger, disappointments, sadness, frustrations, and regrets. Not managing anger only allows it to develop into a more intense form of anger, which is bitterness. Bitterness is a chronic, generalized anger toward almost everyone and everything. It is felt in the present but may have nothing to do with what is happening in the moment. I'm sure you see examples of this: people who you'd describe as bitter, looking for the worst in everything, who never have a good thing to say, who hold anger in their body and express it through their facial expressions, tone, and posture.

Resentment is unresolved anger between people in a relationship. If we let our pain in a relationship turn into anger, and if we do not manage that anger, it can morph into bitterness because the pain in the relationship has not been healed.

In the therapy hour, I hear about bitterness and resentment in motherhood all the time from the women who are living with these shadow emotions: mothers who continuously give to their families, not needing a lot in return but who are barely—and I mean *barely*—getting much in return. And what a mom needs is often so reasonable: a smile, a hug, an *I love you* or a *Thank you*, and compliance with her reasonable requests.

Mothers become resentful toward their child (regardless of the child's age and stage) for a variety of reasons: (1) limited personal freedom, (2) lack of appreciation and gratitude, (3) limited or no cooperation, (4) constant giving, (5) limited support, (6) actions or efforts that don't have the desired outcome, and (7) hurtful words and actions. For example, a new mom, exhausted from sleep deprivation and constantly giving to her baby, is surprised by the amount of anger and resentment she feels hearing her baby cry; she desperately needs sleep (i.e., constant giving). Then there's the mom going through the motions of caring for an infant, feeling resentful from a loss of freedom to do even the simplest tasks—brush her teeth, go to the bathroom, eat, or change her clothes—because she's constantly soothing the baby (i.e., constant giving). The mom with a toddler can't get five minutes to shower, or use the toilet, or even load the dishwasher, let alone do anything without being interrupted by her toddler (i.e., limited personal freedom).

There is the mom who has battles with her toddler to leave the house every single morning and to go to bed every single night (i.e., actions or efforts that don't have the desired outcome). And the mom who is constantly repeating her requests and expectations for her school-age child to clean up their room, do their homework, and take a shower (i.e., limited or no cooperation). The mom of the tween on the threshold of puberty, who snaps at her every morning and challenges every reasonable request without expressing appreciation for all she's doing, wonders where her happy, talkative child went (i.e., limited or no cooperation, lack of appreciation and gratitude). And then there's the mother of a teenager who forgets to do their chores, who barely speaks more than one-word answers when she attempts to connect with them, or who, when they do talk to her, simply ask for things (i.e., lack of cooperation, appreciation, and gratitude).

But one of the best parts of my work in supporting these moms is when a mom shares a positive interaction with her child that she's been waiting for. For instance, when a baby smiled at her intentionally for the first time, it's as if all those sleepless nights were worth it. Or when the toddler unexpectedly says, "I love you." Or when the child listens and cooperates—for the first time in months—when it's time to leave for school in the morning and when it's time for bed at night. When the tween apologizes for their attitude and gives their best effort. When the teen spontaneously expresses gratitude, shares details of their life, cooperates with expected responsibilities and wants to spend time with their mom. Those are some of the best sessions, when I can see how these small gestures from a child melt away whatever resentment may have been there, because what a mother is really asking for is positive feedback from her child that she's doing a good job, that she's appreciated, and that she's loved by her child, and that her child is learning necessary life skills.

While bitterness and resentment often appear in our mother-child relationships, it's important to remember that these shadow emotions can also fester in other relationships and situations related to motherhood. This type of bitterness and resentment impacts our mothering and how we connect with our child. Some examples include the following scenarios:

- A mother wants to work part-time but has to work full-time because she carries health insurance or because her family needs the income. She feels resentful toward her sweetie when they make nonessential purchases, don't follow a budget, or don't want to look for a job with health insurance.

- A mom is resentful for how overwhelmed she feels always taking care of someone or something, without enough support, when she looks around and sees friends with supportive extended family.

- A mom experiences resentment when the division of childcare and household chores is unbalanced.

- A mother may feel resentment when she is the default parent, even when she works outside the home (e.g., when she is the one to care for kids on the weekends or to stay home when a child is sick).

- A mom is resentful with her sweetie's personal freedom to come and go, and she may feel resentment if she feels she has to ask "permission" to go anywhere alone by requesting that her sweetie watch their child.

- A mom may feel resentful of friendships where there is a lack of support during known times of stress.

- A mother may become resentful when her unresolved family-of-origin issues come popping up in full force and she reexperiences them on her own motherhood journey.

All of these are examples of how unresolved anger between a mother and her child, or in other significant relationships in a mother's life, can lead to resentment. Over time, a mom may become vulnerable to bitterness when she is feeling anger from of lot of different places in her life: when she is at odds with her children or sweetie, when she is burdened with responsibilities, when she is feeling overwhelmed and exhausted and unsupported. If she does not manage her resentment, she risks becoming bitter.

The shadow emotions of bitterness and resentment disrupt your health, happiness, and connections with those you love. Underneath these shadow emotions is a heap of suffering and unresolved pain that's been bottled up, asking to be managed and taken care of. However bitterness and resentment show up in your life, the first step is to acknowledge what you're experiencing. Once you do that, you can learn how to manage this form of suppressed suffering and pain, which manifests in the form of anger and keeps you from fully thriving in motherhood.

You Are Not Alone: Alexis's Story

One day, when she was scrolling through photos on her phone to send to a friend, Alexis was shocked to see an image of herself that had been taken by her daughter. Alexis was in the background, scowling at the computer with a tense face and a furrowed brow. She was horrified—when had she become so old and so tired, like a bitter and angry person? Alexis had gone through a lot that year: She lost her brother to cancer, and she found out her husband had had an affair and they had recently separated. She had been feeling angry for some time—for the suffering her brother went through, the loss her elderly parents were going through, on top of her marital issues. Alexis had a lot of beliefs about how unfair things were, as she had always "done the right things" by being a good wife, sister, daughter, and mother. But now, she was feeling bitter and resentful, especially because these shadow emotions were beginning to take away her ability to connect with her daughter.

I encouraged Alexis to be compassionate with herself. She had experienced two incredible losses, her brother's passing and the betrayal from her husband. Underneath these feelings was grief paired with incredibly stressful events. Alexis came to counseling once a week and decided to go on an antidepressant to address her impaired motivation, depressed mood, difficulty sleeping, and weight loss. We created structure and support for her by having weekly scheduled activities to work out with a friend and manage her negative self-talk. I also asked her to focus on the immediate future until she felt less overwhelmed. We also put in place weekly outings with her daughter that were focused on joy and fun as moments to connect, even in the smallest ways.

At the Heart of Feeling Bitter and Resentful

At the heart of bitterness and resentment is unresolved suffering, pain, and anger: the result of being treated poorly or unfairly and not receiving support or appreciation. Feeling bitter and resentful is the result of habitually ignoring pain by pushing it down inside or avoiding it, only to have it pop through in unexpected ways (e.g., intrusive thoughts or replaying history in the present moment) At the heart of bitterness and resentment is a need to acknowledge your suffering and to take steps to heal and forgive. Forgiveness is often the antidote to these shadow emotions. Forgiveness is more than an apology or seeking an acknowledgment of justice. Forgiveness is an act of self-love, of allowing the moment of pain and suffering to be cared for and then let go. Only then can our pain be transformed into growth, understanding, and compassion.

Reframe Your Mantra

Thoughts are powerful. Your self-talk (the things you say to yourself) has a deep impact on what you feel and how you respond. Keep this principle in mind and reframe problematic thoughts that increase your shadow emotions.

SHADOW MANTRA If you're saying this . . .	THRIVING MANTRA Positively reframe to say this . . .
I'm so frustrated that they don't seem to care how much I do for them.	Where is the evidence they don't care? I do a lot for my family, and I want to. They haven't been cooperating or expressing gratitude, and that is super frustrating. I can have a family meeting and express what I need. I can also give positive feedback when they do cooperate and express appreciation.
I give and give, and I just want to feel appreciated every now and then.	I give so much to my family, and I really don't want much in return. Lately, though, I've been feeling this way more, which is a signal I haven't been hearing appreciation or gratitude from my family. I can remind them how I feel and specifically ask for more respect, kindness, and appreciation.
I have no personal freedom anymore. I'm so angry about how unfair and unbalanced it is with my sweetie.	This phase of mothering makes it really hard to go anywhere by myself without a lot of planning. It's not fair how unbalanced it is, and this is a signal to talk to my sweetie and discover ways to fix this. Holding on to this bitterness and resentment will only make me feel worse.
Everyone takes me for granted—I do so much and ask for little in return.	Is it possible I've been stuffing my frustration down inside and not letting my family know about how it has intensified this feeling? What is the one step I can do to improve this situation?
How am I supposed to forgive them for what they did (or didn't do)?	Forgiveness is an act of self-care. I don't have to forget about or agree with what happened. Being preoccupied and thinking about this event makes something in the past live in the present, and that is taking away my joy, health, and well-being.

SHADOW MANTRA If you're saying this . . .	THRIVING MANTRA Positively reframe to say this . . .
I feel angry all the time; everyone gets on my nerves. I'm on edge and I'm going to lose it one of these days.	My anger is showing me there is something in my life that needs healing. I've buried some of these feelings and now it's finally time to manage and deal with my pain. I don't have to lose it—there are other things to do, like take a break or walk away and reach out for support.
I just can't let it go; I'm so angry every time I think about it.	Keeping a running list of the pain and hurt is keeping me stuck. In a way, I'm reliving the event and the pain when I focus on it. Perhaps what I need most is to write out these feelings and let them go. I can't change the past, but I can be mindful of what I do with these thoughts.
If I let it go, then they win. Why should I forgive? I was hurt so much—they did something wrong.	I suffered a lot, and being treated that way was very upsetting. I can't go back in time and change what happened, but I can heal, learn from this, and take care of myself. If a friend came to me and shared with me about a similar situation, what advice or recommendations would I give? Perhaps the support I'd offer to someone else is what I need myself.

Moving Beyond the Shadows

TIP #1: UNDERSTAND WHAT'S UNDERNEATH YOUR PAIN.

Feeling resentful toward others and feeling bitter from pain shows up in a few ways: persistently having negative thoughts about someone, dwelling on past situations pretty regularly (so much so that when you do, it feels as if it's happening in the moment), and brooding about what things should or could be like. Resentments are painful interactions and situations within a relationship that are the result of one or more of the following: (1) limited personal freedom, (2) lack of appreciation and gratitude, (3) limited or no cooperation, (4) constant giving, (5) limited support, (6) actions or efforts that don't have the desired outcome, and (7) hurtful words and actions.

There is a balance to acknowledging your resentments, thinking about them, doing something about them, and then letting them go. Dwelling on resentments is not in anyone's best interest. Holding them in, ignoring them, or avoiding pain and suffering only allows these feelings and thoughts to intensify. To begin healing from your pain, work through the following suggestions and tips. If at any time you feel distressed or overwhelmed, please know it's okay to pause this exercise. Distress and overwhelm may indicate you're not ready, that it's not the right time, or that you need to do this with the support of a counselor—this is all okay and completely understandable.

TIP #2: ASK QUESTIONS TO CREATE SELF-AWARENESS.

As you've read through this section on bitterness and resentment, chances are you're seeing this shadow emotion in a new way. Without judging what you're feeling or thinking about, I want you to create a quiet space of time, if even just ten minutes, and reflect on the questions that follow. Take a minute and list out the people (e.g., your child, sweetie, mother-in-law) or obligations (e.g., work, household tasks), or events or situations in the past (e.g., lack of support, hurtful words, a bad fight) that you reacted to, feeling upset or frustrated. Remember, this isn't about judging yourself or wondering what you may see on the list. This is an exercise of moving pain in your mind and heart to paper, creating awareness in a tangible form, which is one step toward healing and thriving.

Next, as you look at what's written, beside each person, event, or situation, identify which of the seven categories on page 220 this resentment would fall into. Then answer the following questions:

- Reflecting on my relationships, with whom am I feeling upset and resentful?

- What pattern do I notice when I look at my list? Is there more pain and frustration from one person? Is there a theme I can identify that I'm angry about?

- Keeping in mind that bitterness can come across as my being irritable, annoyed, and angry most of the time without a specific reason or situation, do I think these situations and experiences have created a bitterness within me? If so, what do I notice?

- When I feel angry and upset, bitter and resentful, how do I express it (e.g., my words, my actions, my behaviors, or in the ways I treat or respond to my children or others)?

- What are the ways I'd like to work toward expressing and managing upsetting and frustrating things in relationships?

TIP #3: REFLECT AND MOVE FORWARD.

Placing resentful and bitter feelings, thoughts, and situations on paper is taking suffering out of your mind so that you can begin letting this pain go. When you can set aside twenty to thirty minutes, go to a quiet space and, taking the list you created in the previous exercise, reflect on the one relationship, event, or situation that is most in need of healing. Write out the resentment you have by answering these prompts:

- What am I most upset about with this situation?

- Have I expressed this or shared it, or have I been holding on to this? If I have expressed it to someone, did I feel fully heard and understood at the end of the conversation?

- If I imagine what I would say to this person, what would I share? (Write it all out, and remember, it doesn't have to be narrative—you can use bulleted points, a list, and so on.)

- If this person could share with me their pain and suffering, why they act the way they do (which isn't an excuse to justify the behavior), what would it be?

- What is the one thing I want this person to know?

- What is it that I wish I could do to move past this?

- What are my strengths that I've learned about or experienced because of this situation?

- Do I want to let this resentment go?

If you are ready to let this resentment go, after all of the journaling, write this:

I give myself permission to let this anger and resentment go. This suffering I've been carrying no longer serves me and is blocking love, light, and healing. In order to thrive in motherhood and in my life, I'm letting the resentment go.

Now, close your eyes and imagine the pain and resentment in the form of a balloon you are holding in your hand. Open your hand and let it go. Watch in your mind as the balloon floats away from you into the vastness of the sky. Taking your hand and placing it on your heart, keep your eyes closed and imagine white, healing light moving from your hands into your heart, filling your chest and then your body, and radiating out through your arms, legs, and feet and the top of your head. You are light and love, and this resentment no longer resides in you.

When you have the time and space, you can go through each

resentment and do this same exercise. You can go through the next one right now, or you may wait until you have the energy and time to begin working through each resentment.

And practically speaking, if you're feeling resentful and bitter toward your sweetie because you do not feel supported and appreciated, you are constantly giving without cooperation, and there are hurtful fights or conflicts between you both, then you have to talk this out and share these feelings. Resentments that are not healed in a relationship create disconnect and break intimacy. If you have feelings of bitterness and resentment with your child every now and then, talking this out with a supportive friend is a great way to get help. However, if you notice that you feel angry often and you feel at times that you could say or do something to act on this anger, then please reach out to a professional for support and counseling to learn anger management strategies as well as parenting skills to help cope and learn new strategies.

TIP #4: PRACTICE THE SKILL OF FORGIVENESS.

Forgiveness is not always easy. That is why I frame it as a practice, a skill to develop over time. Forgiveness is the act of acknowledging pain, suffering, and wrongdoing; dealing with the aftermath; and letting the pain go, bit by bit, over time. Forgiveness is not suppressing pain or anger or denying a wrongdoing. Forgiveness is not giving someone a pass or condoning or justifying the damaging words or actions. Rather, it is a process of working through pain, much like a person grieves after the loss of a loved one.

There is no one way to forgive, just as there is no one way to grieve. But an important component of forgiveness is working through the suffering to transform the pain into something else, instead of letting the pain live inside you, growing and blocking your health and happiness. Forgiveness can have multiple layers; for example, understanding the motives behind another person's actions and seeing the person as wounded or suffering in some way with limited coping skills to take care of themselves or having a limited capacity to interact with others in a compassionate and caring way. The practice of forgiveness helps chip away at the pain living inside of you, slowly taking care of it and tending to it, so it can be released and transformed into something better.

TIP #5: FIND THE LESSON AND CREATE WISDOM.

Feeling bitter and resentful, while uncomfortable, can teach us lessons and create opportunities for growth. Looking back on a situation or relationship with a person, what did you learn? Perhaps you were too trusting, maybe you didn't see values or personality traits that became problematic, or perhaps you let unacceptable behaviors go on too long without using your voice and you feel upset for not trusting an instinct or seeing certain signs. Or maybe you're bitter and resentful for how someone treated you.

However this feeling of bitterness and resentment came to be, know there is always great potential to learn from any experience. As simple as this may sound, it is powerfully true. I think this wisdom applies to many things in life, including the feeling of resentment. Placing your anger on pause for a moment, ask yourself: *What has this situation taught me? Is there a lesson here that I can use to create awareness and wisdom? How can I help others through my experience?* When we can make meaning of what we're feeling, even in the service of helping others, we often find the wisdom about what to do next and how to move forward and feel better.

Thriving Mama Reflection

Underneath the shadow emotions of bitterness and resentment is unresolved anger, perhaps for an expectation that wasn't met, a need to connect or receive support that was unfulfilled, or a rejection or hurt that created pain in your life. However these shadow emotions came to be, while the incident has passed, the suffering is still living inside of you, impacting your health and well-being. *What does holding on to resentment do for you? Is holding on to pain really the best way to manage and solve suffering? Have you tricked yourself into believing that holding on to pain is a way to keep someone else accountable for the pain they caused you?* If so, think about this carefully: *How is holding on to bitterness and resentment impacting someone else?* More often than not, it is impacting you more, allowing the suffering to continue and blocking joy and calm in your life. One way to move past resentment is to practice forgiveness, as we explored in this chapter. And this doesn't mean what happened was acceptable or justified. Forgiveness is working to heal from the pain and suffering inside of you. It is an acceptance of what is, a letting go of trying to rework the outcome you wanted in your mind. Time is something that cannot be relived or taken back. So what we have left is acceptance of what is, what remains, and the aftereffects. And by facing your suffering, you can grieve, feel the pain, and allow the process to move forward. Suppressing your feelings only transforms the pain into resentment. Often it can seem easier to hold on to the anger of resentment—anger can seem powerful and protective. But that is an *illusion*, because beneath resentment is suffering asking to be released and cleansed.

You may fear experiencing the true pain beneath your resentment, so anger feels like the preferable option. But suppressing pain and suffering is like creating beautiful space for a garden and doing everything necessary for growth, except planting the seeds. Instead, you place the seeds in a drawer but check the garden every day to see if flowers are beginning to emerge. Seeds need the right conditions to transform into flowers. Your bitterness and resentment is similar: When you release these shadow emotions instead of allowing them to take up space, blocking growth, you open up to transforming these feelings into something else—joy, calm, and connection.

highlighting abundance

how feeling jealousy and envy are signals to appreciate your strengths

A flower does not think of competing to the flower next to it,
it just blooms.
—Zen Shin

Jealousy and envy in motherhood are not pretty. These shadow emotions can be awful to experience, especially when these feelings are in reaction to your child. The first time I felt jealousy and envy as a mother was when my twin daughters, who were born premature, needed round-the-clock care in the neonatal intensive care unit for two weeks, with breathing tubes, heart monitors, and feeding tubes.

I didn't feel the shadow emotions of jealousy and envy right away, or even during the first days when I had visitors and was busy spending time with the girls. No, these shadow emotions came in the quiet of the night, when I was alone in my hospital room and my babies were being cared for by a team of nurses down the hall in the NICU. About three nights into our hospital stay, I woke up to the sound of a crying infant from the room across the hall. I felt the shadow emotions of jealousy and envy in full force. The infant's cry was a painful reminder of what I was missing, what was lost, and what was not possible since I had premature babies.

The surge of jealousy I felt was toward the nurses, who were spending more time with my babies than I was, who were bonding with my girls and knew how to care for them better than I did. Complicating my emotional state was my feeling of envy of the mom across the hall, then all the moms on the maternity wing, moms who had their babies rooming-in. This didn't seem right, or fair, and I felt cheated on a peaceful transition to motherhood—instead I had a dramatic emergency C-section to deliver babies born early, and I wasn't even able to care for them.

Breathing into my feelings, I noticed my thoughts and embraced these shadow emotions for a minute or two. Then I reframed my thoughts, fueled by jealousy and envy, and thought, *Get up, go down to the NICU, those are your babies.* And I reframed my feelings to find the gratitude in this moment: *Thank goodness my babies and I have access to medical services. There are amazing nurses, dedicated nurses, who can care for my babies. They'll teach me what I need to know. And I am their mother, my girls already know me. And the new mom across the hall—maybe she wants to get some sleep, or maybe she feels alone, exhausted, and scared. How is feeling envious helping me right now?* I was finally able to push past these difficult-to-manage shadow emotions.

Jealousy and envy are shadow emotions that are often thought to be the same. While they are related, these feelings have significant differences. Jealousy is a feeling of anger we experience in reaction to a perceived threat about a loss of connection or about our being replaced in a relationship. Envy is feeling angry when someone has something we desire, wish to attain, or accomplish.

This can take the form of an attribute, possession, or status that may be lacking in our life. Underneath these shadow emotions is a combination of insecurity, anger, and fear.

Feeling jealousy and envy in motherhood comes in many forms and intensities. For me, those shadow emotions were short and transient—each day, they diminished as I gained confidence in caring for my girls. But these shadow emotions can be more situational or chronic, and they happen throughout motherhood. Universal examples moms have shared with me include feeling envious with how their sweetie can play with their child and tune out the background noise of the house (such as unfolded laundry, a sink full of dishes, and dust and dirt under the table and sofas). Even if and when a mom tries to be in the moment by playing with her child, she has a nagging feeling that she should be doing something else, or she is watching the clock to keep things moving. A mother may also feel envious of her sweetie's personal freedom to take a shower, eat, use the bathroom alone, and go anywhere without being the main caregiver 24/7.

Another common occurrence of these shadow emotions I hear in the therapy hour is when a mom goes back to work after maternity leave. Not only is she stressed about getting ready for work and getting her child ready for daycare or the nanny, she's also feeling these shadow emotions toward her child's caregiver: She's jealous, fearing her child will bond more with the caregiver than her, and she's envious when or if the caregiver may see some developmental "firsts" before she does. Going back to work for new moms isn't as easy as resuming the responsibilities of her job; being a working mother means she's feeling a whole new level of emotions she may have never experienced before.

When a mother can share these feelings, she almost always

feels a sense of relief. I always remind moms, regardless of what "first" happens when her child is at daycare or with a caregiver, *"When your child does this for you, it will be the first between mother and child, and nothing can ever replace the bond between a mother and child."* I also remind mothers that when they work, they are showing many things to their child, one of which is that there are loving people who care for them in the community, which in turn creates a sense of trust and safety in the larger world.

Most applicable to the shadow emotions of jealousy and envy is the concept of abundance, which means that each person has unique qualities, gifts, and abilities meant to be shared with the world. And these gifts that each person has—including happiness, belonging, and love—everyone has the right to. But we often look outward and compare and compete with ours, instead of looking inward knowing there is an abundant (indeed, limitless) supply of all these things. If there is something you want in your life, instead of looking outward so as to focus on what you're not getting, shift your focus and create what you desire in your life. Sometimes envy is an indication that we have *given up on the potential within our life*, and, instead of looking inward to change it, we stay stuck by looking outward with blame.

As with any feeling or emotion, being aware of your emotional state of jealousy and envy is part of thriving in motherhood. When you act out on these feelings, or when you dwell on jealous or envious thoughts, that is what takes you away from thriving. Thriving in motherhood is having strength to be vulnerable and curious about what you're feeling. Once you can recognize and label the feeling—not to judge it, but to understand what's going on—then you can decide on the steps you want to take to manage the feeling. As I've said many times in this book already, learning this skill helps keep mild to moderate shadow emotions from developing into more intense emotional reactions.

At the Heart of Feeling Jealous and Envious

At the heart of feeling jealous and envious is a focus on what's lacking or missing and a feeling of insecurity in a relationship, with fears of being replaced, or not being enough, or not having enough compared to others (e.g., positive qualities or traits, possessions, or opportunities). These shadow emotions are indicators of pain, suffering, anger, and insecurity somewhere in the past that are being experienced and expressed in the present moment.

Instead of acknowledging the suffering and looking inward to heal yourself, you may shift your focus as a distraction or an attempt to avoid what is hurting. You may find yourself looking outward and focusing on comparisons, on what's missing and what is needed externally to feel whole. At the heart of these shadow emotions is addressing the suffering and insecurity you as a mother have felt in a relationship or in regard to your skills and abilities by taking statements of anger—such as *"I want," "I wish," "If only," "Why not me?"* and *"It isn't fair,"* which are actually expressions of masked pain—and healing something that's hurting inside. The suffering or insecurity has to be acknowledged and taken care of; you need to focus on what needs to be healed rather than on what is missing. And healing begins when you as a mother focus on your gifts, abilities, and strengths as well as the people you are grateful to have in your life.

Reframe Your Mantra

Thoughts are powerful. Your self-talk (the things you say to yourself) has a deep impact on what you feel and how you respond. Keep this principle in mind and reframe problematic thoughts that increase your shadow emotions.

SHADOW MANTRA If you're saying this . . .	THRIVING MANTRA Positively reframe to say this . . .
My child spends so much time with their caregiver or teacher—I'm so jealous.	Being able to acknowledge my feelings is so important. My child is taken care of by wonderful caregivers, and it's natural to feel this way. Many working moms have felt this way. Nothing can replace the bond between a mother and child. When I feel this way, I can take care of these feelings by spending quality time with my child.
I worry my child will be upset that I'm not there to see "firsts," that they'll remember their sitter and not me.	It's almost impossible to see every "first" my child does as it happens. I could be at home in the bathroom when a "first" happens. Whenever there is something special, the first time I see it as their mom is what counts. My child will remember loving, caring people in their life, but nothing can replace a mother.
My child doesn't come to me like they used to; I wonder if they're upset with me or prefer others to me.	I'm feeling insecure about how my child feels about me. I need to remind myself that a secure child is a healthy, happy child. Where is the evidence my child is upset with me? Or that they prefer someone else? Chances are, I'm taking my insecurity and putting it on our relationship. I need to consider where my child is in terms of development and stages.

SHADOW MANTRA If you're saying this . . .	THRIVING MANTRA Positively reframe to say this . . .
I wish I didn't have to work and could spend more time with my child like the other moms I know (envy).	Being a working mom has its challenges. Some days I'm so tired and overwhelmed, it's easy to think of how my life would be if I didn't work. Not working has its challenges as well. When I feel this way, where can I focus my energy to make positive changes?
I want to be able to go on vacations with my family like my friends, but we can't afford to (envy).	Comparing myself to other people clouds my sense of abundance and what is possible. I don't know other families' situations, and they don't know mine. I need to focus inward instead of outward and ask myself: What is missing in my life right now? Do I want a break from day-to-day responsibilities and to spend time with my family? How can I set small goals to achieve this that are practical and affordable for my family? Putting my energy toward what is possible is healthy compared to dwelling on what is missing.
She has the perfect life, her kids are amazing, she looks happy all the time—why can't that be me (envy)?	Where is the evidence she has a perfect life and kids? I can never know what goes on in a person's life unless I follow them around all day. What I see is only a snapshot of her life. If I see something in her life, how can I be inspired by her instead of putting myself down in harmful ways?

(continued)

SHADOW MANTRA If you're saying this . . .	THRIVING MANTRA Positively reframe to say this . . .
So much of my time at home is spent taking care of our home, while my sweetie plays with our child. I wish that were me. They have so much fun together. When do I get to have fun (jealousy, envy)?	Many mothers feel this way; the mental load is real and can make it tough to relax, have fun, and connect with my child. Feeling this way can be a signal to delegate some chores to my sweetie and spend that time having fun with my child. If I want to have fun, I can't wish for it—I have to look for small ways every day to make it happen.

Moving Beyond the Shadows

TIP #1: ASK QUESTIONS TO CREATE SELF-AWARENESS.

How do the shadow emotions of jealousy and envy show up in your life? Are these feelings something you experience often? Seldom? Or are these feelings something new you're experiencing? Read on to examine ways these feelings can manifest in your life as a mother.

In Motherhood

What are the triggers of jealousy with my child? Is there a caretaker or family member (or someone else) I feel this jealousy toward? Is there a situation or event that creates jealousy? For example, when I work long hours, not spending as much time as I'd like with my child, or when I see my child bonding with someone else or having fun with them? What are my fears about me and my child during these moments of jealousy? Do I have feelings of envy in motherhood? If so, what triggers, situations, or events bring on this shadow emotion?

With Others (Sweetie, Friends, Parents, Siblings)

What triggers jealousy for me (e.g., not being included, left out of a gathering, feeling like I'm competing for attention)? What are my triggers for envy? (e.g., someone else's pregnancy announcement or talking to a mom who doesn't work, has supportive family nearby, or has more financial resources)? How have these shadow emotions impacted me and my relationships with others?

What's Going on Beneath the Surface?

Underneath these shadow emotions, there's a sense of lacking in your life as you wish for and want what another person has. Looking even deeper, there may be components of fear, anxiety, anger, loss, insecurity, regret, trauma, or pain in your life that are manifesting through your feelings of jealousy and envy. One way to understand these shadow emotions more deeply in your life is to ask yourself the following:

- Is there some kind of unresolved pain, fear, or issue in my life that is showing up as these shadow emotions?
- Do I have certain expectations of what a relationship with my child (or any other relationship in which I'm feeling these shadow emotions) should look like? Where did this expectation come from?
- If I could change something about my relationship with my child, what would I want to add? What would I want to remove?
- What am I really afraid of regarding my relationship with my child? How is this contributing to the shadow emotion I'm feeling?

TIP #2: DON'T BELIEVE EVERYTHING YOU SEE.

When you experience the shadow emotions of jealousy and envy, I want you to notice how much time you are spending on social media, as social media often encourages us to focus on what we perceive in someone's life. It also breeds the fear of missing out and comparison. If you experience these things when you scroll through social media, you need to reduce the time you spend on it or put your social media use on pause. What you see on social media is a well-crafted version of what someone wants you to see—it doesn't tell the full story. This principle applies at school drop-offs, at playgroups, and any other place for that matter. Being aware of your thoughts and how your behaviors and habits increase a shadow emotion is an act of self-care. So practice self-care when you feel these shadow emotions and look at how your thoughts and habits keep these feelings going.

TIP #3: FOCUS ON YOUR STRENGTHS AND GRATITUDE.

The shadow emotions of jealousy and envy can create a cycle of negative thinking, in which you're preoccupied with worry and "what-if" situations paired with behaviors that intensify this feeling—you're constantly scanning for clues and information that your fears could be a reality. This cycle creates feelings of anger and fear that your value in a relationship is diminished, threatened, or could be taken away. When you experience envy, frustration and anger fuel thoughts of what's missing and lacking with your gifts, your abilities, and what you have in your life. Looking outward, comparing yourself to others, creates distress. To manage these feelings, start by looking inward and focusing on the strengths, traits, and qualities you have as a mother, partner, and friend. For each role in your life—person, mother, partner, friend, and professional (or volunteer)—write down five strengths and qualities you have in each relationship. Then make a list of five of your innate gifts and abilities, five people you are grateful to have in your life, and five sources of comfort and joy in your life. Each time you notice that you're experiencing these shadow emotions, take out the list and read it to refocus on the abundance in your life.

TIP #4: BUILD CONFIDENCE AND FOCUS ON YOUR PERSONAL GOALS.

Often, when a mom feels these shadow emotions, beneath the surface is insecurity in herself or her important relationships. One way to combat these insecurities is to strengthen your self-esteem and confidence. This exercise is related to the previous tip of highlighting your strengths, but it also builds on it by asking you to reflect on aspirations, goals, and dreams—all the things you'd love to do or try. Ask yourself: *Is there something I can do to reduce feeling these shadow emotions (e.g., have more fun with my child, be responsible for fewer chores after work so I can spend more time with family)? Is there something I've been putting off that I'd like to do or try? Are these shadow emotions masking my desire to do something more in my life or to change a part of my life I may not be happy with? How can I take this feeling and focus on a goal I'd love to accomplish?* And the reason you need to pursue this exercise is because investing in yourself, in your goals and dreams, is a gift that gives not only to you but also to everyone you are in a relationship with. When we take steps to get closer to our authentic self through following our dreams and setting goals, we create a path of self-discovery, and we experience growth and joy along the way.

TIP #5: GET SUPPORT AND TALK TO A COUNSELOR.

If you experience the shadow emotions of jealousy and envy often, please consider going to counseling and talking about what you're struggling with. As I've mentioned throughout these chapters, emotional patterns that disrupt your life and create distress can indicate a deeper issue that needs to be cared for and healed. A counselor will be able to help you navigate this healing process and learn the skills to manage these feelings.

Thriving Mama Reflection

The shadow emotions of jealousy and envy place the focus on what is missing and perceived as less-than in your life— these shadow emotions tempt you to look outward, believing what others have is better, instead of appreciating the value, strengths, and unique gifts you already have. These shadow emotions spring from a place of fear and insecurity and from ignoring or diminishing your value, gifts, and abilities. When you're feeling these emotions, it is essential to look inward to what is asking to be healed instead of looking outward for what is missing. You cannot heal inner pain through outer comparisons and judgments. Suffering is not healed by adding more suffering. On the contrary, healing happens by acknowledging the pain and taking steps to heal what is hurting.

Focus on your breathing, sit in a relaxed state, and ask yourself, *What am I afraid of right now? What am I angry about? What if, instead of looking outward and seeing what is missing, I look inward and see what is in need of repair?* Listen to your answers carefully. In this moment, focus on the strengths within yourself, and with compassion embrace those parts of you that are in need of healing and are manifesting in the form of jealousy and envy. Focus on appreciating your courage to look within yourself. Acknowledge the incredible gift you are to your child, family, friends, and community. You matter. You have many gifts and strengths to share, and these shadow emotions are blocking not only your ability to see them within yourself, but they are also preventing you from sharing the abundance of these gifts with those you love.

transforming embarrassment and shame into self-compassion

Why can't I relax? I feel so awkward!

I feel so embarrassed when my child has a tantrum—all eyes are always on us, and I don't want to take them anywhere.

I'm so broken, my kids don't deserve to have me as their mom.

I'm a terrible mother.

Shadow moments of embarrassment do not discriminate in motherhood. It doesn't matter whether you work outside the home or if you work at all, whether your child is in daycare or with you during the day, or whether your child is bottle-fed or breastfed, your child will embarrass you, and you will feel awkward, mortified, humiliated, and ashamed in motherhood at some point in time.

If only we could make choices to skip the certain stresses in motherhood. But you can't escape child development, and neither can your child. As children grow up, there's a lot their little brains are trying to do: communicate, learn about the world and understand how everything works, and navigate big feelings that can take them by surprise. This development process lasts for a large portion of their early life, up until age six, and resurfaces again transitioning from child to tween and then to teen and young adult. Which means that being out in public with your child has a lot of potential for their developing brain to respond in unpredictable, unexpected, and sometimes shocking ways, regardless of your parenting style and choices.

241

Nothing can make you feel more exposed than being in public and having a challenging moment with your child, creating the shadow emotion of embarrassment. Embarrassment is feeling exposed, judged, and uncomfortable, as well as experiencing some level of regret (*Why did I even leave the house today?*) in a social context. I'm sure you've been there, questioning how a simple trip to the store can create such chaos and stress between you and your child—a dramatic meltdown by your child in public leaves you second-guessing your parenting abilities.

In its mild form, embarrassment is experienced as feeling awkward. We experience awkwardness when we feel uncomfortable making small talk with other moms, when we're uncertain of how to act at a playgroup, or when we wonder how to bring up an important but uncomfortable conversation with another mom (for example, that your child had lice and shared dress-up clothes, including hats, with their child at the last playdate).

Awkward situations that feel more exposing or intense, in which you feel foolish and self-conscious, create the moderate-level shadow emotion of embarrassment. Feeling embarrassed can be triggered by something you do or say or something your child does or says; for instance, you feel embarrassed when your child tells the teller at the market, "Mommy likes to chat with daddy when he poops"; when you forget to show up to your child's parent-teacher conference; or when you have a conversation with your neighbor only to realize when you go back inside that your shirt has a big wet mark from where you leaked breast milk.

Feeling mortified is the most extreme form of embarrassment. When a mother feels this shadow emotion, chances are she wants to crawl into a hole. For example, you're at the park with a group of moms and kids, and your child points to a duck, saying the name of the animal; but your child can't pronounce the *D*, and it comes out sounding more like a rhyming expletive. Or you're at the market and your child sees a mole on a woman's face and inquires loudly, *"Mommy, why does that lady have a ball of dirt on her face?"*

Within the broader shadow emotion of embarrassment is a more intense form of these feelings, which includes humiliation and shame. Humiliation is being embarrassed and disgraced in front of others. Humiliation most often happens where there is an actual or perceived power differential, such as parent-child, physician-patient, coach-player, teacher-student, or boss-employee. But in reality, being humiliated can happen to anyone in any situation.

Years ago, I experienced a humiliating interaction. I was at a doctor's appointment for a routine checkup with my endocrinologist. My third daughter was fourteen months old, and I was still nursing her (but not during the appointment). As the doctor was taking down updated medical information, he asked if I was still nursing my daughter. When I answered yes, he stopped writing, looked up at me, and said, "How long will you keep doing that? You know she'll go to kindergarten soon and you won't be able to do that anymore." I was humiliated. Mortified. I wanted to get up and leave right then, judged for nursing my daughter. Instead I said, "Oh, I get it—you're angry at your mother, correct?" Then I left. It was the best comeback I could think of in the moment. I was astonished at his words. Of course I found a new physician, but I felt humiliated driving home and for a few days after. To be judged and put down in that manner was infuriating.

When we do not manage the effects of awkward, embarrassing, or humiliating moments, or when we believe these experiences or the mistakes we've made are true and accurate judgments, perceptions, or statements, this is when the shadow emotion of shame takes hold. Shame is the belief that when a humiliating moment happens, it is the result of a personal flaw, shortcoming, or defect. If you have a shame-based reaction, instead of saying, *"I made a mistake or did something wrong,"* even if you feel guilty and remorseful, you also say, *"Not only am I guilty, but I am a bad mom."*

For example, during my doctor's appointment, my doctor asked if I was nursing my child. When I answered, his response was judgmental (shocked that I was nursing my one-year-old), which created a reaction in me (self-consciousness and embarrassment). He followed up on his judgment by shaming me (mocking that I'd have to stop nursing my child before kindergarten), which then created an emotional response in me of feeling humiliated. Here is something important to know about my experience: While I felt embarrassed, humiliated, and really angry, I did not feel shame. I could have, but I did not take his observation to be true or accurate.

My experience is an example of what can increase shadow emotions in motherhood: being judged for our parenting choices and behaviors. When we're out in public, with people we may or may not know, our parenting is on display, ready to be evaluated. And nothing puts our parenting on display more than when our child begins to act out, throw a tantrum, run around, be disruptive, or cry. When their child does something socially inappropriate, many moms, in reaction to the tension and fear of being judged or embarrassed, start an inner dialogue of self-talk: *Am I reacting okay? How do I handle this situation? What are people thinking? Do they think I don't have control over my child? They must think I'm a bad mom.* And the only way a mom could know the answers is if she asked those observing.

The shadow emotions of embarrassment all share a common theme: *How did I come across? What do others think of me?* And, more importantly, *Do I believe their supposed opinions, thoughts, and beliefs of me to be true?* While the shadow emotions are experienced in a social context, they're internally felt and processed—sometimes our interpretations of the shadow emotions are accurate; other times we believe the internalized messages, but they are hardly true.

Mothering a child is personal—it's not about doing everything perfectly and never making mistakes. Often, we make the decision that feels right in the moment with the time, information, and energy we have. Only later can we look back and examine what we could have done differently or why we made a certain choice. Regardless of the outcome of a certain situation or event, here is something I know to be true: Motherhood is more than one moment; it's a series of moments between a mother and her child. And at the end of the day, you have to be comfortable and confident with your choices, decisions, words, and actions.

In this section, the shadow emotions of feeling awkward, embarrassed, humiliated, and ashamed are explored in more detail in the context of motherhood, along with skills and strategies to help you navigate these uncomfortable—and at times painful—shadow moments.

the uncomfortable moments of motherhood

simple ways to bounce back after an awkward or embarrassing moment

Before I became a parent, I swore my kids would never have a tantrum in public with me. Let's take a minute to laugh about this together.
—Anonymous

The shadow emotions awkwardness, embarrassment, and mortification all share a common thread: They are emotional reactions we feel in the context of relationships in a social setting. No role is more social than being a mom! Having a child will force even the shyest and most introverted mama into social spaces and places where she's forced to interact way beyond her comfort zone, all for the sake of her child.

The mildest form of these shadow emotions is awkwardness. All moms at some point feel awkward in motherhood; we all have moments of being socially uncomfortable, feeling out of place, and not being certain what to do or say in a social situation.

Some examples of awkward moments in motherhood can be the following:

- Meeting up at a playdate or on the playground with other moms and kids, only to struggle with finding conversation starters, causing you to feel incredibly awkward teetering between sharing pleasantries and oversharing because most days you don't see another adult.

- Not realizing your child overheard you telling your sweetie how much you despise your in-laws' cooking, only to have your child share this at dinner with your in-laws the next day.

- Being forced to socialize with parents you barely know at a child's birthday. You have no interest in talking with them, so you hang out at the bouncy house as the "supervisor," because making conversations with the adults feels awkward and contrived.

- Answering uncomfortable and unexpected questions you don't feel qualified for (but you're doing the best you can). For example, answering your child's questions about physical processes (e.g., how babies are made, body changes during puberty) or death and our place in the universe.

Feeling awkward is a shadow emotion because it takes away from being in the present moment. Instead of enjoying what is happening (e.g., spending time with other moms), you may have a mental preoccupation of what's happening and what others may be thinking. You may be worrying about what to say or how to act, how to make connections with other moms, or what to do if your child has a challenging and difficult moment.

More intense than feeling awkward, the shadow emotion of embarrassment is a moderate emotional response in social situations when a mother is feeling self-conscious, stressed, and foolish in front of others. I'm sure you've been there: questioning how a simple trip to the market or Target can create such chaos and stress between you and your child, after that dramatic tantrum in public leaves you questioning your parenting abilities. Feeling embarrassed is part of life, especially for mothers. Kids do and say some of the most unpredictable things, and their interpretation of the world is an interesting one!

One of the most common triggers for feeling embarrassed is how your child behaves in social settings. Taking your child anywhere in public, to complete chores and run errands, or to explore parks and museums, or to simply gather at a friend's home, can feel risky and unpredictable depending on the child's age, stage of development, and when the outing happens during a child's routine (i.e., their daily schedule of eating, napping, snacking, and going to bed). All of these variables can create stress and tension for a child and their parents. And when a child is hungry, tired, or wants to leave, chances are they're going to express their desire not through words but through behaviors, sometimes even through a massive tantrum. And those meltdowns are not easy; when your child lies down on the ground, impossible to move, crying, not cooperating and rejecting your attempts to redirect, comfort, and soothe them, the emotions are challenging for both you and your child.

Tantrums like this are tough, and there is often an added layer beneath the surface as you are trying to get your child off the ground: You're feeling embarrassed, your parenting skills are on public display, and you are vulnerable to perceived or actual judgments and opinions. You are wondering: *Did I do the right thing? Did I cave under pressure and give in? Was I too harsh? Is my child okay? I wonder what they're thinking of me and my child?*

In motherhood, there are countless ways and situations to feel this shadow emotion of embarrassment. Tantrums are one way we can feel embarrassment, but there are other situations in motherhood when these feelings arise. They fall into two broad categories: (1) personally embarrassing situations and (2) embarrassing interactions with others.[5]

Personally Embarrassing Situations

There are several types of embarrassing personal situations, including the following:

- **A gaffe or accident:** This category includes falling, tripping, or dropping something in front of a group of people; for example, knocking over a display at a store when you're not paying attention, having something stuck in your teeth or hanging from your nose during a conversation, or using a bathroom while you're out, only to look in the mirror to see that your hair is looking messy, your shirt is stained with your baby's spit-up, snot, or food, and your eyes are puffy.

- **Saying or doing something wrong:** This category includes forgetting someone's name, misusing a word, forgetting what you're saying midsentence, oversharing personal information, eating a food incorrectly, being underdressed for an event, forgetting to show up to your child's teacher conference, or writing down the wrong time for your child's concert and missing their performance.

- **Losing control of your body:** This category includes passing gas, leaking breast milk when you are nursing, leaking through your clothes when you're on your period, and spilling food or beverages while you're eating or drinking.

- **Failures in privacy:** This category includes someone opening the bathroom door when you're on the toilet, thinking an episode of yelling at your child is private but then realizing others can overhear you, and talking about someone and not realizing they're right behind you.

Embarrassing Interactions with Others

Embarrassing interactions with others can include awkward and embarrassing interactions with your child, other moms, your sweetie, family, and strangers.

- **Not being prepared or failing to do something:** This category includes forgetting to send your child to school with a coat so they aren't able to go out for recess; missing a sign-up deadline for your child's sports team, school play, or camp; and being called out by your mother-in-law for having a messy home.

- **Your child losing control of their body:** This category includes your child refusing to walk or stand during a tantrum so you are forced to leave the scene carrying them like a football; your child vomiting or having an accident (peeing or pooping) in a public place; your child burping loudly in a quiet setting; or your child having a screaming meltdown in a store.

- **Accidents or inappropriate behavior:** This category includes times when your child is disrespectful, calling you names or telling you to be quiet or to shut up; when your child spills something in a restaurant, disrupting everyone; when you learn that your child has been repeating curse words at school, although you didn't realize they had heard you use them; or when you yell at your child, lose control, and feel horrible.

- **Truth bombs:** These happen when your child says or asks a question that is embarrassing; for example, when they ask someone who is older why they have lines in their face, when they ask a woman if she's going to have a baby because her stomach is big, or when you overhear your child tell someone something about your behavior (e.g., "My mom was crying last night," or, "My mom loves wine").

Embarrassing moments are part of the landscape of motherhood. And most of the time, when these moments happen, a mother can either laugh it off or let it go after a few hours or by the next day (although sometimes it takes a few days).

A more intense, severe, and extreme form of embarrassment is feeling mortified. Feeling mortified is uncomfortable not only while you are experiencing it but also afterward, when you recall the memories from the situation. The experience of feeling mortified can be so intense that even the memory can make you feel as if it were happening all over again.

My hope is that experiencing this shadow emotion hasn't happened to you. If it has, I hope it's not often! Feeling mortified can come up in small ways; for instance, when we're looking through old photographs from a previous relationship, reading old journals from middle school, or considering some of our hair and fashion choices from the past. Feeling mortified as a mom, however, takes embarrassment to a whole new level and is incredibly upsetting and stressful. One example of mortification is being out in public when your child has a tremendous meltdown. They're not just crying, they're also screaming things like, *"I hate you! Stop it! You're mean!"* They may be acting out in other extreme ways, like hitting, screaming, biting, kicking, or name-calling. Another example is when you're at a playdate and your child says something mortifying, such as asking the host, *"Why is your house so messy?"* Or perhaps they say things like, *"I don't want to be here, I don't like [the name of the child at the house]."* Or maybe they share overheard information: *"You were talking about Mrs. S. to Grandma, saying how she's not nice, but now you're friends?"*

When the shadow emotions of awkwardness, embarrassment, or mortification show up, paired with a sense of diminished self-worth, long after a situation has occurred, it indicates that these shadow emotions aren't being managed. Unmanaged pain and suffering can manifest themselves in our motherhood journey as a more severe shadow emotion: shame. We'll dive deep into shame in the next chapter.

At the Heart of Feeling Awkward, Embarrassed, or Mortified

At the heart of awkwardness, embarrassment, and mortification is feeling vulnerable, exposed, self-conscious, and judged. Whatever the intensity we experience, these shadow emotions are part of the landscape of being a mother; all of us mothers have flaws and idiosyncrasies, and we all make mistakes. No one and nothing is perfect—not you, your child, or anyone else. We're all works in progress at different stages. Which is why, at the heart of these shadow emotions, is being compassionate with yourself when situations create these emotional reactions. Of course it is a moment impacting you, but this experience or shadow emotion does not define you; it's simply one part of you experiencing one moment in motherhood.

Reframe Your Mantra

Thoughts are powerful. Your self-talk (the things you say to yourself) has a deep impact on what you feel and how you respond. Keep this principle in mind and reframe problematic thoughts that increase your shadow emotions.

SHADOW MANTRA If you're saying this . . .	THRIVING MANTRA Positively reframe to say this . . .
Why can't I just relax? I'm so awkward. Why did I say that? (Awkward)	Moments like this can be challenging. But I have strengths and have gotten through difficult times. Creating awareness about what I can do differently is an important focus right now. Being compassionate with myself and learning how to relax and take care of myself would help me figure this out in the future.
I am such a weirdo, so odd and different. I wish I weren't this way. (Awkward)	Labeling myself in a negative way isn't going to help me, and it's going to make me feel worse. If my child was having the same feeling and calling themselves a name, how would I respond? Treating myself with the same amount of compassion I would show my child is important. If I need to develop a skill or do something differently, this is where I can focus my energy.
I can't believe I have to force small talk with moms or people I don't even want to know. (Awkward)	Sometimes I have to do things I don't want to do. I don't have to force conversations, but I can be polite and find ways to be comfortable at these outings without judging myself or other moms harshly.
I can only imagine what they must think of me. (Embarrassed)	Unless I ask someone directly, I can't read minds or know what someone thinks of me. In this moment of feeling upset, I can only be compassionate to myself right now.

(continued)

SHADOW MANTRA If you're saying this . . .	THRIVING MANTRA Positively reframe to say this . . .
I can't believe that happened. I'm so embarrassed—so many moms saw that! (Embarrassed)	Embarrassing moments happen to everyone. Is there something I can learn from this? Instead of judging myself, thinking about the embarrassment in a curious way and trying to understand it would be more helpful.
I'm mortified. I'll never be able to show my face in that group again. (Mortified)	I'm feeling very exposed right now and am wondering what others think of me. Holding on to the belief that I can't show my face in public is not a rational thought. I will, and it may be uncomfortable. Chances are I'm judging myself more harshly right now than anyone else would. What is the one thing I can do to feel better right now?

Moving Beyond the Shadows

TIP #1: ASK QUESTIONS TO CREATE SELF-AWARENESS.

Because these shadow emotions happen all the time in motherhood, sometimes allowing time to pass is all that's needed to recover. Other times, looking a little deeper to understand patterns and how these emotional reactions happen is needed in order for you to make changes. Ask yourself the following questions:

- What are the situations or times when I feel awkward (or embarrassed, or mortified)? List all of the situations that come to mind.
- Is there a pattern or common theme (e.g., situations or people)? What is the trigger?
- Is this feeling creating stress or distress for me? If so, how? Am I limiting an activity? Isolating myself? Using negative self-talk? Starting to feel more anxiety?

- Does this situation or experience remind me of something in the past—unresolved and still creating some suffering—that I need to address?

- When I've felt this way in the past, what has helped me feel better and move forward?

- What has this situation or interaction taught me? Is there a lesson to be learned or a takeaway I can use?

- Is it possible I could reduce how often I feel this way by learning a new skill or preparing ahead of time? For example, if I feel awkward socially, perhaps a book on increasing my self-confidence in social groups or how to make conversations would be helpful.

TIP #2: GIVE YOURSELF PERSPECTIVE.

After feeling any variation of these shadow emotions, it's natural to feel uncomfortable and exposed. And it's also important to remember the following:

- You—not anyone else—are likely the one who is judging yourself the harshest right now. As social as humans are, we also tend to be self-focused, meaning we spend a lot of time thinking about ourselves in the context of a situation *more than others think of us.*

- You are so much more than a behavior or one embarrassing moment. Separate *yourself* from the *behavior.* You are not the behavior, nor can you be responsible for someone else's behavior. Don't create negative self-talk that leads you to believe something is wrong with you. Don't generalize this moment into an attribute about your worth as a person. For example, let's imagine your child had a meltdown at an event, and you feel embarrassed because you had to leave early or your child hit you as you tried to console and comfort them. If on the way home you keep repeating to yourself, *I'm an awful mother*, then this is an example of what I *don't* want you to do.

Instead, shift your perspective and realize that the moment was quite stressful and, despite your best efforts, things did not go as planned.

- If what just happened to you happened to someone else, what would your response be? Chances are you'd be compassionate and understanding to that person. Which demonstrates the point: When embarrassing things happen, the one who thinks about it the most is the one who it happened to; more often than not, those who saw it move on quickly. And for those who dwell on it, well, chances are they're not your true friends and they just revealed something about themselves. Would you want to be friends with them or know them anyway?

- Using humor and being direct about embarrassing moments is often the best response. When something embarrassing happens, there are really two ways to deal with it: (1) act like it didn't happen and ignore it or (2) address it right then and there. Often addressing it right as it happens can help you cope with the moment, and humor, calling attention to what just happened, can be incredibly helpful to mitigate your discomfort from embarrassing situations. But the key point with humor is this: Make sure it's not aggressive or harmful humor to yourself or another, and keep the humor light and playful instead of insulting or harmful.[6]

TIP #3: BE AN OBSERVER TO YOUR EMBARRASSING MOMENT.

Experiencing an embarrassing moment or situation is uncomfortable. And this feeling of embarrassment often continues long past the actual moment. One skill to embrace in order to work past an awkward or embarrassing experience is to put yourself in an *observer role*. When a person has been in an embarrassing situation, they often think about themselves in the situation as the *actor*—or main participant—in the situation, meaning they perceive themselves to be on a stage and narrate the event as if they were in the actor's shoes, evaluating themselves and imagining what everyone is thinking (or could be thinking). In contrast, researchers have found if a person places themselves in the *role of the observer*, they are more likely to see the situation differently, as less emotionally intense.

In the role of the observer, a person does not put their views on or try to predict what the observer thinks. Instead, the goal is to place themselves in the shoes and perspective of the observer's experience. As an observer watching the embarrassing situation, the person actually feels better and less stressed. And the reason is this: *Individuals have a tendency not to take into account the observer's empathy for them during the embarrassing situation.* When a person takes on the role of the actor (i.e., uses a self-focus), they experience more distress compared to taking on the role of the observer. Taking the focus from themselves and using imaginal thinking, feeling, and perspective, taking into account what another person thinks, can create empathy, tolerance, and kindness.[7]

Let's imagine this concept in a scenario lots of mamas encounter: A mom is in public, and her child is acting up and acting out. The mother likely feels stressed, overwhelmed, and physically tense, embarrassed by the attention her child's screams are drawing to her and the situation. She just wants to get out of the store, but her child is in a heap on the floor, refusing to get up. As the mom feels embarrassed, she may think to herself, *I can feel everyone's eyes on me, judging me. I bet they're thinking, "This mom has no control. It's too late in the day, and her child should be home in bed. What kind of mom takes her child out this late?"* The mother is taking the stance as the actor. In contrast, taking the role as the observer, this mama may find alternative ways others may have felt and thought about the situation. Let's

257

examine how this mom could reframe her perception of each person's viewpoint:

- The mom shopping with her teenager. She looked at me and thought, *Oh, I remember those days—some days were so hard. I don't miss those meltdowns and how challenging it was to go places, but I do miss those years.*
- The man in his mid- to late thirties. He could have thought, *I really need to be the one to do the shopping. My sweetie has been talking about how hard it is to shop with our kids. I wonder if this is what she goes through each time? Goodness, no wonder she hates going to the market with the kids.*
- The mom with a newborn. She likely thought, *This newborn stage is challenging, but I don't envy the terrible twos ahead! I hope I hold myself together as well as that mom when it happens to me.*

Imagining how others may perceive you through a compassionate lens, instead of a critical or judgmental one, will help you develop the skill of being the observer, which is one way to move from this shadow emotion into thriving in mothering.

TIP #4: LEARN FROM THE SITUATION AND MOVE ON.

Sometimes, it's important not to overthink or overanalyze a situation or interaction. If you've spent some time thinking about what created this shadow emotion and can't seem to make sense of it, it may be time to accept what happened and move on. In other words, don't dwell on it—let it go for a bit. Perhaps going for a walk or doing another activity will give you some space from the situation and, with some distance, you'll have a fresh perspective and be able to move on.

If you have an insight from the situation and want to do

something differently next time, focus on what you learned. Start with asking yourself, *What, if anything, could I have done differently?* If your child had a meltdown, and you made the correlation that it was close to lunch or naptime, then knowing this helps you plan future outings around your child's best time of day. If you or your child said something awkward or overshared, leaving you feeling embarrassed, then sometimes the best thing to do is simply apologize in the moment and move on. Later you can talk with your child about ways to be more sensitive and thoughtful to others' feelings, especially when it comes to appearance, shapes, sizes, and other differences. And if you forgot to hand in a form or sign your child up for a sports team or play, maybe the new habit to form in order to avoid this in the future is to put a reminder on your smartphone.

Practicing this skill—determining what you learned and what you can do differently—is not supposed to make you feel more shadow emotions like shame and start a cycle of self-blame! Be sure to look at the situation as an observer, being curious about what unfolded, instead of passing judgment. And one of my favorite skills to use is to ask yourself: *If my child or friend came to me and had just gone through the same situation, what advice or recommendation would I share?*

TIP #5: REACH OUT TO A SUPPORTIVE FRIEND.

After an embarrassing moment or situation, if you find yourself still preoccupied with replaying the event, then an act of self-care would be to reach out to a caring person in your life for support and help in processing what happened. If you had an awkward or embarrassing moment at the playground with another mom, and you're feeling like you can never go back (even though your child has friends in the group), then reaching out and talking it over with a friend will not only help you feel better, but you may also get some ideas on how to handle the next playgroup instead of simply never going back. When you feel stuck and don't know what to do after trying a lot of these tips, then chances are that after sharing what happened with a supportive person, you'll feel better and have a new perspective.

TIP #6: START COUNSELING FOR SUPPORT AND SKILLS.

If you feel awkward, embarrassed, or mortified often, or these shadow emotions are pervasive and repetitive in your life, then working with a mental health professional to heal, get support, and learn skills to reduce these feelings would be beneficial. In my practice, many moms begin counseling to strengthen their parenting skills and strategies, which is incredibly empowering and helpful; we all need support on this journey through motherhood, and my belief is that the strongest people are the ones who reach out for support and go to therapy.

Thriving Mama Reflection

Feeling awkward, embarrassed, and even mortified happens to everyone at some point. When it does, it can feel as if the world is judging you. But more often than not, this is a *perception of fear* instead of reality. The only way you could know what others thought is to ask them, and as a busy mama, do you really have time for that? Instead, when you feel exposed and vulnerable and you wonder what others think, recenter and refocus on these questions: *What does it matter? Truly, what does it matter?* Because the reality is that you've judged yourself more harshly than anyone else, and those who witnessed what happened likely had more compassion for you than you could imagine. As mothers, we've all experienced these shadow emotions, and you are no exception. For a moment, reflect on this: How does the moment you experienced feeling these shadow emotions define who you are? And if you saw another mother going through exactly what you experienced, would you judge her the way you're judging yourself? This moment does not define you at all. Awkward or embarrassing moments in motherhood are not meant to be held on to. All you can do is learn from them, hold yourself with compassion in your humanness as a mother, let the shadow moment go, and move forward.

the hidden suffering in motherhood

how letting go of humiliation & shame creates space for joy & happiness

If we can share our story with someone who responds with
empathy and understanding, shame can't survive.
—Brené Brown

Being a mother means being incredibly vulnerable, not only
because you are responsible for caring for and raising a child, but
also because the challenges of motherhood will shine a light on
all the places in your life where suffering hides, asking to be paid
attention to, to be taken care of, to be healed. And there's no more
powerful example of these places of suffering than the shadow
emotions of humiliation and shame.

Under the umbrella of the shadow emotion of embarrassment
is humiliation, which is the feeling you experience when a
person treats you in a harsh, cutting, demeaning way. Shame, on
the other hand, is believing that *you deserved* the humiliating
treatment. If *humiliation* is someone's poor treatment of you,
shame is your belief that you deserve to be treated this way and

that you are not worth better treatment. Let's look at an example scenario to illustrate these concepts.

Imagine your child goes to school in mismatched, torn, and stained clothes. When you pick your child up at school, one of the teachers points out the dirty clothing your child is wearing.

If you feel *embarrassed*, you may feel uncomfortable having this pointed out, but you then explain to the teacher that you and your child had a battle of wills over their clothing choices and that you eventually gave in. After a few hours, or a day or two at the most, you have let this moment go.

If you feel *humiliated*, you may feel this way because another mom heard the teacher say this to you. You see her laugh, furrow her brow at you, then roll her eyes. You also notice her child, who is impeccably dressed.

If you feel *ashamed*, you believe your child wearing ratty clothes and the teacher and mom reacting this way reinforces a core belief of yourself: *I am a horrible mom. My kids deserve better than to have me as a mother. This is yet another example of how I'm not like other mothers, how I am failing as a mom.*

Shame is an emotional cocktail of embarrassment on steroids, guilt bred from taking the blame, sadness cemented in worthlessness, and self-worth measured in shortcomings and flaws. Shame often develops in childhood through experiences and messages we receive from important people, messages that create a sense of being less-than, worthless, unlovable, or unvalued.

Humiliation and shame often show up in a few ways: criticizing or highlighting vulnerabilities in front of others (*"What's wrong with her? She shouldn't be having tantrums like this at her age," "You've been working so much, and I can't help*

You Are Not Alone: Olivia's Story

Olivia described her self-talk as two distinct things: (1) herself and (2) the bully in her head. The bully was the self-critical voice shaming her for all of her flaws and insecurities, calling her a fraud and impostor, and that it was only a matter of time before she was found out at work and with her friends. Olivia was incredibly ashamed about her upbringing. Her mother, an alcoholic for most of Olivia's childhood, was her sole parent; her father had abandoned the family and had significant gambling issues. Growing up in poverty, Olivia had the role of taking care of her sister when their mom worked, cooking meals and doing laundry at age seven.

Olivia started counseling to get support on how to navigate her relationship with her mom, who was newly sober and wanting to reconnect with Olivia and her three children (ages nine, six, and four). Beneath the surface of this practical issue (if and how to reconnect with her mom), Olivia had to address the bullying in her head, a firestorm of shaming thoughts stemming from how she grew up and how she'd been treated by her mom. On top of it, Olivia struggled with feeling like the life she built—a great job, a healthy marriage, and economic stability—could go away at any moment, and that underneath she was a fraud. We worked on addressing her childhood trauma, managing negative thoughts and setting firm boundaries and conditions so she could possibly be willing to reconnect with her mother. Throughout our work, we focused on Olivia developing self-compassion as well as highlighting her strengths and her resiliency to take these difficult childhood experiences and make healthy choices as an adult to become the amazing mom she was.

wondering if that's why he's having trouble in school"); comparing a loved one to others (*"Why can't you be like so-and-so?," "I never felt those things when you kids were young"*); sharing vulnerable or embarrassing moments in front of others (*"All I wanted was to drink my coffee, but someone had an accident and peed, so that didn't happen"*); mocking or teasing (*"Do you ever do anything right?," "You're going to eat all that?"*); and sharing personal details, struggles, or issues in social settings or in public (*"Well, we'd have been here on time if someone hadn't had an epic tantrum"*).

When a person has been humiliated, they may express upset about how they were treated, only to hear defensive responses and dismissive comments such as, *"You can't take a joke. What's the big deal? You're overreacting!"* Or, *"Oh, you're too sensitive. That's not what I said; you heard me wrong. You need to move on."* Another tactic is using personal information to continue the humiliation, such as, *"Yeah, who asked you? Your mom is an alcoholic."* Or, *"Oh, it's that time of the month—watch out!"* Over time, the person comes to believe the humiliating comments and messages, turning an embarrassing moment of put-downs into the shadow emotion of shame. The shamed person comes to believe that *"I don't matter."*

These shadow emotions are often buried deep, pushed down in an attempt to forget the painful messages from parents, siblings, partners, or others. Words are incredibly powerful. And the most powerful words are the ones spoken between a parent and child—words are internalized in a child's mind, etched in their heart forever.

A child's relationship with their parent is the first place the child learns about the world. And a parent shows a child through their actions and their responding to the child's needs and struggles what the world thinks of that child, setting up the framework from which all other relationships in their lifetime will be measured and compared, including the relationship a child has with themselves.

The parent-child relationship creates a mosaic of core beliefs about oneself, others, and the world; for example, *I am smart, I'm creative, I'm loving and very much loved.* Or perhaps these beliefs are: *I'm a burden. My needs don't matter. I'm not smart. I don't deserve good things, because I'm not a good person.* This is not to put pressure on a parent with the expectation to be perfect, to never say something unkind or react in a less than nurturing way. Parents are human and they make mistakes, sometimes many mistakes. But it's the *consistency* in how a parent cares for and interacts with the child daily, over the span of their childhood and life, that makes the difference. Hopefully, the parent and child have more loving, positive, and affirming interactions than harmful, humiliating, and shaming interactions. But when the majority of the interactions and experiences between parent and child are hurtful, stressful, and judgmental (or abusive and neglectful), then the shadow emotions of shame and humiliation develop and thrive.

In the work I've done over the decades, I've observed that when parents treat their child this way, it is *always* because the parent has unresolved pain or unmanaged mental health issues; instead of taking care of *their* suffering, they transferred it to and acted it out in their relationship with their child. It is not a child's job, role, or responsibility to carry the emotional pain and suffering of and from their parents. There is a *sacredness* between parent and child; a parent's words, actions, and interactions with their child will be the most influential relationship across that child's lifetime.

Challenging moments in motherhood with our children can create a wellspring of these shadow emotions: you as a mother take blame, feel like you are less-than, as if you're failing as a mom. In fact, these shadow emotions are a white flag of compassion asking you to pause, pay attention to your suffering, and find the place within you that needs to be healed. But this is not an easy path to take. In motherhood, the shadow emotions of humiliation and shame are difficult to talk about, often because these feelings are so deeply intertwined with our self-worth and value.

It's important for us as mothers to recognize humiliation and shame within ourselves, because it can affect our relationship with our child in a very intense and vulnerable way. If we believe we are not a good mom and that we're a failure when we're going through a tough phase with our child, what happens when our child gets upset, doesn't listen, isn't cooperative, and expresses anger toward us? *We're going to see our child's reaction as proof that we're failing at mothering: We believe that our child doesn't respect us and that we don't matter.* And our child's behavior may remind us of some important person in our life who hurt us long ago, hitting a nerve of pain and creating another shadow emotion—anger. And we respond to our child's behavior with expressed anger, perhaps through yelling or name-calling, unintentionally humiliating and shaming our child. We do this not because we're a bad mom, but because we are unaware of the depth of our suffering and our own buried shame. And when we calm down later, more shadow emotions emerge—sadness, guilt, regret, and fear—which reaffirm our negative thinking as accurate and true: *I'm not a good mom.* Once we come into awareness that this is what's happening underneath our behaviors and shadow emotions, then we can take steps to heal and allow ourselves to feel without acting on or expressing our shadow emotions and harming ourselves or our child.

Being a parent is to be in a position of authority. Parents care for their child and make decisions on their behalf, taking into account what they believe is in their child's best interest, for years before their child is developmentally ready to articulate, request, and seek out their own preferences and interests. And in those moments, children often protest and display preferences and desires through expressing behavior. These behaviors are not easy for a parent or a child—tantrums and power struggles are often developmentally appropriate and can be expected during separation and independence. How a parent and caregiver handles these challenging parenting moments is significant and impactful to the child. Some examples of how parents and caregivers can humiliate a child, which creates the potential for shame to develop, include:

- embarrassing the child, or reacting to the child in a way that dominates—via size, power, or words—and lessens their voice and shuts them down;

- name-calling, mocking a child's behavior, or making fun of the child;

- highlighting the child's struggles, flaws, or mistakes in front of friends, peers, or siblings; and

- taking pictures or videos of the child's tantrums or other behavior and using them to gain power, mock, or control, including posting the pictures or videos to social media or sharing them with others.

Children who have experienced humiliation and shame as a form of discipline or as a pattern of routine behavior face greater challenges with their mental, social, and academic well-being. And often, those who've been treated in humiliating and shameful ways in turn act them out on others or within themselves, or they seek out friends and partners to keep this pattern alive, unless they receive intervention, support, and healing.

Humiliation and shame are not discipline tactics; *they are intimidation tactics, control tactics, and abuse tactics.* Nothing makes it acceptable to humiliate a child (or anyone else for that matter). If any of these behaviors are what you do, or another parent or another caregiver has done to a child, please seek support from a counselor or therapist for yourself or take steps to educate these other caregivers on how to be loving, healthy, and supportive to the children in their care through professional support and help with learning parenting skills and strategies.

If you've humiliated or shamed your child, please know: You need to change this, and you *can* change this. You can move forward, heal yourself, and repair your relationship with your child. This is some of the most important work I do and healing is possible.

And if by reading this chapter you recognize that you are in an unhealthy relationship where there are ongoing patterns of humiliation, know that this is a form of abuse and signals an unhealthy relationship, work environment, or family system and serious intervention and support from a mental health professional needs to happen. Or if you realize that you have been the victim of humiliation and shame tactics from earlier in your life that are now coming to light through thoughts and feelings of shame, it's time to heal that hurt.

Motherhood has a funny way of taking all the coping skills that you developed earlier in your life—the ones that helped you push down these feelings and hide them from others—and making them less effective (even useless), allowing these shadow emotions to surface in unexpected and unpredictable ways that can no longer be ignored. Becoming aware of your feelings of shame—including negative self-talk that says you are a bad mother, something is wrong with you, you are failing your children, or everything is your fault—will shine a light on all the places that need attention and healing.

When you as a mother experience shame, there is often a deep belief that you are unworthy, unlovable, and less deserving compared to others. Shame is a painful, disruptive emotional response and experienced appraisal of yourself that hides beneath the surface, breaking through and showing up in the most unexpected ways in the role you cherish most: being a mother.

When you feel ready, I want you to follow any personal shame statements you notice in your life (some of which you may recognize in the table on page 271 or the Feelings Mantra on page 273) and truly understand how the path of pain was created in your life. I want you to see and understand what you currently do in the present moment and in motherhood to maintain this shadow emotion (e.g., using negative self-talk, not prioritizing self-care, spending time with shaming people). You can get off the path of shame. You can create a new path that is encouraging, loving, and compassionate and turn all of that shame into something else.

The Ways Shame Manifests in Motherhood

Some examples of feeling shame in motherhood include:

- not being able to forgive yourself for mistakes you made in the past;

- for the family you grew up in and how they treated you;

- about having been sexually assaulted or sexually abused (which can manifest as low self-worth and problems in sexual intimacy);

- for not being able to nurse your baby;

- about your body or about not being able to lose weight;

- for making mistakes as a parent (e.g., not being able to change the past and wondering about the impact of your behavior on your child, fearing you damaged them);

- about your looks, intellect, or abilities;

- because of a secret you have that no one knows and that you think about almost every day;

- when your child does something socially inappropriate and you worry about what other people will think of you as a parent or how they will judge you;

- because of divorce or marital issues (such as infidelity) or because of your or a family member's substance dependence;

- when people in your community know about something personal and painful happening in your family and you know people are gossiping about the situation; and

- when your child has a mental health issue, because you think other people will judge you, your child, and your success or ability as a parent.

At the Heart of Feeling Humiliation and Shame

At the heart of feeling humiliation and shame is a deep wound where negative messages you have received from important people in your life become internalized and believed, such as *I don't matter*, *I'm less-than*, and *I'm not important*. These messages or interactions create a sense of diminished self-worth and value and foster a belief that you do not deserve things such as love, security, connection, peacefulness, health, and happiness. At the heart of these shadow emotions is taking in another person's judgments, negative appraisals, or behaviors and believing they were true and deserved, which leads you to feel less-than, not good enough, or flawed. Believing such things is an incredible error; any person who has treated another this way made the mistake by ignoring and not managing their pain, by choosing to take their suffering out on another person. Regardless, humiliating and shaming another person carries the consequence of harming that person's most tender self, planting a negative belief and appraisal that will destructively grow.

Reframe Your Mantra

Thoughts are powerful. Your self-talk (the things you say to yourself) has a deep impact on what you feel and how you respond. Keep this principle in mind and reframe problematic thoughts that increase your shadow emotions.

SHADOW MANTRA If you're saying this . . .	THRIVING MANTRA Positively reframe to say this . . .
I'm a bad mother. I feel bad for my kids.	Where is the evidence I'm a bad mother? Perhaps I've made some choices that were not good, but that doesn't make me a bad mother. Right now what I need to focus on is learning from my mistakes and making a commitment to do better. I can get support to manage my behavior and learn the skills to parent in a more peaceful way. I have strengths and gifts that have been crowded out by my stress and actions. I can repair what's happened with my kids and move forward.
I don't matter—my kids don't need me like they used to.	I feel like no one cares and I don't matter, but my thinking is influenced by what I'm feeling, which is not accurate right now. I do matter, especially to my kids. They may not show it, but they love me. I matter very much to my children. My suffering is blocking my ability to see this; reaching out to a supportive friend would be helpful.
I deserve to be treated this way.	Being treated poorly or in an abusive way is never okay. That was wrong. I need to release this belief that I'm not deserving of respect and kindness. My actions do not justify being humiliated. I need to take care of myself and talk to someone about this for support.

(continued)

SHADOW MANTRA If you're saying this . . .	THRIVING MANTRA Positively reframe to say this . . .
I don't understand why I'm being treated this way by my kids. What did I do to deserve this?	Being treated this way is upsetting. I need to talk with my kids about kindness and respect, what I expect from them and what they can expect from me. I can also set consequences in place for unkind behavior. And it's possible my kids are going through something, but they need to understand that it isn't okay to treat me this way. Regardless of how people treat me, I am worthy of love, respect, and kindness.
I wish my kids knew how lucky they are; I wish that when I was growing up I'd had the family they do.	Shame creeps up in unexpected ways. I suffered a lot growing up, and I do wish things had been different. I've made amazing progress in my healing, and I've created a family of my own that's loving and supportive. Maybe one day when my kids are older, I'll share my experiences with them. Right now, I can focus on how my kids don't have to know how lucky they are, because all they know is a loving home, and that's because of what I've created through healing some of my pain.
I'm so damaged, and being a mother is so hard. I feel worthless; my kids deserve to have a better mom than me.	I'm not damaged, I've been impacted by situations and history. This is part of me, but not all of me. Responding to myself with love and compassion and knowing I've suffered is the first step to healing. Can I let go of the thought that I'm not damaged and instead recognize that part of me needs love and healing?

Moving Beyond the Shadows

In this chapter, where we're dealing with some pretty sensitive feelings, we'll pass over reflection questions and instead dive right into ways you can address and heal feelings of shame and humiliation. I recommend exploring deeper parts of these shadow emotions with guidance and individualized support from a mental health professional.

Often, we hold ourselves to unrealistic standards and compare ourselves to others. No one is perfect and everyone makes mistakes. But the problem is that these shadow emotions of humiliation and shame, if left unmanaged, change the way someone thinks, creating deep patterns of critical and negative self-talk, which means that person may maintain these feelings long after the interaction or situation has passed. Make sure to spend time in reflection transforming your shadow mantras into positive thriving mantras (see page 273).

How to Manage and Heal Feelings of Shame and Humiliation

TIP #1: INCREASE YOUR SELF-COMPASSION.

Shame and humiliation are toxic emotional responses that suffocate self-worth, health, and happiness. These shadow emotions are the ultimate tricksters, creating a false sense that you don't matter, or deserve joy, or aren't enough compared to others. Which is why learning the skills to heal from humiliation and shame are essential for any person (but especially mothers).

Self-compassion is the antidote to shame. Self-compassion is giving to yourself what you so desperately needed in the past and what you still need now in motherhood: empathy, love, understanding, and acknowledgment of your suffering or struggles. You need to extend these things to yourself just as readily as you would extend them to your child. Often when mistakes are made, or difficult situations arise, we have a tendency to judge ourselves harshly instead of extending the same compassion to ourselves that we would extend to someone else. When you make mistakes or errors, instead of igniting negative and critical self-talk, meet yourself with self-compassion and a curiosity to understand what happened and what you could have done differently. Instead of blaming yourself, shift into a *curious* and *empathic* mindset.

You were created enough, and the only thing that has changed since you were born is your growth and experience. At the core, you are you, part of the divine creation, deserving of love, worthy of happiness, and already enough. Respecting yourself, your goals, and your dreams and finding meaning are critical to your purpose. No one can tell you what your purpose is; it is for you to discover on your journey.

Remember, you are more than what others think of you, and no one has authority over you. Of course, there are rules and expectations in our society and culture, but no one can tell you how you "should" be as a person. That is for you to determine.

TIP #2: RECOGNIZE THAT BEING TREATED ABUSIVELY IS WRONG.

Years ago, when I was working in a community mental health center treating adolescents and their families who were struggling with substance dependence, I learned a great metaphor about how our surroundings and environment can be harmful and sometimes we do not even know it. The metaphor is graphic, but it illustrates a great point: If you put a frog in a pan of hot water, the frog will feel the heat immediately and jump out of the pan. If you place a frog in a pan of lukewarm water and slowly increase the heat, the frog won't jump out, even as the water begins to burn it, because it gets used to the conditions and doesn't recognize what is causing its pain.

This is a perfect example for humiliation and shame. If someone treats you poorly one time, chances are you'll be able to recognize it and move away from this person. But if humiliation is a tactic that starts off in minor ways that build over time to more moderate then severe and extreme treatment, it can be hard to recognize it as such because you've been conditioned to the behavior, situation, or interactions. And if all you know is an environment filled with humiliating and shameful interactions, then when the humiliation and shaming happens in another relationship, you're so accustomed to the conditions—they're so familiar—you don't see them as problematic.

Disrespecting, teasing, or putting another person down is wrong, as is any other kind of behavior that leaves a person feeling humiliated or ashamed. If you experience this, or treat other people this way, now is a great time to pause, reflect on what has happened, and take the steps to change this behavior.

TIP #3: SHIFT YOUR PERSPECTIVE.

At the core of shame can be feelings of being less-than, undeserving, or worthless. Which is why shifting your perception is a key component in addressing shame. We are all created equal, and no one person is better or more important than another. Of course, there are those who hold prestigious jobs or titles and education, but those are merely a person's *experiences* and *achievements* and do not qualify them as being better or more valuable than another person. You are deserving of peace, health, harmony, love, and happiness, and you don't have to prove that fact—it just is. Experiences or messages that create humiliation and shame and cause you to question your self-worth are not accurate. You are as worthy as anyone else. Looking at yourself through the lens of these shadow emotions will hold you back, block your joy, stifle your happiness, and prevent you from sharing your gifts and abilities with your children and the world.

TIP #4: FOCUS ON POSITIVE MEMORIES AND PERSONAL STRENGTHS.

After experiencing a humiliating moment (or any shadow moment discussed in this book), it can be tempting to replay the situation long after it's happened. Doing so will maintain and intensify your feelings of distress. When we replay scenarios from the past that are filled with pain, suffering, anger, or sadness, just thinking about them creates a reaction in our brain telling our body this scene is happening in the present moment. That's how powerful our thoughts are: they create feelings and sensations, and chemical reactions by just thinking about an emotional event, so much so that even though it happened in the past, just by thinking about it, we can feel some of the reactions as if it were happening in the present.

When you notice yourself thinking about and replaying a shadow moment, I want you to do one of two things. First, if you can, think of and replay a pleasant and happy moment in motherhood or in your life. Notice how you feel. Imagine the moment is happening right now; close your eyes if you need to visualize this moment. After playing this pleasant scene in your mind, notice how you feel. Hopefully less stressed and more relaxed!

The second activity is to write down on a piece of paper

at least five of your personal strengths (you can write down as many as you like). If you can't think of your strengths, then ask a supportive, caring person to share five with you. Read your list throughout the days that follow. And when you have a thought about the humiliating moment, go to the list and remind yourself of who you are and the strengths you have.

TIP #5: RESET YOUR CENTER.

Engaging in activities you enjoy and that bring you comfort is a great way to ground yourself after an upsetting incident. Find ways to ground and center yourself in the moment—remember who you are rather than allow yourself to be defined by this moment or experience. Resetting your center can happen in a number of ways: going for a walk, spending time working on a hobby, playing a musical instrument, calling a friend, playing with a pet, or doing something you enjoy that boosts your health and well-being. In moments when you're treated poorly, it is critical to remind yourself of who you are and what you love to do and to center yourself in what you know about yourself versus what someone thinks of you or how they have treated you.

TIP #6: SHARE YOUR STORY.

Sharing your story about these shadow emotions is an important part of healing. Sharing your story can come in many forms: through writing, art, theater, and talking about it with another person. An act of self-care when you're feeling shame and humiliation is to seek support and share your experience with someone who is emotionally available, safe, and caring, such as a friend, loved one, or mental health professional.

TIP #7: REACH OUT TO A COUNSELOR.

Everyone has been humiliated or shamed in some way. If you experience these feelings often, going to therapy and talking with a counselor can help you heal and work on strengthening your self-confidence as you learn strategies to limit the people and situations that maintain this emotional state. Counselors are trained to help you identify patterns, teach you skills, and encourage healing by helping you reconnect with your authentic self. When a person has endured chronic humiliation and shame, they learn to protect themselves emotionally in order to survive. The person may protect themselves by people-pleasing, overfunctioning, being afraid to make a mistake, and trying to be perfect—all the while, they do not believe they matter or that they are entitled to a voice or opinion. This in turn creates doubt, insecurity, low self-esteem, sadness, anger, and frustration. Working with a counselor is an incredible act of self-care. I think one of the most precious gifts of being a psychologist is being a witness to the transformative power of sharing one's story. Often, the simple yet courageous act of sharing the hurting parts of ourselves with someone can be the first step in healing, because it shifts the energy that has been buried in darkness and brings it into the light of hope.

How to Reduce and Eliminate Enacting Humiliation or Shame

TIP #1: IDENTIFY THE PAIN IN YOUR LIFE.

If, after reading this chapter, you've become aware that your behavior toward others has been harmful and hurtful, creating humiliation in someone else, I want you to give yourself a whole lot of credit here for taking responsibility for your words and actions. Taking responsibility is a great first step in not only healing yourself but also in helping protect and repair relationships with those you love. Here is what I know after decades of work supporting clients: *When one person is treating another person this way, there is unresolved pain and suffering somewhere in their life.* You have likely endured similar treatment by someone you cared about. The next step after coming into this awareness is to get help to manage and understand the pain and suffering in your life.

TIP #2: GO TO COUNSELING.

I see treating people in humiliating or shaming ways as an expression of anger, sadness, frustration, and pain from the past that's been buried and is now coming out in the present through words and interactions. *Pain and suffering does not give anyone permission or the right to harm another person.* Going to counseling and working with a therapist is a great way to understand yourself in a larger context to see patterns and learn coping skills you may not be able to gain independently. Therapists are trained to understand mental health, the impact of early childhood experiences on one's life, as well as teach healthy coping skills to use as you raise a family. I believe therapy is one of the greatest acts of self-care you can give yourself.

TIP #3: LEARN PEACEFUL PARENTING SKILLS.

There are a lot of books on parenting—so many, in fact, that it can be confusing to know where to start and what to focus on! One suggestion I share with parents I work with is to find a parenting style and framework that is easy to understand and applicable to modern life. Two of my favorite resources are the Peaceful Parenting model encouraged by Dr. Laura Markham (www.ahaparenting.com) and research-validated information from the American Academy of Pediatrics (www.aap.org). If you want to learn more about all things parenting from experts, these two sources will provide solid, trustworthy information.

TIP #4: BUILD EMPATHY AND COMPASSION.

Empathy and compassion are key traits needed to thrive in motherhood, both for yourself as a mother and for your children. In motherhood, chronic stress and overwhelm from caring for everyone and everything without support or cooperation from others can leave you feeling frustrated and resentful. In turn, over time, these shadow emotions can then block your ability to think of how your behavior is impacting someone else—not because you don't care, but because you've been pushed beyond the point of exhaustion. Instead of thoughtfully anticipating how your words and actions will impact another person, your distress and overwhelm can create an automatic reflex to relieve tension by saying or doing whatever comes to mind, which, at the extreme, is harmful. In moments where you feel this distressed and overwhelmed, put a pause between you and the reaction. Before you speak or react, ask yourself: *How would I feel if I were in the situation of the other person? What would I experience?* Taking another's perspective and imagining how they feel is a helpful skill to learn, so try to pause before you react.

The second part to this skill is to understand the destructive nature and long-term effects of humiliation and shame. Being on the receiving end of these shadow emotions impacts every part of a person's life, whether that person is you or your child. As you know, the messages of humiliation and shame impact an individual for a very long time, especially when the humiliation and shame comes from an important person whose role is to nurture, love, and protect (e.g., parents, dating or life partners, extended family, teachers, peers, coaches, and so on). How we treat our children teaches and informs them on what behavior is acceptable (or unacceptable) in the relationships they form throughout their lives.

TIP #5: ASK FOR FORGIVENESS.

When you treat someone in a hurtful way, saying "I'm sorry" is only one part of the apology. I believe an apology needs a genuine tone, both in voice and body language. When you offer an apology, take into account how your actions have impacted the other person on an emotional level (i.e., show empathy), express concern and remorse by not making excuses, and take responsibility for your behavior. An apology isn't simply checking something off a list. A heartfelt apology has a component of remorse, shows an awareness of the consequence your action had on the other person, and makes an attempt to repair the relationship and be mindful to not repeat the harmful behavior. For example, an apology to a loved one could sound like this:

> *I'm truly sorry for the way I treated you. Not only was it not okay but I can also see how my words and actions hurt you. Relationships are built on trust and I imagine that as a consequence of what I did, it could be hard for you to feel safe and trust me. I'm going to use this incident as an opportunity to look at myself and understand what is going on inside of me to cause me to think it's acceptable to treat you or anyone else this way. That's not yours to worry about; I'll take care of that. Please accept my apology for how I hurt you. I'm truly sorry. Is there something you need from me right now or something you want to share?*

Here is an example of how to phrase an apology to a child:

You feel sad, and I am very sorry. The way I treated you was not okay. I'm going to make sure I don't do that again, and I'm going to learn from this. Words and actions are ways we show people how we love and care for them. My words and actions weren't kind at all, and you didn't do anything wrong. To treat you that way was not okay, it was wrong, and I love you very much. Is there something you want to talk about, or do you need something from me right now?

TIP #6: COMMIT TO MAKING CHANGE.

As an act of kindness to yourself, try not to dwell on your mistakes or actions from the past. Overfocusing on what happened could create more stress and leave you feeling stuck and overwhelmingly guilty and ashamed. Instead, take a moment to regroup and focus your efforts on what you can do going forward, which is to learn from your behaviors, create awareness as to what brought you to this place, and use healthy skills to manage your emotions.

And when you're so frustrated and overwhelmed with your child, feeling the urge to say or do something harmful, remember this: You always have the option to walk out of the room for a moment. If you feel the tension getting so powerful in your body that you know you're about to say or do something hurtful, take just *two seconds* and remember this: *You can never take back words, phrases, or actions—ever.* You can apologize, you can learn from your mistakes, but you can't undo the words and actions that enter your child's mind and heart. You can walk to the bathroom, close the door, take a minute to regroup, wash your hands or face, and take a few deep breaths. Then, if you still don't feel better, pick up your phone, call someone you love, and tell them you are hurt, frustrated, and angry, that you need them for a minute, just to talk with you or distract you or to listen to what happened between you and your child.

I promise you that the first time you try this skill, it will be hard. But if you are able to use those two seconds to stop your words or actions and step away to calm down, you will feel empowered to know that even when you feel incredibly angry or stressed, you don't have to share it in unhealthy ways with your child. You will see how you have the power to pause in the small space between your thoughts and actions, to step away and choose a different course.

Thriving Mama Reflection for Humiliation

Words are intention with energy, in spoken form through sound and physical form through letters on paper or a screen. Actions and behaviors are energy through movement. All of these—words, actions, behaviors—have the power to communicate positive, neutral, or negative messages to yourself or another person. Being on the receiving end of humiliation means you are the target of words and actions that someone else is using as a weapon against you to cut to the core of your self-worth. In moments when you've felt this way, know that it is not only wrong for another person to humiliate you, it is harmful to the core and essence of what makes you you. There are many ways to handle being humiliated, as we discussed earlier, but right now what I want you to do is close your eyes for a moment and, placing your hands over your heart, take a deep breath in and remind yourself that to be treated this way is wrong. As you do, visualize healing white light entering your heart from your hands and radiating through your body, then going back out into the world. Say a loving and compassionate statement to yourself such as: *Regardless of how someone treats me, I matter. I am worthy of love, respect, and kindness. In this moment, I can pour love and light into my heart, reminding myself that I matter and that I have gifts and beautiful things to share with the world.*

Thriving Mama Reflection for Shame

Shame blocks your growth, happiness, and ability to thrive. Shame is an emotional reaction in need of healing and transformation. One way to begin the healing process is through sharing stories and experiences through expressive writing, art, movement, acting, and ritual. There are two rituals that can help you let go of your shame. Both involve a way to concretely measure the amount of shame that's taken up residence in your heart, mind, and soul.

LETTING GO OF SHAME RITUAL

Create a quiet space where you can sit for up to fifteen minutes uninterrupted and bring with you a Mason jar, pen, and paper. Sit quietly, closing your eyes for a minute as you focus on your breath, inhaling while you count to three, holding your breath while you count to three, and exhaling while you count to three. As you do this for a few minutes, remind yourself that you are loved, that you are worthy, and that it's time to let go of your shame. It no longer serves you and is trampling on your right to experience happiness, contentment, and thriving. Open your eyes and begin writing all the shame beliefs and thoughts you have. You can write them out any way you'd like (e.g., in a numbered or bulleted list or a narrative). Write for the sake of expressing, not for grammar or correctness. When you've finished writing, fold the paper into the smallest form possible. Hold it in your hand and, looking at the small shape, remind yourself that this is shame in physical form. And this small piece of paper symbolically has the power of enough written words to hold back your joy and self-worth. This paper no longer serves you, nor does the shame. Place the paper in the Mason jar. Let go of the shame, and whenever shame pops back up, write it down and place it in the Mason jar. Close the lid and let this be a reminder that shame can't survive if it isn't living inside of you.

RELEASING AND TRANSFORMING SHAME RITUAL

Go for a walk. As you walk, collect sticks or kindling you see on the ground. Walk in silence, reflecting on your innate worth and value with all the strengths you have to offer. Pick up as much kindling as you have shame. As you walk, pick up a stick and say, "This is for the shame I hold for_____." State it, label it, then carry it. Bring all of this kindling to a firepit, campsite, or fireplace where it's safe to burn. As you prepare the fire, pick up each piece of kindling and place it in the fire, saying out loud again one shame belief or thought you have (or you may just place the kindling in the firepit or fireplace). Keep adding the kindling, as many pieces as you need to fill the firepit or fireplace. Then start the fire. And as you watch the kindling burn, let this be a symbol of releasing the shame that has lived in your mind, heart, and soul. As you watch the sticks burn, feel the warmth from the fire and look at how the matter is being transformed, just as you are. The shame you held on to is no longer needed in the form it came in, and by using it for growth and letting it go, the shame provides an opportunity for you to be changed for good, just as the fire provides warmth.

PART VI

using disgust and self-judgment as chance to heal

Being a mom is so gross—I had no idea how
much poop was involved.

I want to throw up some days with all the gross
things I have to do.

If I have to do that again, I'm seriously going to lose it.

I feel like an imposter. If only others knew how much I
despise and hate myself.

In motherhood are many opportunities to experience situations that are gross, disgusting, and downright repulsive. If you carried your child, the shadow emotion of disgust started long before your baby is placed in your arms. Most likely, it started in pregnancy with food aversions, nausea, and an incredibly heightened sensitivity to smells, all of which are nature's effort to protect mom and baby.

And birth, while beautiful and truly a miracle, is *not* a clean or neat process. Whether a baby is delivered vaginally or through Cesarean section, birth includes a lot of body fluids (as does post-delivery and post-partum). And if pregnancy and birth didn't have moments that exposed you to disgust, once you take care of your baby, you'll have plenty of opportunity to experience it! From meconium to spit-up, snotty noses, projectile vomit, and blowout diapers, having a child will give you plenty of chances to experience moments of disgust, repulsion, and just-plain-gross things, all in the name of love and motherhood.

In motherhood, regardless of your efforts to keep things

neat and orderly, you will be exposed to gross things. Mothering at times seems like a contact sport with your child's bodily fluids. You'll wipe tears and snotty noses with your sleeve or the bottom of your shirt if you can't find a tissue, and you'll gag when you find a collection of "boogies" smeared on the side of a car seat or on a pillow. You'll smell things to figure out what they are, including little bottoms, and wear clothes with the sour twinge of your child's spit-up. There will be smells whose sources you can't locate—in the car, in your purse, in the toy box, under the sofa, and in the bedrooms. You'll finally discover the origin, often moldy or decomposing food, sometimes unidentifiable, in car seats and under beds, in bags, lunch boxes, and backpacks that have been forgotten about over weekends and school breaks.

Cleaning under your child's bed or beneath their pillow, you'll find dirty laundry, papers, and "nature" collections (bugs, acorns, rocks, for example). Your child may harbor a fascination with burps and speaking while belching, sometimes attempting to get through the alphabet, and passing gas or replicating this sound in a variety of ways. And if you haven't already, you'll eventually deal with blood and infections, scabs and scrapes, and do so all in the name of comforting your child. And your child will pick up things that gross you out: bugs, dirt, trash on the ground, chewed gum stuck in random places, and decaying objects. It can all be so gross.

And as your child gets older, there will be smelly socks, shoes, clothes, and underarms so putrid, you'll be begging them to shower, use deodorant, and wash their greasy hair. Count yourself lucky if you've never had to deal with lice, pulling nits and lice out of your child's hair, and laundering and vacuuming everything you can. I bet your head started to itch as you read that one!

We'll explore the shadow emotion of disgust in those classic ways in the next chapter, but one thing many moms may not consider regarding disgust is an emotional response many mothers hide but often feel: self-loathing or self-hatred. Pregnancy, exhaustion, getting older, and lack of time for self-care often creates a lot of changes in a mother's appearance, body image, energy, and activity level. When these changes happen, mothers can feel gross and disgusted with them, a feeling that manifests as the shadow emotion of self-loathing in minor or more intense ways. For moms who struggle with disgusting situations, or with feelings of disgust toward themselves (which can become as severe as hatred of their bodies or their deeper selves), this section is going to help you understand these feelings and provide tools to help you manage them.

handling the disgusting moments of motherhood

keeping perspective and a sense of humor

Motherhood is always with you, usually in the form of
something gross on your clothing.
—Anonymous

The shadow emotion of disgust happens so much more often in motherhood than any of us would care for it to. I can guarantee that if you're reading this book, you've experienced disgust by now! Disgust is an emotional response hardwired in our brain with one goal in mind: *to help us survive*. This shadow emotion is an instinctive reaction repelling us from risk or danger, keeping us safe from exposure to something or someone that is a real or perceived threat to our health, well-being, and survival. But when we're a mother and our child is the trigger for this shadow emotion, even if it's potentially risky or harmful, we push past it to respond to what our child needs. Many of us mothers are very sensitive to feeling disgust, but our instinct to protect and care for our child will override even our survival instinct, placing our child's well-being and safety first.

Disgust is experienced through the five senses: what we

see, hear, touch, taste, and smell. Disgust is often triggered by *contamination* (such as colds, the flu, infections, stomach bugs, or lice), *body fluids* (expelled when our children vomit, sneeze, have a runny nose, or blow out their diapers), or *decay* (such as spoiled or rotting food under cushions or in car seats, lunch boxes, and backpacks).

Disgust is an emotional response closely related to contempt, anger, and fear. For example, let's imagine you're at the park with your child, and they see a blob of chewed gum under the bench. They pull it off, place it in their mouth, and begin to chew. You see this and respond with disgust, "Oh, how gross!" You probably follow up this response by saying, "Get that out of your mouth" or sticking your finger in their mouth and pulling the gum out. Not only are you reacting to disgust (chewing gum that has been stuck under a bench), you're likely feeling some fear (*Could my child get sick from this?*), and anger (*How thoughtless to leave gum on a bench!*).

If you were telling the story to one of your friends, chances are she'd understand right away what you were feeling—the shadow emotion of disgust. But suppose you were to ask your child later in the day, "What was Mommy feeling when you put the gum in your mouth at the park?" Chances are, if your child was under the age of eight, they'd say you were angry. And from a child's point of view, this is quite accurate. The reason is that, developmentally, children eight years old and younger do not understand the emotional reaction of disgust in others, unless it's quite obvious. Instead they interpret disgust as anger, which is important to know as a mother—when disgusting moments happen, responding in a way that clearly shows you're disgusted is less scary to your child than showing anger. For instance, if your child has ever eaten a cookie that was on the floor or that had a bug on it, that is totally normal and developmentally understandable for certain ages. Children (especially children ages one to three) put a lot of things in their mouths and pick up almost anything. When a child under the age of four picks up an item or places something in their mouth, parental or caregiver responses such as facial expressions of disgust paired with phrases like *Ewww*, *Gross*, *No touching*, and *Yuck* will cue them as to what is disgusting and adverse.

Disgust Through Your Child's Eyes

- Up to two and a half years of age, children are attracted to many things that adults find disgusting.

- Children who are between three and a half and five years old demonstrate adultlike responses to disgusting objects.

- Children who are five to six years old actively reject disgusting objects offered to them.

- Children up to eight years old scrunch their noses when they experience disgust, but when they are looking at another person they can only infer disgust if it's obvious in the context; otherwise, children interpret disgust as a sign of anger.

- Children around the age of nine and continuing through the teen years gradually learn to identify what disgust looks like in another person.

Further along on the continuum and more intense than disgust is the shadow emotion of repulsion. If you've never felt repulsed in motherhood, count yourself very lucky! The most memorable time I felt repulsed was when one of my daughters had lice. (If you've never experienced lice, my wish for you is that you never do—my head is beginning to itch just thinking about it!) I thought I was one of the lucky ones, having avoided lice for fourteen years of motherhood. The night before my birthday, after all the girls were in bed, I settled into a lavender Epsom salt bath, only to have my soak be cut radically short when I heard a horrific scream then a muffled "Mom!" that cut through the sounds of sobbing. I opened my bathroom door to find one of my daughters on the other side, dry heaving and hysterically crying, "I have lice!"

In denial and disbelief, I calmly responded, "Are you sure?"

"Yes, get them out! I saw one crawling!"

Checking her head, I saw that it was clear: She had lice, all right. I checked the other girls and two of the four had lice. My husband went to the all-night pharmacy and picked up four treatments. While I waited for him to get home, I tried to calm my girls, who were beyond disgusted—they were repulsed by having bugs not only living in their hair but laying little eggs and hatching nymphs. My daughters were experiencing pure, repulsed horror. I kept using phrases like, "Really, it's okay—this happens to families all of the time," and, "We need to count ourselves lucky we've gone fourteen years and avoided lice." When those didn't work, I tried, "We'll do the treatment, wash the linens, and the lice will be gone—take a deep breath."

I'm sure you've seen via posts on social media and texts that spread like wildfire that when a child has lice, there's a mix of anger, disgust, support, embarrassment, and humor among mothers, who are checking their children, wondering when or if they'll get lice, and feeling repulsed by the thought.

These shadow emotions, disgust and repulsion, are part of motherhood. We can't avoid experiencing these situations—raising children is messy, gross, and wildly unpredictable. The only thing to do at times is use some good coping skills and strategies, find the humor in those disgusting moments, and remember that, eventually, children grow up and out of these disgusting phases.

At the Heart of Disgust and Repulsion

At the heart of disgust and repulsion is a need for you and your child to feel safe, secure, healthy, and comfortable. Experiencing any intensity of disgust creates a natural response to recoil. However, when you're a mother caring for your child, love, compassion, and the drive to help or protect your child will push you to do whatever your child needs you to do, no matter how gross. At the heart of disgust in motherhood is a powerful current of empathy, connection, love, and the desire to help your child move back into a place of safety and security, which in turn becomes security for you.

Reframe Your Mantra

Thoughts are powerful. Your self-talk (the things you say to yourself) has a deep impact on what you feel and how you respond. Keep this principle in mind and reframe problematic thoughts that increase your shadow emotions.

SHADOW MANTRA If you're saying this . . .	THRIVING MANTRA Positively reframe to say this . . .
I never thought being a mom would be this disgusting!	Being a mother has a lot of disgusting moments. I won't always feel this way; this is just for right now. Things will get back to normal soon. To take care of myself, I can do something soothing and relaxing.
This is so disgusting. Yuck, I can't believe I have to do this.	It's hard to find the energy to take care of this right now. I may need some help on this, and I may need to ask for support. Anything I think about when I'm feeling disgusted or experiencing something gross is going to increase negative thinking. Using humor right now could help me get through this.
Ugh, I'm so repulsed; I feel like I am going to be sick.	I'm on sensory overload, and this is intense! I may get sick or I may not. Perhaps taking a minute to ground myself, focus on my breathing, and imagine something lovely would help. Smelling something like peppermint or citrus could help me feel better in this moment.

Moving Beyond the Shadows

TIP #1: ALLOW YOURSELF TO FEEL THE REACTION.

Experiencing strong emotional reactions can be uncomfortable. When you feel disgust and repulsion, give yourself some space between experiencing the shadow emotions and making a decision about what to do or how to respond. (Of course, if there's a need to do something right away and it can't wait, then this advice doesn't apply.) Giving yourself space between the situation and what you are experiencing can be as simple as asking for a minute or two and focusing on regulating your breathing. When you become stressed, your breathing pattern changes, your heart rate goes up, and your body releases adrenaline so you can protect yourself and respond. You may not be able to override all of these sensations, but you can ground yourself by taking a few minutes and regulating your breathing. Focusing on your breathing will regulate your nervous system, helping it relax and come down a few notches, and taking this space of time will allow you to regroup and problem-solve.

TIP #2: ASK QUESTIONS TO CREATE SELF-AWARENESS.

When you find yourself feeling a lot of disgust (or feeling intensely repulsed) from a situation or experience, ask yourself the following questions:

- What disgusts me and grosses me out?
- How do I express disgust through my behaviors?
- How do I show disgust through my facial expressions?
- Do I experience fear when I feel disgust? If I always or sometimes do, how does this fear manifest itself?
- Do I experience anger when I feel disgust? If I always or sometimes do, how does this anger manifest itself?
- How do I take care of myself when I feel disgust?

TIP #3: PROBLEM-SOLVE AND SET GOALS.

There are some moments in motherhood so gross and disgusting they can't be anticipated or prepared for—you just have to go through them and get to the other side! After going through these moments, ask yourself, *What, if anything, did I learn from this situation?* Reflect on the following questions:

- Is there something I could have done differently knowing what I know now? If so, what could I do differently?

- How can I teach my child and prepare them if this situation were to happen again?

- Do I need to set up a system that is more organized? For example, no eating in the car or bedrooms? Do I need to establish the routine of emptying lunch boxes and backpacks right after school? Do I need to check my child's hair for lice, put her hair in a braid, or use a preventive product in her hair?

- What have I learned about my child (or another person) from this situation? What have I learned about myself?

- How does my child's age and development influence and impact what happened?

TIP #4: REMEMBER THAT PERSPECTIVE AND HUMOR GO A LONG WAY.

Keep perspective that you may feel alone in these shadow moments, but find comfort that all moms have gone through similar situations. Thankfully, motherhood is defined by so much more than these moments—if motherhood was all about these shadow emotions all the time, no one would have children!

Motherhood is going to be disgusting. But thankfully, it's not disgusting all the time. And when you're in the midst of stripping beds and laundering towels and linens, think of mothers from previous generations. They had to deal with gross and disgusting things without the conveniences that make life easier in modern parenting. I can't even imagine what moms did a hundred years ago when their babies had projectile spit-up or their child got sick and vomited. How did those moms do the laundry without modern washers and dryers? Cleaning up the messes may have taken days!

And remember, connecting with other moms is a great way to decompress, get support, and find humor in these moments. Reach out to a supportive mom and share what you just went through. I'm sure she'll not only give you perspective and support but also share with you moments of disgust she's experienced. If you can find the humor in disgusting moments, embrace it—humor is a great coping skill and stress reliever. Those gross and disgusting moments in parenting may just become funny family stories to share!

TIP #5: REPEAT A CALMING AND SOOTHING MANTRA.
In a moment like this, it's important to not only focus on your breathing to help reduce your stress but also to repeat a calming and soothing mantra. Some examples that may be helpful include the following (and be sure to create a few meaningful ones of your own):

- Yes, it's gross, but I've got this. I'm a strong mom. I can do this!
- Other moms have handled this, and I can handle it too.
- I've gotten through challenging times and can do so again.
- This is gross and is disgusting, but it will pass, hopefully quickly.

Thriving Mama Reflection
Feeling disgust is often related to one or more of the five senses. And disgust can also include feeling variations of fear and anger. One way to ground yourself after a gross interaction or experience is to take care of yourself through one of your senses. Doing so creates a pleasant environment and helps bring you back to a comfortable state, creating some distance between you and the

offensive moment. This can be *listening* to something positive or inspiring, like an upbeat song. It may include *smelling* something that calms you (like lavender, vanilla, or cinnamon) or clears your nose (like peppermint). And it can also be taking a minute through *touch* by massaging a soothing cream or lotion into your hands or washing your face. You may also need to *look* at photos that bring a sense of calm and peace to your heart or close your eyes and imagine different soothing places that bring you peace. Try to imagine the different sensory experiences that would be in those places. For example, imagine yourself sitting on the beach listening to the waves and smelling the salt in the air, feeling the sand on your feet and the warm sun on your face. Or imagine that you're walking through a lovely garden filled with blueberry bushes. As you walk barefoot, feel the grass beneath your feet. Stop to pick a blueberry, perfectly sweet and slightly tart. And if you're more in the mood to *taste* something, take a piece of chocolate, a piece of gum, or a mint and savor it slowly and with intention, breathing into a relaxed state.

chapter 19

the feelings moms have but don't say out loud

how transforming self-hatred to self-love is the key to joy

Butterflies can't see their wings. They can't see how truly beautiful they are, but everyone else can.
People are like that as well.
–Anonymous

I love the quote that opens this chapter. But I would go a step further to say that mothers especially are like butterflies—they are so beautiful, strong, and amazing, but they often can't see it themselves. One of the greatest joys and rewards in my life is helping moms see what they so often can't: how much they matter.

As a psychologist, when I sit with a mom and she begins sharing her feelings of self-loathing, I always hold my breath. I'm bracing. Bracing for the honest thoughts and feelings she's about to share and knowing that I'm the first person to hear these words aloud. She's kept these shadow emotions, so complex and layered, in her mind and in her heart. I know there will be tears—lots of them. I also know she's going to leave the session feeling lighter, supported, and hopeful. But I'm certain that for the next forty-five minutes, I'm going to see her suffering pour out. So I hold my breath and sink into my chair, bearing witness to her pain.

I want to take her hurt away, but I know this is not the path of healing. She has to move through this suffering. No one can do it for her; she's been carrying her pain, and now she's ready to unpack it.

My role is to help her sort through her pain and suffering, looking at it from all angles, especially how this shadow emotion of self-hatred and self-loathing shows up in motherhood. And as we sift through the suffering—situations, experiences, and messages layered in her heart and mind—through humiliation and shame, I remind her of what she can't see: those beautiful colorful wings, delicate and vulnerable, yet brave and powerful enough to soar to incredible places. Then I ask her to see herself through her child's eyes: eyes of love, comfort, and acceptance. She is the entire world to her child, and she matters more than she could ever know or imagine.

The shadow emotion of self-hatred and self-loathing can be one of the most tender of all the shadow emotions. In this chapter, I want you to reflect on your suffering, what you've been carrying and what you're ready to unpack. I want you to know that you are just like the mom in my counseling room. You matter so much.

Feeling disgust in motherhood is not limited to experiences with our children. Self-loathing is a shadow emotion with a combination of feelings, most often anger, sadness, guilt, regret, shame, and unresolved trauma and pain. The shadow emotion of self-loathing and self-hatred is one of the most delicate to read, write, and talk about. But make no mistake, this shadow emotion is being experienced by many mothers—you are not alone. In the therapy hour, so many mothers share with me how they feel mild forms of disgust toward themselves, to moderate feelings of self-hatred, to intense feelings of self-loathing. The reasons are varied but tend to be in reaction to changes in body shape, size, and appearance; personal habits and behaviors; and unresolved childhood stress and trauma that have become amplified in motherhood.

In milder forms, the shadow emotion of self-hatred and self-loathing shows up when we feel ugly or unattractive or when we overfocus and highlight our flaws and insecurities. Being human means that at some point we'll have moments of self-criticism or judgment, moments when we do not feel good about ourselves. But when there is a persistent pattern of self-loathing, when we feel bad about ourselves more than good, we are in an unhealthy place.

Nothing changes a mother's body more dramatically than pregnancy. It's miraculous how a mother's body rapidly transforms to carry life, intuitively knowing what to do to grow a baby over the span of nine months. The changes continue postpartum and long after, especially when a mother nurses her baby. From stretch marks on her breasts, abdomen, and legs to the changing size and shape of her breasts (not to mention the scars and incisions from birth), a mother's body is like a map revealing on the outside that she's been forever changed. And if a mother's body didn't change due to pregnancy and birth, then it's only a matter of time before, in the course of caring for her child, she loses sleep and becomes so exhausted she hardly recognizes her reflection in the mirror.

A mother may get more regular sleep as her child gets older. But self-care is too often far down on her priority list, because

You Are Not Alone: Brigitte's Story

Brigitte was preoccupied most days with constant negative self-talk, hating so many parts of herself—her face, body, and almost everything about her appearance. No one knew this inner turmoil; she hid it from her husband, her children, even her closest friends. Brigitte spent a lot of time in the morning putting herself together in order to look perfect, which was a ritual she developed in college—flawless hair, expertly applied makeup, coordinated outfit—in order to suppress what she believed, and had been told: that she was ugly and worthless.

Brigitte grew up with parents who had untreated mental health issues, who verbally abused and berated her throughout her childhood and into her young adulthood. Bright, motivated, and focused, she knew there had to be another way. She worked to put herself through college, securing her independence. Brigitte came to see me after a cosmetic surgeon recommended counseling; Brigitte was planning to have significant plastic surgery to fix all of her perceived flaws. Our work focused on addressing the pain and suffering she had suppressed since childhood. We focused on highlighting her strengths, reframing negative and abusive self-talk, and postponing any cosmetic treatments for a period of time, so she could heal her suffering and make a clear decision without seeing her body through the lens of pain. As her treatment progressed, Brigitte wanted to let go of the need to look perfect every day. We worked to increase her self-acceptance and self-compassion, and she was able to achieve all of these goals. Ultimately, she decided not to pursue the radical surgical procedures.

there's always so much to do—exercising, showering, styling her hair, and even changing her clothes seem impossible. So to cope with her stress and exhaustion, she creates habits to comfort her, like scrolling on her phone, staying up too late mindlessly watching TV shows, or using the quiet time at night to indulge in snacks, treats, and sweets. She's filling a void, ignoring what's really going on: She's missing the part of herself that has been crowded out by motherhood.

In the morning, before her feet hit the ground, she begins to use critical self-talk: *Why did I eat that? Why did I stay up too late? I should be exercising more.* As she makes her way to the bathroom, she looks in the mirror and is disgusted by what she sees—a puffy face, tired eyes, and a body she doesn't recognize. As she gets dressed, the tension rises as nothing she wears makes her feel good. She's starting to loathe her body, wishing she looked and felt different.

These shadow emotions of personal disgust, self-hatred, and self-loathing share the common theme of constantly finding fault with what you do and how you look, tearing you down in any and every area of your life—seldom is anything off-limits. In milder forms, this shadow emotion manifests as negative self-talk, but left unmanaged, it can escalate to inner criticism, a dialogue sounding more like a bully than you: *You're not good enough. Why bother? You look disgusting, you're so fat. You can't do anything right.*

Self-loathing can also be focused on the future, with foreboding warnings of doom. Self-loathing comes in the form of critical self-talk that taunts the most tender and cherished parts of a mother's life: her children. You may use internal statements like, *You may not see it now, but you're messing these kids up. No one would like you if they really knew who you are.* And you may make harsh, cruel comparisons like, *I'm not like other moms. I bet my child wishes I were different.*

Self-loathing is emotional pain that is stuck, and is often based on your past and showing up in the present. This may sound strange, but think about it this way: Self-loathing often develops from unresolved past pain that is asking to be taken care of in the present moment, showing up in full force with the incredible changes and vulnerability brought on in motherhood. Some possible reasons behind self-loathing are unresolved childhood trauma, such as emotional neglect and physical, verbal, and emotional abuse. Self-loathing can also be rooted in childhood or family interactions with parents who were regularly overwhelmed, unavailable, or had unhealthy or poor coping skills or who relied on critical parenting styles and interactions. Certain personality traits can create a vulnerability to self-loathing; those with perfectionistic standards and individuals who are emotionally sensitive, taking blame for situations and things that have nothing to do with them, may be at greater risk of experiencing this shadow emotion.

Unresolved pain and suffering often comes out in unexpected ways. A common theme I've observed is when a mom comes to therapy to manage stress or cope with a parenting or relationship issue, only to realize she first needs to heal part of her past suffering, which she may have never addressed but is now showing up through her mothering. Self-loathing, and any variation of this shadow emotion, is important to identify and manage, because a deeper part of you is asking for support to heal.

At the Heart of Self-Hatred and Self-Loathing

At the heart of self-hatred and self-loathing is the desperate desire for self-acceptance, love, compassion, and understanding, elements that often have not been given to a mom by an important person in her life (e.g., her parents, siblings, or sweetie) and that she perceives as impossible to give to herself. Beneath the surface of this shadow emotion is pain and suffering surrounding a situation, event, or criticism that wasn't challenged or taken care of, something that is accepted as true in a mom's heart. When this shadow emotion is present, the path of healing begins with developing awareness, then managing pain and replacing critical self-talk with self-compassion, which is a gift a mother not only gives to herself but also to her children and the generations that come after.

Reframe Your Mantra

Thoughts are powerful. Your self-talk (the things you say to yourself) has a deep impact on what you feel and how you respond. Keep this principle in mind and reframe problematic thoughts that increase your shadow emotions.

SHADOW MANTRA If you're saying this . . .	THRIVING MANTRA Positively reframe to say this . . .
I wish I were like other moms. I don't have it together like they do.	Comparing myself to others is not healthy. I have strengths and right now, I'm not feeling great. Some days I have it together, other days I don't. If I could do one thing to improve how I feel about myself as a mom, instead of focusing on what's not going well, what would I do? And if a friend came to me and said she felt like this, how would I respond?

SHADOW MANTRA If you're saying this . . .	THRIVING MANTRA Positively reframe to say this . . .
I can't stand the way I look after having had a baby.	My body has changed in ways I'm not comfortable with. Instead of focusing on what my body looked like before, how can I embrace and accept my body as it is right now? I can try to see the beauty of, and take pride in, the amazing thing my body has achieved through pregnancy and birth. What are the things I can do to take care of my body, so that I can be the healthiest version of myself emotionally and physically?
No one knows what an impostor I am; if they only knew what I experienced growing up.	I'm having a tough moment, and I feel insecure. I'm not an impostor. I have strengths and great qualities, but right now my negative thinking is blocking me from seeing my strengths and abilities. I had some challenging experiences that impacted me, but they don't have to define me. I'm strong and loving, and my child loves and needs me.
My kids don't deserve to have a mother who is this broken. I'm so afraid I'm messing them up.	I'm not broken, I'm having a tough moment. Hating myself is not going to make me feel better, but it's a coping skill I learned a while ago that I need to change. I'm not messing up my children—I'm doing the best I can, and while this is a fear right now, where is the evidence this is true? Reaching out for support is what I need to do. I don't have to go through this moment alone.

(continued)

SHADOW MANTRA If you're saying this . . .	THRIVING MANTRA Positively reframe to say this . . .
I think I'm repulsive and disgusting.	Is this kind? Is this true? Is this a loving statement to myself? In this moment, what do I need to feel better, to take care of myself, and to give myself compassion instead of judgment? How would I respond if my child said this exact thing about themselves? I need to do the same for myself.
I am not a good mother.	Right now I don't think I'm a good mother, but I am; I love my child and am doing my best. The way I'm feeling is coloring my thoughts and what I focus on. I am the best mother I can be right now, and I have to remember that motherhood is not one moment but a series of moments. The judgment that I'm not a good mother is untrue. If a dear friend were going through exactly what I am right now, what advice would I give her?

Moving Beyond the Shadows

TIP #1: ASK QUESTIONS TO CREATE SELF-AWARENESS.

Identifying any intensity of self-loathing is an important part of thriving in motherhood. No matter how pained or vulnerable you feel, I want to remind you how incredibly brave and strong you are. You can get through this and you will—with time, dedication to yourself, and the support of a therapist. But first, I want you to ask yourself the following questions:

- What event or situation in motherhood has triggered my feeling disgust, self-hatred, or self-loathing?

- Was there an event or situation in my childhood that impacted the way I feel about myself now? What was it?

- What positive messages did I learn about myself as I was growing up? What positive messages were told to me and by whom?

- What negative messages did I learn about myself as I was growing up? What negative messages were told to me and by whom?

- Is there unresolved trauma or a traumatic event that impacts the way I feel about myself in motherhood?

- Do I compare myself to others and have high, unrealistic, and perfectionistic expectations of myself? Am I afraid to make mistakes? If so, when did this start?

- And am I overly concerned or preoccupied with how people think I should be or act?

- Do I feel as though I'm living an authentic life, one that I chose and am happy to be in? If not, how would I like to live? What does my authentic self need to be happy, to be content, and to live with purpose and meaning?

TIP #2: BE INSPIRED BY OTHERS, BUT DON'T COMPARE.

Self-loathing is a shadow emotion fueled by intense negative and critical thoughts that focus on deficits, flaws, and hurtful personal insults through comparisons with others. Comparison is the enemy and thief of joy, happiness, contentment, and thriving. Don't compare yourself to others; it will only bring you down and feed the beliefs in the cycle of shame and self-loathing that you are not good enough, that you are less-than, and that you are undeserving. When you catch yourself comparing yourself to others, remember to stop and challenge yourself by keeping in mind that what you see in another person is only a small portion of their reality—it's what you *perceive* but is not 100 percent accurate. Instead, I want you to look at others through the lens of inspiration: What do they do (or what do you see) that inspires you? What qualities do they have that you'd like to cultivate in your life? When you think from a place of inspiration instead of comparison, you may find yourself encouraged to create a more authentic and meaningful life.

TIP #3: PRACTICE SELF-COMPASSION.

Self-compassion is a practice of self-love and understanding that every mom deserves to feel, including you. Self-compassion starts with an awareness that you deserve to feel happy, loved, and secure. Next, self-compassion is giving yourself the same kindness and understanding that you give to others. Finally, self-compassion is about being aware of your suffering, pain, and insecurities and being intentional not to judge, criticize, or harm yourself with the words or actions you direct at yourself. Self-loathing, on the other hand, is a shadow emotion fueled by negative thinking and self-talk; harsh, critical, judgmental statements of yourself; and highlighting the mistakes you make or the challenges you face as character flaws, all of which contributes to diminished self-worth. As simple as it sounds, you can start this moment by making a commitment to talk kindly to yourself, as you would a friend and your child.

Learning the skills of self-compassion will help you heal patterns of self-loathing and foster more health and well-being in all areas of your life.

TIP #4: NOTICE PATTERNS OF SELF-LOATHING.

The shadow emotion of self-loathing is often triggered by certain situations, people, or events. In order to heal and move forward, it's essential to understand when, where, and why these feelings occur. Do you have more self-loathing thoughts when you spend time with certain people? Do you notice that spending time on social media increases your feelings of self-loathing? If so, how? Do you have more self-loathing thoughts when stressful situations arise? Is there a behavior or habit that you're doing (or not doing) that could be encouraging this shadow emotion? Pay attention to the patterns you notice, and then take steps to reduce, limit, or put a pause on these behaviors, habits, situations, or relationships.

TIP #5: REPEAT A CALMING AND SOOTHING MANTRA.

In a moment of self-loathing, practice this very simple and quick exercise: Close your eyes and focus on your breathing for a few moments to help reduce your stress, then repeat a calming and soothing mantra. Some examples that may be helpful include the following (be sure to create a few meaningful ones of your own as well):

- I am worthy of love and happiness.
- I am enough.
- I have beautiful and unique strengths.
- My body has changed and will continue to change, and I am more than my body.
- Becoming a mother has changed me on the outside; and on the inside, my heart has grown in the loveliest ways.

TIP #6: GET SUPPORT AND START COUNSELING.

An important act of self-care is knowing when the right time is to begin or resume counseling. When self-loathing shows up often and regularly, negatively impacting your life and taking away from your personal well-being and happiness, then it would be beneficial to pursue counseling and support in order to learn skills to transform your self-loathing into self-compassion. Self-loathing is often ingrained and intertwined with your personal history, beliefs, and experiences in such a way that working through it on your own to heal is possible, but a trained mental health professional will get you there sooner and in ways that are more helpful than you could ever imagine.

Thriving Mama Reflection

When we look at our child for the first time, what we see is a baby or child who is vulnerable, helpless, and in need of our care. But what we can't see is the wisdom in a child's heart and mind, a love pure and free from judgment and faultfinding. When we meet our child, we meet a little radiant being, shining with unadulterated joy, love, curiosity, and awe. Only as our child gets older, and the demands to care for them become higher, do we begin to lose the essence of that first encounter of incredible awe, unconditional love, and immense gratitude for our child.

We are no different than our child. We came into the world, a bundle of pure, unconditional love for ourselves, others, and the world. But along the way, for whatever reason or because of whatever situation, we began to receive messages, learning about who we are through what significant people in our life thought or believed about us. Perhaps these messages were loving, supportive, and encouraging; but most often, when the shadow emotion of self-loathing is present, we received critical messages saying we were less-than, not good enough, or full of flaws and deficits.

Over time, these messages get layered on top of one another, dimming the radiant truth we once knew with certainty. But the reality is that the harmful messages and beliefs that create these shadow emotions are never accurate. The heart of a child is so open, vulnerable, and trusting, and it has no mechanism of defense to challenge these messages and beliefs. Instead, a child takes these messages in whole, embracing every word as an accurate belief of the self. It is only when the child grows that they have the potential to understand that these messages are inaccurate, that they are holding back the individual's potential for growth, health, and happiness. But some never even consider that these messages are inaccurate and can be let go of.

Healing the deep pain of self-loathing is a tender journey of unpacking pain and suffering, as well as discarding beliefs and messages you've received that have weighed you down. As you begin the healing, know that the messages you received are not accurate—they were a reflection of what was going on in the inner world of those who gave you their pain to carry.

For a moment, close your eyes and imagine yourself as a baby with an open heart—wise, all-knowing, ready to share your joy, awe, and curiosity with the world. Breathe into the truth that your heart and mind are still the same as when you were a baby years ago. The experiences and messages you've received have dimmed the awareness you once knew, but you still have the pure, radiant, loving light you came into the world with. Your job now is to let go of the suffering you've been carrying, others' as well as your own, so that the unconditional love in your heart can shine brightly, as it was always meant to do.

PART VII

conclusion

revealing your true motherly state of joy, calm, and confidence

At the time of writing this conclusion, my oldest (twin girls) are seventeen and have a little more than a year before they finish high school and move on to the next phase of their independence, which means I will move on to a whole new phase of mothering. In another seven years, my third daughter will be on the threshold of independence, and two years after that, my youngest will be preparing for the same. Lately, my mind has been focused on the here and now, enjoying the time we have with all six of us together in one space—as it's been for a long time—before our family goes through a monumental shift and enters uncharted territory. I think that is the one part of motherhood I'm most humbled by: how it's always changing, in small and large ways. Just as we get used to a developmental phase and stage, it seems as if there is a new one beginning to emerge, forcing us moms out of our comfort zone, ushering in new experiences for everyone as children develop and mature to independence.

I think what has been preparing me, and all moms, for this natural progression of separation and independence on the horizon are all the small steps along the journey of motherhood, nurturing and caring for my children as they grow up and away. At the core, what has helped me adapt to these never-ending changes is caring for myself—my emotional health and well-being—and embracing the shadow emotions as they show up in my life.

Motherhood is a constant and ever-evolving journey. Just as your child is growing, so are you as a mother. I am not the same mother I was when I first became a mom almost two decades ago. Nor am I the same mom I was when I began writing this book. Perhaps that is the beauty of motherhood—the constant undercurrent of change, the plethora of opportunities for growth, connection, and healing.

One active way to embrace motherhood is to accept and acknowledge all of your experiences, even the ones that catch you off guard. If you are to thrive as a mother, you need to allow yourself to feel the shadow emotions of sadness, fear, anger, disgust, embarrassment, and all the variations between. As you've read, suppressing, ignoring, or denying these shadow emotions only creates an environment where the shadow emotions get louder and more pronounced, asking for you to take care of yourself, until you're forced to address what you are experiencing emotionally.

There's no denying that motherhood is an emotional journey. As you've seen through this book, sometimes your shadow emotions are showing you what needs to be healed from your personal past that is now being played out with your child on the stage of motherhood. Embracing the parts of ourselves we are trying to hide, allowing them to be seen and acknowledged and given a chance to be healed, is the path to joy. Thriving in motherhood is a matter of learning to acknowledge and meet these shadow emotions with openness and compassion instead of judgment. It's not what we feel emotionally—it's being mindful of how we choose to respond when we have feelings that matters most.

I don't know where you were when you first picked up this book. But my hope is, now that you've read it, you have a deeper sense of how to be more loving, compassionate, and understanding toward yourself not only as a mother but also as a person.

Now that you've completed the book, know that the work continues for you, work to keep practicing the skills of managing your shadow emotions and shadow moments and to actively create more positive mood states and experiences so that you can thrive in motherhood. And this journey begins by:

- monitoring your thoughts and reframing your negative self-talk;
- practicing physical, emotional, mental, social, personal, and spiritual self-care;
- doing activities that bring you joy;
- finding and highlighting the meaning and purpose in your life;
- maintaining and creating connection through relationships;
- expressing gratitude and highlighting your personal strengths; and
- being compassionate with yourself in motherhood.

And if at any time you need a reminder or some encouragement to know how much you matter, or to know that you are not alone on this journey in motherhood, remember that this book is always available to you. Let it remind you that in your most challenging shadow moments of motherhood, there is always hope to cultivate joy, calm, and connection in your life.

Final Thriving Mama Reflection: You Are Already More Than Enough

You matter more than you will ever know, and you are already more than enough—even during your most challenging moments and days in motherhood. To know how much you matter, you'd have to see yourself through the unconditionally loving eyes of your child and the heartfelt presence they feel when you enter a room. When they are tired, sick, or going through a tough time, you and your presence of love and energy is what they know and what brings them comfort—whether you speak words or not, it is felt and sensed through the unbreakable bond between the two of you. Regardless of what you may be going through in this moment or stretch of time, nothing can take away how much you matter.

Whether your child was born in your heart or from your body, no one can take your place or sever the bond that is unique to you and your child; it is sacred, it is unbreakable, and it is the foundation from which all of your child's future relationships will grow. And for you as a mother, no matter what age or stage your child is in, you will be forever their mother, all the days you walk on this earth. Embrace the beauty and uniqueness of this role with your child (or each of your children) and take in how incredible this bond is.

Motherhood is not only embracing your child but also embracing all parts of you, including the shadow emotions as they arise. In doing so, you make a declaration of self-acceptance and self-compassion, knowing that you are already more than enough, more than a shadow moment or a shadow emotion. You are defined by something greater than anything else: you are a mother. Remember this when you question whether you are enough, or you fear you're failing your family, or you worry that you may not be doing the right thing. When you come from a place of love and acceptance and the desire to help and nurture, there is no wrong. Know that you matter so very much.

Breathe into how sacred you are, how the agreement you made to care for and love your child is immeasurable and goes far beyond any shadow emotion or shadow moment. Yours is a sacred bond that is forever and more vast than what may be happening in the present.

Holding one hand to your heart and one on your stomach, breathe in the power of this sacred bond and role you have embraced as a mother. As you inhale, imagine the truth of this knowing as a white light fills your heart, expanding your lungs, opening and radiating throughout your body. Hold this light for a moment in your breath and body, and then slowly exhale the beauty and love of all that is within you. In shadow moments, you need to be reminded that the shadow emotions cannot dim your knowing of this truth, that you are love. As you exhale, visualize gold and white light radiating from you, manifested love that you send into the world, a love beginning with accepting yourself and radiating to your child, a love that fills your home and that you share with all you meet. This is what is true, and you matter more than you can ever know.

Get in Touch

I want to thank you for bringing this book into your life, for taking in the messages and skills we've discussed. It is my hope that the words on these pages have touched you, impacted you, and healed parts of you that perhaps you didn't even know needed attention. I'd love for you to reach out and share how this book has affected you and what your takeaways are. *You* are the reason I wrote this book. I wanted to reach moms I may never have the chance to meet, so that I could share this message of compassion, acceptance, and appreciation I have for you as a mother.

There are many ways to connect, and I'd love to hear from you. You can sign up for newsletters and announcements at MomsWellBeing.com. And you can join our community of thriving mamas on social media for more skills, pieces of wisdom, and perspective to support you on your motherhood journey @MomsWellBeing on Instagram and Facebook and the Thriving Mama Community Group on Facebook. Please share with me your thoughts, your experiences, and how this book has inspired and impacted you. I want to hear from *you*!

With love and light,
Dr. Claire

endnotes

1   "Raising Kids and Running a Household: How Working Parents Share
the Load," Pew Research Center, November 4, 2015, https://www.
pewsocialtrends.org/2015/11/04/raising-kids-and-running-a-household-
how-working-parents-share-the-load/.

2   "Raising Kids," Pew Research Center.

3   Check out HealthyChildren.org, a website from the American Academy
of Pediatrics, an online resource that will help answer all of your safety
concerns with facts, expertise, and research.

4   Tom Bunn, *Soar: The Breakthrough Treatment for Fear of Flying* (Guilford,
CT: Lyons Press, 2013), https://www.fearofflying.com.

5   Brent Robbins and Holly Parlavecchio, "The Unwanted Exposure of
the Self: A Phenomenological Study of Embarrassment," *Humanistic
Psychologist* 34, no. 4 (2006): 321–345.

6   Jeffery Hall, "Is It Something I Said? Sense of Humor and Partner
Embarrassment," *Journal of Social and Personal Relationships* 28, no. 3
(2010): 383–405.

7   L. Jiang, A. Drolet, and C. A. Scott, "Countering Embarrassment-Avoidance
by Taking an Observer's Perspective," *Motivation and Emotion* 42, no. 5
(2018): 748–762.

acknowledgments

I have incredible gratitude and appreciation for the supportive, encouraging, and loving people in my life, as well as those I've met along the way, who believed in me and assisted me in bringing this book to you. I am forever grateful.

To my Regina Brooks of Serendipity Literary Agency, I so appreciate everything about you! I'm so fortunate to have crossed paths with you years ago and am grateful for your support, encouragement, and faith in me. You believed in my work and message and helped me navigate this journey. And oh, what a journey it has been!

To Sarah Monroe, my editor at Page Street, working with you has been an incredible joy and gift. Your expertise to refine my manuscript is incredible. You are truly amazing.

To Nichole Kraft, my copyeditor, thank you for your thoughtful review and knowledge of the craft to further polish this manuscript.

To the team at Page Street Publishing, collaborating and working with you as a first-time author has been an amazing experience. Thank you.

To the entire team at Alter Endeavors, Teylor Schiefelbein, Megan McGrath, Nick Alter, and Aubrey Berkowitz, who handle so many details in the background with skill and ease, thank you for your ongoing support and encouragement.

And this book would not be possible without the greatest gift and role I could ever have imagined: being a mom. Sophia, Grace, Anna, and Lauren, your support, love, and understanding through this journey has been incredible. Each of you have shared words of encouragement, sweet notes, and thoughtful snacks when I was writing all day and for long stretches of time at night. You've also contributed ideas and feedback for this book. To be the mother to each of you is the greatest blessing in my life—it's what dreams are made of. I love each of you so very much. And to my son, Kevin, who never took a breath but changed my life and helped me find my voice and continue writing, sweet angel, I love you. Thank you for your presence and inspiration.

And to my husband, Jim, for supporting and encouraging me, believing in all of my dreams, and caring for our girls when writing days were long and deadlines loomed, thank you. I am blessed to have a loving partner on this journey.

To my mom and dad, who throughout my life—whenever there was an obstacle or a challenge—were there to cheer me on and encourage me to follow my dreams and persevere for what I believe in, thank you. You have been my greatest teachers of love, perseverance, and growth. I am inspired by you both, and I believe anything is possible because of you both. And to my sister Ann, whose wit, wisdom and support has carried me through the highs and lows of life, and motherhood. You are a true blessing!

And to my dear friends, thank you for being there, always. Thank you, Lynn Rakowsky, Bethany Fain, Meryl Goldhaber, Daniel Golding, Julie Pearson, Jay Reily, Melissa and Andrew Chernick, Tracey Palmer, Sharon McMahon, and Steven and Michael Dixon-Weisbrod.

And a special thank-you to the clients I've supported along the way—it has been a gift to be part of your journey of healing. And to the MomsWellBeing community and Thriving Mama Community, I am so grateful for your support and encouragement. Thank you for giving me a platform to bring moms together and share my writing.

about the author

Dr. Claire Nicogossian is a licensed Clinical Psychologist in private practice and a Clinical Instructor in Psychiatry and Human Behavior at Brown University. Passionate about all things related to modern parenting, she is the founder of MomsWellBeing. com, a site supporting parental mental health, self-care, and well-being from a psychologist's perspective. She is the creator of the popular online quizzes "Are You a Burned Out Mom?" and "Are You a Burned Out Dad?" Her podcast, *In-Session with Dr. Claire*, focuses on mental health, self-care, and well-being for parents. You can find her writing on MomsWellBeing.com as well as on sites such as Scary Mommy, Motherly, Thrive Global, *HuffPost*, and TODAY Parenting Team. Dr. Claire lives in Rhode Island with her husband and four daughters.